HST
Silver Jubilee

Colin J. Marsden

Ian Allan
PUBLISHING

Contents

Front cover:
Not a usual location for a Virgin HST, or any HST for that matter, is Dent on the Settle & Carlisle route between Leeds and Carlisle. On 4 January 1997 the first Virgin Trains-liveried HST set, prepared by Leeds Neville Hill, was transferred to Edinburgh for the official Virgin launch on 6 January. The transfer move was scheduled to operate via the East Coast main line, but due to bad weather north of Newcastle it was agreed to divert the train via the S&C and Carstairs. En route some official pictures of the train were taken at Blea Moor and Dent. The train is seen at Dent in this view, led by power car No 43063, which was named *Maiden Voyager* two days later. *CJM*

Back cover top:
The use of HST power cars as locomotives to haul another train is very rare. However, on 10 December 2000 power cars Nos 43019/182 were coupled back-to-back and used to haul a failed IC125 set, complete with its power cars, from Exeter to Plymouth Laira. The movement took place when no FGW or Virgin locomotives were available at Laira. Train number 5Z77, the 12.00 Exeter-Laira, which looks like a triple-headed IC125, is seen passing along the famous South Devon sea-wall at Dawlish. The formation, from front to rear, is power cars Nos 43182, 43019 and 43042, trailer vehicles Nos 44049, 42145, 42144, 42143, 42268, 40745 and 41136, and power car No 43024 at the rear. *CJM*

Back cover bottom left:
The stylish body lines of the prototype HSDT are clearly visible in this view of the train on the WR main line, being overtaken by a 1967-built English Electric Class 50. *CJM collection*

Back cover bottom right:
In the original squadron colour of yellow and blue for power cars and blue and grey for passenger stock, set No 253007 passes Savernake on the Berks & Hants main line on 28 August 1979 with the 11.05 Truro-Paddington additional. *CJM*

Endpapers:
One of the most picturesque locations in the UK to capture HSTs on film is at Cockwood, between Starcross and Dawlish in South Devon, here trains cross over a causeway between the River Exe and the little village of Cockwood, with its small inner harbour. On 5 June 1993, No 43191, painted in InterCity 'Swallow' livery, heads west at Cockwood with the 10.18 Manchester Piccadilly-Penzance working. *CJM*

Title Page:
Led by power car No 43149, painted in InterCity 'Swallow' livery, the 2+8 formation of the 16.40 Penzance-Paddington crosses Bolitho Viaduct east of Liskeard on 22 June 1996. *CJM*

First published 2001

ISBN 0 7110 2847 8

© Colin J. Marsden 2001

Published by Ian Allan Publishing

an imprint of Ian Allan Publishing Ltd, Riverdene Business Park, Hersham, Surrey KT12 4RG.

Printed by Ian Allan Printing Ltd, Riverdene Business Park, Hersham, Surrey KT12 4RG.

Code: 0110/B1

Foreword

FUTURE railway historians will be able to summarise the development of the InterCity railways during the last quarter of the 20th Century by writing just three initials - HST. The High Speed Train, first introduced in 1975, revolutionised express train travel in Britain. The introduction of clockface departures and reduced journey times by operating at speeds up to 125 mph, winning back lost customers who had taken to the motorways or the airlines.

This book, however, deals not with some long lost class of traction, but of trains which after 25 years are still going strong and remain in front line duty on First Great Western, Great North Eastern Railway, Midland Mainline and Virgin Trains services.

Below:
On 12 May 1997 a close bond was formed between the RAF Red Arrows display team and Virgin Trains, when power car No 43155 was named *The Red Arrows* in a ceremony at York station. At this event it was agreed that a special photographic shoot would be arranged to capture the Red Arrows flying display and their HST in the same picture, with the author of this book asked if he would undertake exclusive photography of the event. Various attempts were made to arrange the meeting of the 'Reds' and a mass of locations reviewed, with eventually a spot south of Aberdeen at Colsea Yawn selected. On 15 July 1997 the Red Arrows were in Aberdeen to start the Tall Ships race, and the following morning the 09.10 Aberdeen-Plymouth was led by No 43155 and this picture was captured. The timing of the Red Arrows' then Team Leader 'Red 1' Squadron Leader Simon Meade and Traction Inspector John Thompson was perfect to the second. *CJM*

It is hardly surprising that having clocked up such phenomenal mileages throughout their service that the HST's are now beginning to be replaced by the next generation of High Speed Trains. When I first joined the railway, some annual locomotive mileage returns could be measured in just hundreds of miles, for the HSTs these figures now read over 300,000 miles per year.

On Virgin Trains, our new generation high speed trains, the 'Voyagers' and 'Super Voyagers' are now leaving the production lines and entering passenger service. These too have the remit of increasing passenger numbers by winning back passengers from the motorways and airlines. For the first time CrossCountry services will benefit from a regular interval clockface timetable and this allows us to double the number of trains we can run. Most of our current HST fleet will then return to the leasing companies and will no doubt go on for a few more years with other operators. This will allow our new generation trains to operate the longest distance trains in Britain between the North of Scotland and the West of England.

The HST story was without doubt the greatest success story of the British Rail era. I congratulate Colin for recording it so far - for the story is far from finished and no doubt a second volume will follow in years to come. I for one will look forward to reading it.

Chris Green
Chief Executive, Virgin Trains

Introduction

It is almost impossible to believe that the HSTs have now been working on the rail network for 25 years — it seems only yesterday that the striking new lines of the High Speed Train sets were first seen parked in carriage sidings at Old Oak Common before entering passenger service on the London-Bristol route.

When most followers of trains and locomotives were mourning the demise of main-line loco classes such as the 'Western' Class 52s, nobody could have ever imagined the impact that the HSTs would have on the rail system. For many years it had been known that a modern, efficient and reliable high-speed rail network was required in the UK to win back traffic erosion by car, coach and air travel. However, all growth expectations were exceeded when the stylish HSTs entered service.

Public acceptance of the new form of travel, the fastest diesel-operated service anywhere in the world, saw major new journey opportunities become possible, with, for example, the chance to make a day return from London to Edinburgh for the first time!

The high-speed train revolution started as a project to provide a short-term modern train to stand in while the then British Railways Board (BRB) developed and refined the train of the future, the Advanced Passenger Train (APT). It was when this project was seen to be falling well behind in timescale and reliability that the Derby-based engineering team decided to seek BRB and Government authority to build a sizeable fleet of modern diesel-powered high-tech multiple-unit-style trains using the latest Mk3 long-wheelbase passenger coach already authorised for trial development.

Although a much larger fleet of HSTs was originally proposed, the eventual build of 197 production power cars and over 700 passenger trailer vehicles, which modernised our railway, have now clocked up a staggering fleet mileage of over 800 million miles, the highest number ever accumulated by any passenger stock in the history of railways.

Under their original remit, the fleet was operated by BR under its InterCity business banner. Upon privatisation of the rail industry the fleet became split between several owner/operators, with two new lease companies, Angel Trains and Porterbrook, becoming 'owners' of the trains and leasing then to four principal operators — Virgin Trains, Great North Eastern Railway, Midland Mainline and First Great Western — each of which has now put its mark on the trains in terms of livery and interior furniture.

The HST fleet is presently the mainstay of the post-100mph main-line passenger railway in the UK, a distinction it has held for a quarter of a century. In the very near future some major changes will take place, with the sets currently operated by Virgin Trains on its CrossCountry network being displaced by new diesel multiple sets also capable of 125mph running. The future of these displaced sets is still far from settled; some will be offered to other operators, which frankly will be those that make the largest financial bid to the owning lease company. However, as this book went to press, Virgin announced that 14 HST sets would be retained for use on the Paddington-Birmingham route. In the longer term, modernisation of the Midland main line *could* see further displacement of sets, and developments on the GNER route from King's Cross to Leeds, Newcastle and Scotland largely depends on the awarding of new franchises. On the Great Western no electrification is planned and diesel train sets will be needed for the foreseeable future. Although a handful of new Class 180s are due to enter service, some form of major upgrading of the Great Western fleet will be needed over the next few years; whether this will consist of a major refurbishment project of both passenger saloons and power cars or the building of new diesel or gas turbine power units, we are likely to see the HSTs remaining in front-line service for many years to come.

On a personal note, I was privileged to be one of the passengers on board the first passenger run of the prototype and production HSTs in the UK, and since then, by virtue of living in the West of England, I have clocked up almost a million miles of HST travel. The ride and on-board ambience of the HST fleet is, I consider, one of the best high-speed train environments in any country, and has given me much inspiration for railway writing.

The production of this title would not have been possible without amazing co-operation from former and current railway staff involved in the HST operation, as well as fellow railway journalists and photographers, to whom I am most grateful. Without providing an enormous list of 'thanks', a few people deserve to be thanked individually: Darren Ford and Brian Morrison for supplying illustrations; John Heaton and Brian Perren for undertaking the authorship of individual sections; Peter Sharp, Charles Woodland, Ashley Butlin and Geoff Hudson for supplying information; the public affairs officers of the former BR InterCity business as well as the privatised operators who operate the HST fleet, for assisting with information; and Chris Dixon LBIPP for printing many of my older black and white negatives.

I personally hope that readers and viewers have as much enjoyment browsing through and reading the pages of this title as it has given me to produce, and long may the HST fleet grace the rail lines of the UK.

Colin J. Marsden
Dawlish, August 2001

Left:
The two icons of 1970s high-speed travel could frequently be seen in the Filton area of Bristol, where the prototype Anglo-French Concorde, registration G-BSST, taking part in flight trials under the captaincy of test pilot Brian Trubshaw, operated from Filton airport while training runs with the prototype HSDT were undertaken from Old Oak Common to Bristol via Badminton. Filton, December 1974. *Terry Nicholls*

Above:
How the 1960s modernised BR network looked, with Class AL6, later Class 86, No E3109 working on the 1966-introduced electric service between Euston and Birmingham, Manchester and Liverpool. Behind the loco is a mixture of Mk2 and Mk1 stock. *CJM collection*

Centre left:
In Japan the modernised railway became the envy of the world from 1964 with the opening of the Tokaido line between Tokyo and Osaka on 1 October, allowing the 310-mile journey between the two cities to be completed in just 3 hours, with timetabled speeds of up to 125mph for the first time. One of the original Japanese 'Shinkansen' electric sets is seen between Kakegawa and Shizuoka, passing a Japanese tea field, in April 1994. *Mikio Miura*

Lower left:
In France the new revitalised high-speed railway used existing and purpose-built lines on which TGV fixed-formation electric sets operated. Painted in the original orange livery, Sud-Est set No 11 passes Montgeron-Crosne on the outskirts of Paris on 31 January 1996 with the 10.30 Paris-Lyon-Marseille service. *CJM*

Those Pre-HST Days

In the years after the end of world hostilities in 1945, the quest and desire for travel throughout the country considerably increased. While the UK had a major railway network, it had suffered seriously from the ravages of the 1939-45 conflict and was unable to provide a high-speed service, even between the main cities and conurbations. The rapid development of the motor car and the introduction of quality high-capacity road coaches was able to fill this gap in transportation.

The 'Modernisation Plan' for our railway network, announced in the mid-1950s, which eventually led to the withdrawal of steam traction, saw the introduction of 'modern' diesel and electric locomotives and new passenger stock, and this did a lot to win back patronage. However, this modernisation led to a general maximum top speed of between 80 and 90mph, with quite often averages as low as 50mph over longer distances, which did little to improve city-to-city times and did not attract the estimated passenger growth.

The opening and rapid expansion of the UK motorway network was another nail in the coffin of the rail industry, and saw motor cars able to cover distances between many cities and towns quicker than or on a par with the train, and thus the railway lost out again. The development of UK domestic air services, linking locations such as London with Manchester, Birmingham, Leeds and Edinburgh/Glasgow, also made serious inroads into long-distance rail travel, especially winning the lucrative business market.

The infamous Dr Beeching, in one of his many reports, almost accepted that road and air competition would see the end of some major rail routes. However, following the departure of Beeching and the appointment of Stanley (later Sir Stanley) Raymond as Chairman of the British Transport Commission (BTC), a lifelong railwayman and a man with immense vision of how the railway *should* be developed, came new marketing strategies, aimed at attracting huge levels of new business. In one of his early addresses he made mention of the major 'Inter-City' routes and how he saw that these could and would be developed into a major modern railway transport network. Indeed, it was Stanley Raymond who launched the now legendary 'Inter-City' brand name, and developed a marketing campaign devised to win back air and road travellers to rail.

One of the keys to Raymond's early success was the mid-1960s modernisation of the West Coast Main Line (WCML), with electrification between London (Euston) and Birmingham, Liverpool and Manchester, long route sections being authorised for 100mph operation. Once opened, these routes saw immediate success and impressive growth. The connection between central London and central Manchester was now down to just 2hr 37min, with an average speed of over 70mph. However, on other routes no such modernisation was under way, and the only, if one can call it so, 'High

Speed' locomotive class operating was the fleet of 22 100mph 'Deltic' locomotives on the Anglo-Scottish expresses on the East Coast Main Line (ECML). This high-speed operation was a little tenuous as most of the stock used on the route was restricted to 90-95mph.

An early pre-empting of the modern high-speed railway came in July 1960 when a small fleet of multiple-unit, fully air-conditioned 'Metro-Cammell' Pullman sets, usually referred to as the 'Blue Pullmans', was introduced on the St Pancras-Manchester route. These superior trains, very similar in many ways to the HST train of the 1970s, had streamlined power cars and high-quality passenger stock. The new diesel Pullman service was able to cover the journey between London and Manchester in just 3hr 10min, far quicker than services on the West Coast route from Euston. This time saving on the important and growing London-Manchester corridor did much to retain rail passengers on the route prior to the modernisation on the West Coast route in the mid-1960s.

Other Metro-Cammell Pullman sets were delivered to the Western Region, where they were deployed on the Paddington-Birmingham and Bristol routes. When the Midland line's 'Blue Pullmans' were superseded by the West Coast electrification, all the sets were transferred to the WR, operating on the London-Birmingham/Bristol/Swansea corridor.

These Metro-Cammell Pullmans were the first to exploit high-speed (90mph) running using a push-pull system; having driving controls within their own formation at both ends, no turn-over engine was needed at a terminus.

By the mid-1960s most developed countries in the world were upgrading and improving their rail infrastructure and trains, but sadly the UK was lagging well behind. In Germany, France and Italy the electrification of principal routes was ongoing, with high-quality track and stock being introduced to allow enhanced speed. The greatest change anywhere, and the basic seed for the 'new' railways throughout the world, was in Japan, where the new purpose-built Tokaido line was opened between Tokyo and Osaka on 1 October 1964, completing the 310-mile journey in just 3 hours, with timetabled speeds of up to 125mph. To operate on this new railway, purpose-built trains were

Right:
Prior to the agreement for new state-of-the-art high-speed trains in the UK, some upgrading and general modernisation of the loco-hauled fleet was made. One of these initiatives was the XP64 stock, fitted with sliding doors and improved interiors, which operated for a short while with blue-liveried Brush Type 4 No D1733. *CJM collection*

Left:
In many ways the forerunner of the High Speed Diesel Train (HSDT) was the early 1960s 'Blue Pullman' stock built by Metro-Cammell for the St Pancras-Manchester and Paddington-Bristol/Birmingham routes. One of the Midland Pullman sets, with power car No M60093 leading, is shown during early tests. *CJM collection*

introduced offering a high quality of travel with enhanced amenities on board.

In the UK, although gains were seen from the 'Inter-City' marketing campaign and the cleaning up of the existing services, the lack of Government conviction about rail travel and the almost total lack of real investment seriously slowed down what few plans were on the table. The anti-rail Government of the period put the cap on many plans to develop home-market 'modern' diesel and electric locomotives and stock. Perhaps of even more significance was that plans were drawn up to build a UK version of the Japanese dedicated-high-speed-line network, linking the most important and largely used centres. This was totally rejected, even though the cost per mile at that time of a new twin track railway was *less* than that of motorway construction.

It was quickly realised that without any central Government support for an improved or new railway in the UK, the country was to be left with an antiquated network. Considerable effort was therefore needed to try and raise speeds as high as possible on the existing railway without causing any danger or increased passenger discomfort. Major track works were authorised at a number of locations; in some places the 'ironing out' of restrictive curves allowed a moderate speed increase, while in other locations 'canting' was adopted whereby the trains leaned over slightly on curves, which were then able to be taken at marginally increased speeds. However, even with this infrastructure

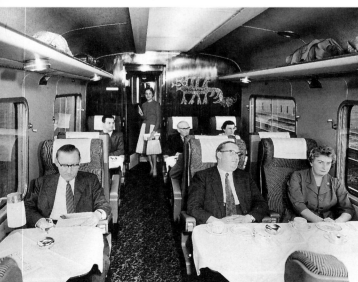

Centre left:
One of the major differences between the 'Blue Pullman' and the subsequent design of the HSDT was that passengers travelled in the power cars, with two bays at the inner end separated from the engine compartment by a soundproofed wall. One of the Midland Pullman trial runs is seen near Bedford. Note that an oil tail light was used — at this time electric tail indicators had not been introduced. *CJM collection*

Left:
The interior of the Midland Pullman, all 1st Class, was of a very high standard. A 2+1 low-density layout was followed, with well-spaced individual seats, each reclinable. Pullman-style marquetry was found on the end bulkhead walls and each seat had an attendant's call button and table light. *CJM collection*

work and the tweaking of bogie equipment on earlier Mk2 stock, speeds above 95-100mph were not really possible.

Looking towards even higher speeds, of between 125 and 140mph, engineers claimed in March 1968 that increases of above 125mph were not practicable on the present UK infrastructure and that higher speeds would have to be achieved on a new railway. However, in the closing years of the 1960s a consistent speed of 100mph was viewed as a major advantage over previous top speeds. Subsequent orders for the Mk2 design stock, fitted with improved bogies, electric heating and pressure ventilation, together with hugely improved interior designs, including double glazing, updated seating, new vehicle lining materials and upgraded toilets, were specified with a 100mph top speed.

At around the same time as the final derivative of the Mk2 passenger stock was emerging from the then BREL Derby Litchurch Lane Works, engineers in both London and Derby were working on a new design for a longer-wheelbase passenger coach of around 75ft in length, with superior bogie layout, which *would* be able to operate at speeds of up to 125mph as a norm on conventional track. These plans paved the way for the later-built Mk3 design.

The technical plans for the new Mk3 passenger carriage were furthered with the assistance of British Rail Engineering Ltd, which jointly undertook an engineering study into the provision of traction to power these proposed fast, or high-speed, trains. Various propositions of 'high-speed' diesel or electric loco were studied, including further development of push-pull operations, and all this eventually led to the High Speed Diesel Train (HSDT), which we see running today and which is celebrating 25 years of operation in the true Millennium year.

However, before we look further into the High Speed Train story, we must consider what else was going on at the Railway Technical Centre (RTC). The UK's most important railway engineering research site, located in London Road, Derby, was developed from the previous LMS/BR research base, and opened in 1962. At that time led by Dr Sydney Jones, who trawled all areas of engineering to staff the new centre, it became principally staffed by scientists and engineers recruited from an aviation background who found themselves out of work at the time, plus a considerable number of other young, university-trained engineers from all engineering disciplines. Thus for the first time some extremely clever young engineers were able to put

their minds to railway operations, which had in the past been viewed as a less glamorous side of science. These new engineers and scientists had a supreme vision of new state-of-the-art railway engineering and were not steered by past knowledge of the 'old' railway.

One of the new sections of the BR Research Division commenced a major study on the behaviour of vehicle ride and the science of the interface of steel railway wheels on steel rails; this work included the very serious phenomenon of 'bogie hunt', which was seen as a significant problem and would restrict much post-100mph running. In the early 1960s some sections of recently laid continuous welded rail, installed to give a clean ride and higher speeds, were the subject of serious freight train derailments, where old four-wheeled wagons just leapt off the track.

In the course of the research into these derailments, in 1966 Dr Jones set up the Advanced Projects Group within BR Research to study and develop new forms of passenger and freight stock, able to travel at faster speeds. This work included development of a new suspension system, which was installed on a four-wheel freight vehicle for development running. On the power rollers at the Derby RTC the vehicle attained a speed of over 140mph, while dynamic testing on the main line was carried out at up to 100mph. The design of the suspension was such that a good-quality ride was found at virtually any speed on any type of track — canted, continuously welded, jointed, on crossings or through junctions. In the 24 months that the

Above:
During the quest for a superior suspension system design that would allow higher speeds on conventional track, the engineers at Derby developed a High Speed Freight Vehicle. This was a modified four-wheel wagon on to which a fixed load (of rails) was fitted, and various suspension and wheelsets were evaluated. *CJM*

Left:
In 1971 the East Coast main line was working with some of the newest Mk2 air-conditioned coaches, powered by Class 47s and 55 'Deltic' locomotives fitted with electric train supply. With six new Mk2e vehicles (three 1st and three 2nd Class), a buffet car and two half-brake vehicles, Class 47 No D1501 is seen near Hatfield on 5 February 1971. *CJM*

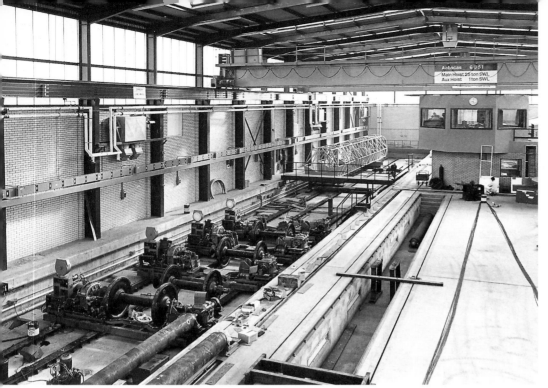

Left:
Most of the research undertaken into post-100mph train running was carried out at the Railway Technical Centre, Derby, where specialist facilities were built. This view shows the advanced project or vehicles laboratory where most of the HSDT and APT work was carried out. In the background one of the prototype APT development vehicles, POP, can be seen, while on the left is the wheelset test rig. *CJM collection*

wheel/rail interface team had been working together more had been learned on the subject of ride than in the previous 50 years.

The Derby boffins, as they were called by much of the operational railway, were now far more confident that passenger train speeds of up to 125mph could be attained without serious problems, and in November 1966 talk was rife of taking research even further into the unknown to explore characteristics of passenger train running at speeds of up to 140 and even 150mph. This plan is worded into a memorandum submitted to the BRB for a new design of fast passenger coach, referred to as the Advanced High Speed Passenger Train, or APT; this, as early as the end of 1966, was the birth of the APT project. By late the following year the scheme had been refined and an APT team formed. Funding for this totally BR research project would require an investment of around £4.8 million, which the rail industry could not fund from its own resources. Dr Jones, who was the kingpin of the project, went to the Government and eventually won 50% funding, provided that the other 50% came from the rail industry. The scheme finally got agreement in December 1968.

Although much of the detail work from 1967 on high-speed-train technology was supported by the APT project, considerable work was still being carried out by the Director of Mechanical & Electrical Engineering (DM&EE) function, also based at the RTC Derby, on the development of a traditional train to travel above 100mph, looking for a 25% speed increase to 125mph. In the main, BR's long-distance routes were restricted by their Victorian infrastructure, which generally could not be changed. The 'running envelope' or loading gauge was a pre-defined measurement stipulated by clearances between tracks, tunnels, cuttings, bridges, viaducts and, to a lesser extent, stations. Any new design of passenger train had to fit this space, as well as comply with the stopping distances of existing 100mph trains while potentially travelling 25% faster; the most important factor here would of course be the sighting distances of fixed signals.

In terms of infrastructure, a 25% speed increase would take its toll on track wear; the engineers at Derby were quite confident about ride at higher speeds, but the effect on the track and increased damage was a different matter. The assumed weight mass of a new vehicle would,

for example, give a heavy axle load in terms of strike weight on a dipped rail joint.

The APT team at Derby, working at arm's length from the DM&EE team, was, however, planning for a 50% potential speed increase for its new-generation train, and a vast amount of its research went into the effects of travelling at speeds of up to 150mph. It was accepted that the new design of bogie could hold the rail at such speed, but what effect curvature would have on passengers travelling at this speed was very unclear. Research showed that the maximum amount of track cant had already been used on trials, and any further vertical correction would have to be carried out on the train's body in degrees of tilt.

Further coverage of the Advanced Passenger Train falls outside the remit of this title, except to state that eventually, with huge Government assistance, a prototype four-vehicle gas-turbine-powered Advanced Passenger Train was built and, after many years of testing, a small fleet of pre-series electrically powered APTs was unsuccessfully introduced incorporating tilting bodies and many other novel features.

In 1967 the DM&EE plan for a high-speed diesel train finally took a major step forward, with the appointment of Walter Jowett as Director of Design. Jowett came from a railway engineering background, having worked with English Electric, and was not afraid of making his points known at BR Board meetings. He was charged with looking at BR's traction needs for the 1970s, and soon into his reign he aired his views on the APT project, considering that the plans for the desired APT were not advanced sufficiently for a quick introduction and that this was not the only way forward, and that more traditional forms of 'new' traction should be exploited — these comments eventually led to the HST project being authorised.

In the summer of 1968 Terry Miller was appointed as the new Chief Engineer of Traction & Rolling Stock at BRB. A lifelong railway engineer, having trained under Gresley at Doncaster, he was a keen supporter of a high-speed diesel train, and viewed this as the quick answer to further the railway; later, if an APT train was developed, it could take over on electrified routes. Both Jowett and Miller were steering the project towards a high-speed diesel train at the end of 1968, with many rough plans drawn out.

In early 1969 concern over the APT project emerged; late running on the original timescale was obvious and the DM&EE team under Miller immediately stepped in with a formal submission for their HSDT project. The submission was very detailed, promising a fully operational prototype train for passenger-carrying in 22 months from official order. The submission also contained plans for the first tranche of production sets.

This surprise submission for authority was endorsed in March 1969 by the then BR Chairman, Henry Johnson, who gave the HSDT project his blessing, going on public record as saying that if the APT project did not prove itself in four, five or even six years, the rail industry would need a state-of-the-art train to fall back on. Although these comments did not provide authorisation for the HSDT project, they moved it forward. In the period March 1969-August 1970 the project was refined using much previous research and development,

Above:
The aerodynamic stress and resistance on the mainly slab-front ends of traction units generated much research in 1970, which resulted in an early version of an HSDT front end being attached to Class 86 No E3173 for trials on the West Coast route. The fibreglass front end had a central square window and a roof horn grille, and two rather unusual non-usable buffers. *CJM*

Left:
In addition to aerodynamic research, Class 86 No E3173 was fitted with a new design of Flexicoil bogie of a type to be developed for the HSDT. With two Mk1 vehicles, the test formation is seen at Tring on 25 October 1970. Note that no windscreen wiper was provided, so what happened if it started to rain during test running is unclear. *Colin Gifford*

including the 75ft 4in Mk3 coach design and BT10 bogie technology. Power was to be provided by either one or two locomotives or power cars.

May 1970 was a major turning point for the project, when the BRB Investment Committee authorised £70,000 to be allocated for the development of a high-speed multiple-unit. In the following August this funding was cancelled and a massive £800,000 set aside for the design, development and building of a prototype train. This was without doubt the most significant decision taken by the British Railways Board during its existence from 1948 to privatisation, and frankly without it the main-line railways of the UK could well have been closed down.

At this time the HSDT project was officially made public, and the BRB said that the development of modern diesel trains would be a 'stopgap' measure until new Advanced Passenger Trains were ready for introduction in the early 1980s. Pre-September 1970 research and ongoing development work enabled a quick start to the HST project, and before the end of the year an announcement was made that a fully operational pre-production HST would be built for launch and testing in 1972. Meanwhile, for many months prior to the official announcement, teams were being put in place in Derby, for it had been known several months earlier that the only possible

way forward was to develop the project devised by the Director of Mechanical & Electrical Engineering (DM&EE). As part of this huge research much groundwork had been undertaken in the two preceding years; this included the installation of a trial streamlined nose-cone on LM Class 86 electric No E3173 to evaluate aerodynamic drag and effects. The loco was also fitted with Alsthom Flexicoil bogies. With its streamlined nose section and hauling Mk1 stock, No E3173 attained a speed of 125mph on the WCML, and the power bogies eventually fitted below the HSDT power cars were a development of this Flexicoil design. It is interesting to record that three months prior to the official announcement of the HSDT project, the BRB had authorised the construction of three Mk3 passenger vehicles for testing, which then formed part of the HSDT project.

Official papers issued by the BRB media machine in 1973/74 spoke of the 'short-term' use of HSDTs on principal services, and that by the early 1980s APTs travelling at 150mph would be working on the main routes and that the 'stopgap' HSDTs would then be displaced to secondary and branch-line use. At one press conference attended by the author it was said that the production HSDTs would have just a 10-year main-line life, after which they would be worn out after such intensive use!

Many criticised the decision to build an operational prototype train, but time was to prove that it was the right decision. It kept the public aware, by good manipulation of the media machine by a top-ranking BR public affairs team, that new trains were on the way, while serving as a huge design and test tool for the Derby teams. It gave passengers the chance to see a train of the future, whereas the APT project fell from public thought for many years, and when it did return it was little short of a total failure.

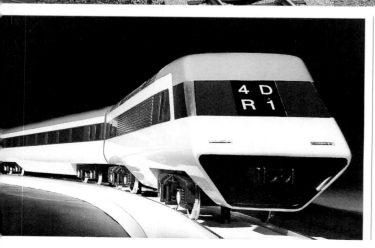

Right:
In the period March 1969-August 1970, when the HSDT project was being refined, many proposals were put forward for the new Mk3 passenger coach, based on an overall body length of 75ft. This mid-1970 drawing shows a developed version of the coach, even showing Inter-City branding and livery. The gangway doors appear to have a much deeper window than those adopted, while the toilet area window is of a different design. *CJM collection*

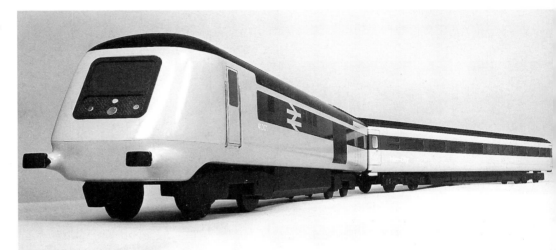

Centre right:
Just before production was finally authorised for the HSDT, this illustration of a model was released by the BRB. It shows in virtually every respect how the finished train looked, except that drawgear was not included. Even the livery, numbering and branding were basically followed for the production train.
CJM collection

Right:
After the BRB decided that the APT project was going to be a long-drawn-out affair, and building commenced at Crewe and Derby of the HSDT project, construction of the APT continued at the Advanced Projects Lab within the RTC. Owing much of its design and construction to the aeronautic industry, one of the APT driving cars is seen under assembly with two of the development POP vehicles adjacent. *CJM collection*

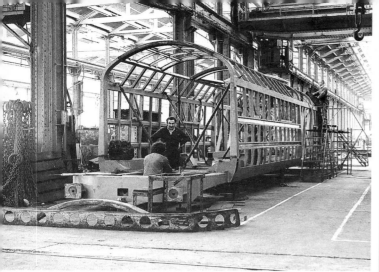

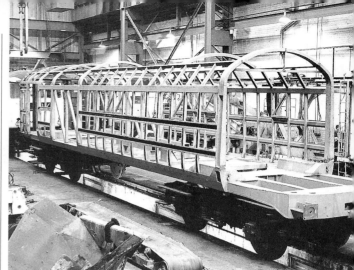

Above left:
The HSDT is born: the skeleton frame for the first of the two prototype power cars takes shape in the BREL Crewe fabrication shop in March 1971. *CJM*

Above right:
Mounted on a pair of old van bogies, the first complete frame is seen inside the main assembly bay prior to being placed on stands for fitting out. At this stage, April 1971, the frame had no exterior plating and was literally a skeleton. *CJM*

Left:
Some eight months after the previous picture was taken, the first HSDT power car is seen skinned and having internal equipment installed in the main assembly bay at BREL Crewe. In the foreground is the first power unit and alternator group delivered as an operational 'set' from Paxman of Colchester. *CJM*

Below:
Another of the many pre-production drawings of the HSDT: this one, produced concurrent with the assembly of the prototype vehicles, shows a ribbed roof section over the non-power equipment end of the vehicle. *CJM collection*

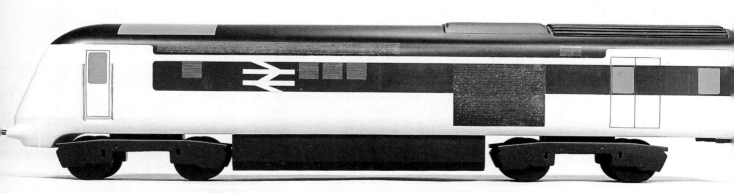

2. The Prototype Train

As discussed in the previous chapter, the turning point in BR's main-line transportation, or 'Inter-City', story came in August 1970, when the BRB sanctioned the production of a prototype High Speed Diesel Train (HSDT), the prototype set due to emerge from BR/BREL in under two years in 1972; the target date for passenger introduction was mid-1975. At the same time as Derby was undertaking the train's design, the civil engineers and signal engineers had to decide what was needed in terms of fixed equipment to allow high-speed operation, without major new works having to be undertaken.

The Derby design office was entrusted with the structural design of the train, which was to be based on two self-contained power cars or locomotives, one marshalled at either end of a rake of high-quality passenger saloons, classified as Mk3. The power cars/locomotives would be of an entirely new design, mounted on a Bo-Bo wheel configuration. The outer, leading end of the body would be fully streamlined, while the inner end, coupled to the passenger saloons, would have a slab coach-end design. The decision to use a power car at both ends of the train formation was steered by two main considerations: first, no single lightweight power unit was available of around 4,500hp, deemed as necessary for the type of train projected; and second, the provision of a driving facility at both ends gave huge benefits in operating flexibility.

The Power Cars

Assembly of the framework for the two power cars for the prototype train, at this stage identified as Nos 41001 and 41002, was undertaken at BREL Crewe Works, then transferred to Derby for detail completion. The power car body styling incorporated two oval buffers in air-smoothed shank housings, while the drawgear, in the form of a main reservoir and brake pipe and a coupling hook, was housed underneath a hinged plate, so when it was not required the front end had the appearance of having no external coupling. In the centre of the raked-back front end, formed of GRP (glass reinforced plastic) over a steel frame, was a large vertical rectangle split in two by a central cross member; the lower glass panel covered two sealed-beam marker lights and a central headlight with a central tail light above, while the top glazed panel formed the cab windscreen, fitted with a single windscreen wiper. In the roof line above the cab front were the warning horns.

The wrap-around style of the cab end did not incorporate any cab-side windows, as the driving position was a break from tradition and in the centre of the cab. Drop-light windows were provided in the cab doors. The cab design was new to the UK and regrettably was seriously criticised by the trade unions at the time. The actual driving desk fitted 'around' the driver, who operated the train's power with his right hand via a push-pull stump control, and worked the brake with his left hand by a similar controller. All indications and switchgear were mounted in easy to see and reach locations to his front and on both sides. Provision was made for a driver's assistant, but only in the shape of a fold-down seat on the rear bulkhead wall.

A soundproofed door, opening into the driving cab, gave access into the equipment room. The cab and equipment bays (engine room) were separate modules with sound insulation between in an attempt to give an improved working environment for the driver. Directly behind the cab was the electrical equipment cubicle, also housing the pneumatic control equipment and bodyside air louvring for traction motor ventilation. The next section of the power car housed (in order from the cab) the exciter and traction rectifier, traction alternator and train supply auxiliary alternator. The hydraulic parking brake and other pneumatic equipment was housed on the side walls in this area, while in the roof was the main silencer unit. Two hinged doors, opening towards the cab, gave access to the next bay housing the main Paxman 'Valenta' power unit. Two more division doors, one on either side of the body, separated off the cooler group bay, driven directly by a shaft off the engine. The cooler/radiator group area had large bodyside air louvres and roof-mounted ventilation. Inward from the cooler/radiator compartment, separated again by doors, was the guard's (conductor's) office, with a full-width luggage area having traditional hinged inward/outward opening doors on each side. On the left-hand side of the inner end was a small doored compartment housing the auxiliary or slab-end driving cab, with basic controls to enable the 'loco' to be used for shunting work, rather than train operation. Only the first two power notches were available from this cab.

On the power car underframe, towards the outer end were located the air compressor and spillage tanks. Towards the centre, below the power unit, was the main fuel tank with a capacity of 1,250 gallons. The battery boxes were located just in advance of the rear bogie, and air reservoirs were mounted at the inner end of the same bogie.

At one point in the early design stage it was considered to bunch all the power equipment towards the driving end of the power car and install passenger accommodation at the inner end, thus making the vehicle in excess of 60ft in length. This plan was dropped in the early days as part of the attempt to maintain a high standard of passenger environment with low noise/vibration.

The Power Unit

At an early stage in the design process, when it was agreed that an HSDT formation would typically be of seven or eight trailer carriages with a passenger capacity of around 400, to provide the top speed of 125mph on the routes specified in the original plan (the East Coast main line and the routes of the Western Region, plus the Midland main line and eventually the then developing Cross Country network), an installed all-in power of 4,500hp was needed.

The problem with selecting such a single high-output diesel and associated equipment was one of weight, the HSDT in its earliest design specification dictating that minimum vertical dynamic forces between wheel and rail were very important to gain certification to operate at 125mph over existing tracks; thus the axle load and unsprung mass on each power car axle had to be kept to an absolute minimum. It was quite obvious that no single lightweight diesel engine or gas-turbine unit was available to meet this criterion. Gas-turbine power was quickly dismissed; the main supplier, Rolls-Royce, was quickly departing from the rail traction field, and the design, build, operation and maintenance cost of such equipment was far in excess of conventional diesels. It is interesting to point out, however, that in 2001, Bombardier, in partnership with Turbomeca, was

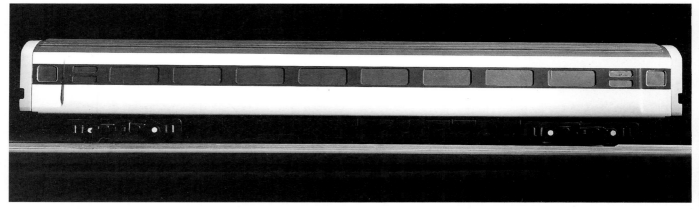

developing a new-generation gas-turbine-powered 'Jetrain', which could well be tested on First Great Western and even replace some of the production HSTs.

With no single diesel available with a proven track record to give the desired 4,500hp, a decision was made in the first few weeks of the project to use two power cars or locomotives, one at each end of the train; two units of 2,250hp would be more readily available. Previous development of through-train line control made it possible for both power units to be used for traction and auxiliary power at the same time under the control of the leading driver, one power car or loco technically going in reverse!

Paxman, based in Colchester, was able to offer off-the-shelf power units of the required output, which would also meet the strict weight guidelines and already held rail application certification. The chosen unit was the 12-cylinder Paxman 'Valenta', which was a derivative of the previously used Paxman 'Ventura' unit, and indeed used a number of common parts.

The 12-cylinder 'Valenta' 60 deg 'V'-form unit, set to deliver 2,250hp at 1,500rpm, had a cylinder bore of 7¾in and a stroke of 8½ in, the same as on the earlier 'Ventura', but with design improvements it gave increased power and greater reliability. The new engines sported improved fuel injection, redesigned crankcase, cylinder heads, connecting rods, pistons and bearings, improved piston cooling and a water-cooled exhaust manifold.

Official records show that during the immediate post-authorisation period of the chosen 2,250hp 'Valenta' engine, Paxman made an offer of a 16-cylinder 3,000hp version, which it is understood would have fitted into the HSDT body shell with little problem. However, nothing further was heard of this scheme.

Engine Cooling

From the 'free' end of the engine, a cardan shaft drove the radiator fan through a bevel gearbox and hydraulic coupling. This high-pressure axial-flow fan sucked in air through bodyside louvres, then through secondary radiator panels before expelling the air through roof-mounted primary radiator panels that catered for the engine and exhaust manifold cooling. The majority of the cooler group was formed of aluminium to reduce weight, with some hollow sections used to transport coolant instead of using separate pipes. To ease maintenance the entire cooler group could be removed as one module, having its own roof section.

Electrical Equipment

Coupled to the drive end of the engine was a compact but highly efficient Brush alternator group, formed of a main alternator, train supply alternator and auxiliary alternator, all units being of the brushless type. The main alternator, used for traction purposes, was rated at 1,480kW at 1,500V and the train supply alternator was set to supply 420kW at 850V; one train supply alternator was sufficient to meet an entire train's demand if one power car failed. The auxiliary alternator, providing supplies to the power car, was set at 33kW at 110V. Until the development of the prototype HSDT power cars, all diesel locomotives in the UK had been equipped with direct current generators, but the futuristic HSDT broke new ground in using ac alternators with output converted to dc for traction by silicon rectifiers. An ac traction alternator group had previously been tested in the UK on the Brush prototypes *Hawk* and *Kestrel*.

The traction motors, also supplied by Brush, were of the self-ventilated type; in order to achieve the necessary low unsprung mass per wheelset, it was agreed to mount them within the bogie frame, with a drive to the actual wheelsets.

The main power from the traction alternator was controlled by varying the excitation current fed to the exciter mounted on the end of the alternator group; since this current was relatively small, it could be handled by simple electronic devices. Auxiliary voltage regulation was made by means of an electronic regulator.

The driver's power controller was based on a 'Westcode' digital system, governing both power cars from either driving position. An automatic short-circuiter with an operating time of less than 50 milliseconds was activated in case of a traction motor flash-over or power earth fault.

Brakes

The special design of the brake system was a fundamental part of the design for the HSDT concept. A design specification was that a train travelling at 125mph *must* be able to stop in the same distance as a conventional train travelling at 100mph. This was achieved by the use of Girling disc brakes, working against cast-iron check-plates bolted directly to the webs of the wheels. In addition, on the power cars a single cast-iron brake-block was fitted for 'track conditioning', installed in order to maintain a clean wheel/rail interface during braking. The same block was also used for the hydraulic parking brake.

Train brake operation was initiated by means of a Westcode system, in which the driver's brake controller was basically a switch energising

or de-energising a sequence of wires that sent a 'brake demand' to the underslung brake control unit, thus regulating the brake cylinder pressure. This avoided the need to bring heavy air pipework into the cab area. An emergency brake application plunger was positioned on the desk, which, if depressed, gave a direct venting of the brake pipe. Electronic wheel slip/slide equipment was fitted throughout the train, with brake cylinder pressure reduced if wheelslip was experienced during speed retardation.

Bogies

As part of the general lightweight design, the power car bogie frames weighed less than 30cwt, although their fabricated assembly was one of the strongest ever used. Tests carried out with a prototype pair of bogies under Class 86 No E3173, which was used in 1969 for high-speed bogie development work and subsequently at the Research Centre, Derby, confirmed validity of the design and fatigue life. The bogie's primary suspension used coil springs and Alsthom links, while the secondary suspension used Flexicoil springs and Koni dampers, specially designed for traction purposes; this new suspension system was used to control primary and secondary vertical movement, lateral movement and bogie yaw. Traction and braking forces were transmitted between body and bogie via two laminated rubber and

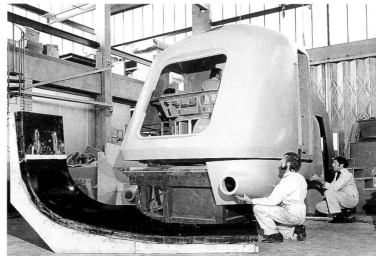

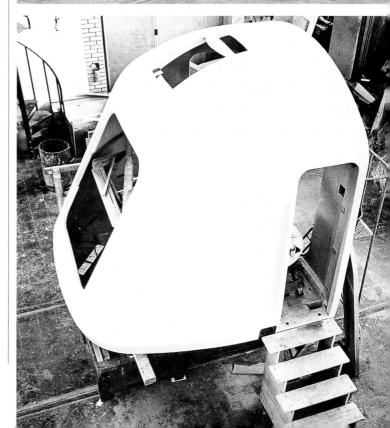

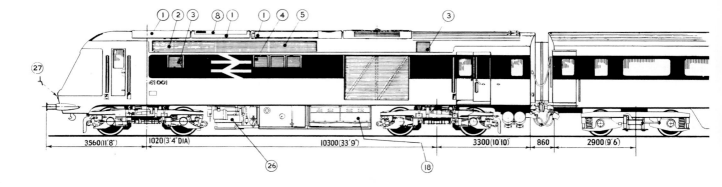

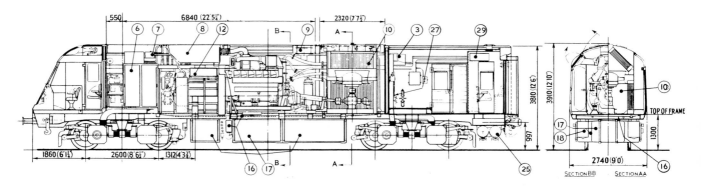

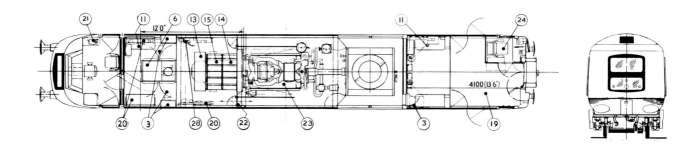

Class 252 motor coach

1. Translucent roof
2. Filtered air vent for interior and electric machines
3. Air for ventilating traction motors
4. Air for ventilating engine compartment
5. Filtered air for engine combustion
6. Electric equipment cubicle
7. Resistance unit and short-circuiter
8. Silencer
9. Engine room ventilating fan
10. Radiator group
11. Flexicoil spring boxes
12. Train supply and auxiliary rectifiers
13. Exciter and traction rectifier
14. Train supply and auxiliary alternators
15. Traction alternator

16. Spillage tray and collecting tank
17. Fuel tank 4,546 litres (1,000 gallons) capacity
18. Batteries
19. Luggage accommodation (1-ton capacity)
20. Pneumatic and miscellaneous equipment
21. Fire equipment
22. Clean air compartment partition
23. Paxman Valenta 12RP 200 engine
24. Guard's and auxiliary driving position
25. Main air reservoirs
26. Air compressor
27. Emergency equipment
28. Hydraulic parking brake
29. Audio navigator

steel plate assemblies in the centre well of the bogie frame transom, located in front of and behind the main centre pin.

The Driving Cab

The driving cab was a separate glass-fibre reinforced plastic module, constructed to 50mm thickness, thus affording train crews the best possible protection at maximum speed, where even a piece of flying ballast could cause serious damage. The large single front windscreen was of laminated high-impact-resistant glass, capable of withstanding a 2lb block of steel impacting cornerwise on the screen at up to 300km/h (186mph). The surrounding GRP structure was able to withstand a 4lb missile at 300km/h without penetration.

The interior of the driving cab — fully detailed in the illustration on page 21 — was designed to reduce driver fatigue and provide an enhanced working environment. It was separated from the main body structure by sound insulation and housed its own heating and ventilation system.

The Passenger Stock

From day one of the HSDT project is was announced that a totally new design of passenger coach was to be used. To accommodate more passengers per vehicle, as well as giving an improved ride, it was decided to design what became the Mk3 vehicles at 75ft 4in in length, in place of the previous Mk2 standard length of 66ft. A basic body shell would be used for *all* designations of vehicle, with slightly different window arrangements on catering cars. The body structure was formed of a steel frame to which was attached a welded stressed steel skin. The design of the vehicles, carried out at Derby, used the latest computer-aided systems to optimise the structural design and obtain the best possible strength/weight ratio. Each coach design was based around a 32-ton overall weight. Compared to a Mk2, the longer design gave one extra seating bay (six 1st or eight 2nd Class seats) per vehicle.

The internal layout of the vehicles was based on a full-length seat-fixing rail permitting any configuration of seats to be installed into any body shell. Problems did exist in the use of vehicles 75ft 4in long on

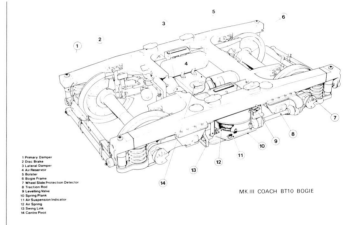

1 Primary Damper
2 Disc Brake
3 Lateral Damper
4 Bolster
5 Air Reservoir
6 Bogie Frame
7 Wheel Slide Protection Detector
8 Traction Rod
9 Levelling Valve
10 Spring Plank
11 Air Suspension Indicator
12 Air Spring
13 Swing Link
14 Centre Pivot

MK III COACH BT10 BOGIE

the UK infrastructure, and the passenger doors at the vehicle ends had to be specially shaped to avoid fouling on curves.

To maintain the air-smooth and streamlined aesthetic appearance of the train, all underside equipment between the bogies was mounted in easy-to-remove modules with either hinged or detachable exterior doors.

The passenger environment was most important in the design of the HSDT and this led to the use of double glazing, full air-conditioning and superior interior sound insulation. A high-quality public address system was incorporated, controlled by either the guard or catering staff. In terms of seating, the latest 'Inter-City 70' design was used, similar to that installed in the final tranche of Mk2 vehicles. With hindsight a number of major initiatives that *could* have been incorporated in terms of passenger comfort were not fitted, including retention toilets and sliding or plug doors; both were available but not incorporated. The decision not to explore the use of automated sliding or plug doors is one that was seriously regretted at a later stage.

In an attempt to show a visible difference in the new HSDT and lift its quality image, it was decided not to apply the then conventional

Left:
By the early summer of 1972 the passenger cars for the HSDT project were emerging from BREL Derby Litchurch Lane works and being sent to the adjacent Railway Technical Centre for various tests, inspections and trials. Vehicle No E12002, a 2nd Class saloon, is seen here. At this stage the coach is far from complete with no interior and some underside modules missing. For some reason the door handles are not fitted and the coach's running number is fitted in the lower window section of the toilet compartment. This coach was later renumbered to 42002, then rebuilt as 'production' train FO vehicle No 41173; it was subsequently rebuilt to TSO No 42356 and is currently working for FGW from Laira. *CJM*

Centre left:
During 1972 a number of tests were operated with the prototype Mk3 vehicles on the Derby-Leicester-Cricklewood route for certification of ride, and many operated prior to the delivery of the HSDT power cars, being marshalled with conventional loco-hauled stock. Sporting the Inter-City name on the near end, the first of the 2nd Class cars, No E12000, technically one of the three 1970-ordered loco-hauled coaches, is seen at Derby on 24 March 1972. Note the large '2' on the coach side adjacent to the door; although clearly indicating 2nd Class, its size was somewhat overpowering and it was removed before the set was tested on the main line. *P. A. Brown*

Lower left:
The two prototype train refreshment vehicles followed the saloon coaches through the assembly process at Derby Litchurch Lane. No 10100, the TRUK full kitchen vehicle with 1st Class seating at the far end, is seen here in the works yard at Derby. Note the opaque windows in the kitchen area; these were provided to give natural light. *CJM collection*

rail blue and grey livery, but to use Pullman colours of pearl grey and blue (the reverse of standard blue/grey), although the designation 'Pullman' was not applied.

For the prototype train a construction order was placed with BREL Derby Litchurch Lane for four Trailer First (TF), four Trailer Second (TS) and two refreshment vehicles, one classified Trailer Restaurant Second Buffet (TRSB) and the other Trailer Restaurant Unclassified Kitchen (TRUK). The plan was to operate the train with three each of the 1st and Second Class saloon vehicles and the two refreshment cars.

The TF vehicles, numbered 11000-11003 and ordered under lot Nos 30833 and 30848, accommodated 48 seats and were set out in the 2+1 seating style; each coach had eight bays of seats, laid out with the seats facing across a fixed table. Each seating bay coincided with a full window position. In the mid-length position a full-height divider or draft screen was positioned on either side. Both vestibule ends housed a toilet on the four-seat side, accessed by a hinged door from the vestibule area. The main vestibule was separated from the passenger saloon by a single-leaf sliding door, operated by foot pressure plates on both sides.

On a drawing dated 4 February 1971 one of the 1st Class coaches is shown as a compartment vehicle, with eight six-seat compartments accessed from a side corridor. However, nothing appears to have come of this plan. The same document also refers to the inclusion of sleeper vehicles and mixed sleeper/day formations. For many months during the design stage it was projected to use the HSDT stock as conventional loco-hauled vehicles if required.

The TS vehicles, numbered 12000-12003 (lot Nos 30832 and 30847) had seats for 72 passengers based on the traditional 2+2 configuration, with most seats grouped around tables. On these vehicles, as the standard body structure was used, the window positions did not match up with the seat positions, causing considerable passenger criticism. Vestibule ends were the same as on the TFs.

The TRUK coach, allocated the number 10100 of lot 30850, was roughly divided half as a seating vehicle and half as a kitchen/pantry with no designated customer serving area. The seating end was laid out in the 1st Class 2+1 style with 24 seats in four bays. The vestibule at the seating end was fitted with a kitchen waste disposal unit in place of a toilet. A sliding door separated the seating and catering areas.

The catering equipment was housed on the two-seat side of the vehicle and from the midway point of the coach there was a staff compartment with lockers, followed by a 13ft 11in-long kitchen. Ovens and fridges were located on the bulkhead adjacent to the staff accommodation, while the food preparation area was along the outside wall, which had two sinks towards the pantry end with two narrow frosted windows above them. Along the corridor side of the kitchen were fish fryers, boiling plates and food preparation areas. A narrow sliding door led from the kitchen into the corridor, and a food servery was also provided, consisting of a square hole with a door. On the bulkhead between the kitchen and pantry was a work surface with storage cupboards below. In the pantry area, a work surface and cupboards were provided adjacent to the kitchen bulkhead. The BR standard Stills hot water unit was housed on the corridor side, while on the outside edge of the vehicle were sinks, fridges and a bottle cooler. A sliding door led from the pantry into the main corridor, and a small serving window was located facing the vestibule end. Passenger external doors at this end were for emergency use only; no external handles were provided, and an emergency egress handle was on the inside. The TRUK was principally designed to provide a full meal service and was marshalled within the 1st Class segment of the train.

The other refreshment vehicle, TRSB, numbered 10000 and ordered under lot No 30849, was again divided into half catering and half seating. The seating section was set out in the 2+2 Second Class style and was designated to be used as normal 2nd Class accommodation. Four bays of seats were provided on either side of a central gangway, with groups of four seats round tables. In the centre of the coach three seats, two on one side and a single on the other, were provided, with their backs facing the mid-length division screen, giving increased gangway width leading to the buffet area. From the middle of the coach a sliding dividing door separated the seating and catering area, with a small staff office and locker room abutting the seating area. Next was the kitchen, which was 10ft 8in long and housed the basic cooking and food preparation area, including the Stills hot water system, sinks, fridge and an oven. Adjacent to the kitchen was a 13ft 7in-long service area, with a bar front facing the corridor side of the coach. This was laid out as a passenger serving area with food display, a counter, sinks and

originally 'taps' for the provision of draught beer. The final 8ft 2in of the coach was a circulating area. Passenger external doors at this end were again for emergency egress or loading of stores.

When the prototype HSDT was built, conventional buffing gear was used, with the inner end of the power cars and trailer vehicles having standard pneumatic buffers.

Testing and Introduction

Production of the two power cars, classified at the time as locomotives of Class 41, numbered 41001 and 41002, was carried out at BREL Crewe. The frame and structural assembly was quickly started, and by mid-1971 the outline of the vehicles could be seen. When structurally complete, both were transferred to the Advanced Vehicles Laboratory at the RTC Derby, the first vehicle arriving at the end of May 1972, where testing and detail finishing work commenced. Assembly of the passenger cars, first the all-saloon vehicles followed by the refreshment cars, commenced at BREL Derby Litchurch Lane in early 1971, with the majority of coaches being finished by June 1972, when for the first time the train was formed up in the carriage works yard. It would have been possible to commence testing within a few weeks, but sadly the railway trade unions, especially the driver's union ASLEF, began a period of industrial action and blacked both this and the gas-turbine-powered APT-E train. In essence the union did not want its members to operate high-speed trains for the standard rate of pay prevailing at the time, and they also argued that for trains travelling in excess of 100mph two fully qualified drivers must be in the cab — quite why has never really been established, as only one could drive the train at a time, and talk and intervention by the other would have been a serious distraction for the person controlling the train.

After the unions inspected the prototype train's cab, a number of objections were made to its design, even though there had been union representation in early design meetings. They did not like the fact that no side windows existed, and while accepting this on the prototype train, demanded that these be a feature of the subsequent production

trains. Also the lack of provision of a proper second driver's seat was not acceptable. Additional windows could not be incorporated into the two prototype vehicles due to the design of the body structure, but an additional seat was provided.

The delay in testing the complete train was not, however, time wasted, as a large amount of on-works testing and trials were conducted; indeed, during the period of industrial action the set did see one or two local trials in the Derby area. The industrial dispute ended in December 1972 with some basic agreements, that drivers would be given three weeks' HSDT training, two drivers would be in the cab when running, and that the maximum 'normal' speed would be 100mph, with dispensation given for higher-speed testing. Dynamic testing commenced on the East Coast main line from January 1973. At this time, as the production of the train's own refreshment cars was slightly late, a Mk1 RKB, No 1524, was

Right:
The full HSDT formation was used on 2 August 1973 to form a press special between King's Cross and Darlington and return, during which passengers were treated to the first runs at 125mph in the UK. The train, led by No 41002, is seen departing from Peterborough returning to Darlington after the run. *P. H. Wells*

Below left:
Dinner is served: the interior of the prototype HSDT TRUK, showing the 1st Class seating layout. The interior of the TRUKs, prototype and production, are always recognisable from FOs by the omission of reading lights and the mid-length sliding door. *CJM collection*

Below right:
The interior of TRSB No 10000, showing the 2nd Class 2+2 seating layout. This posed picture is taken from the coach end looking towards the catering end, with the sliding door in the mid-length position. *CJM collection*

Right:
After testing of the HSDT design concept was complete on the Eastern Region, the prototype train was transferred to the WR to pave the way for the production sets then under construction. On 17 December 1974, just 13 days after arrival from Derby and now carrying its set number, 252001, the HSDT passes Bristol East signalbox on a test run to Old Oak Common. *G. Roy Hounsell*

Left:
Even during the period when the HSDT was officially 'blacked' by the trade unions, some local moves between the Railway Technical Centre and Derby works and depot were made, usually piloted by a loco. On 25 August 1972 power car No 41001, wired for instrumentation, and a TS coach are hauled through Derby station by Class 20 No D8047. *David Canning*

Left:
Formed with two 1st Class saloons at the far end, the TRUK, a Trailer 2nd, the TRSB and two further TSs nearest the camera, No 252001 passes Victoria Park, west of Bristol, on 4 July 1975 with the 13.48 Weston-super-Mare-Paddington. *Barry Nicolle*

Below right:
Literally just a few days after arrival on the Western Region, a 2+3 Class 252 formation is seen pulling away from Swindon with a Swindon-Reading test and staff training run on 12 December 1974. *Terry Flinders*

Above left:
Once in timetabled service on the Western Region a huge number of passengers re-arranged their travelling to be able to sample the train of the future; through a well-controlled media operation based at Paddington, the public were made aware well in advance of what services would be HSDT operated. On 28 July 1975 the full prototype set is seen east of Box Tunnel with the 14.15 Bristol Temple Meads-Paddington. *J. Brennan*

Right:
By the spring of 1976 the prototype HSDT was deployed on some Swansea line services, frequently operating a Bristol-Paddington duty in the morning peak, a return Paddington-Swansea service during the day, and returning to Bristol with a westbound evening peak service. On 12 April 1976 the set storms through the centre road at Reading with the 11.52 Swansea-Paddington express. *David Canning*

modified with B5 bogies and control jumpers and repainted into the train's 'Pullman'-style livery for testing.

It should be recorded that during the early 1970s, when the prototype train was under detail design, it was considered that the use of the high-speed power cars should *not* be restricted to daytime use with passenger train formations, and that at night they could be easily detached and used for overnight sleeping car services, a plan that was furthered some way, especially with Mk3 sleeping cars, on the drawing-board. Another option was to utilise the power cars for high-speed freight operations, with some form of variable gearing; this is mentioned in a number of minutes around 1970-1, but thereafter appears to have fallen from favour. If this plan had been progressed, a pair of power cars would have operated back to back, providing a 4,500hp traction unit, and it was for this reason that conventional drawgear was originally incorporated. This was another reason for the inner-end small cab, which would have been used when attaching the pair together. Another suggestion that went into the melting-pot was to use one power car at either end of high-speed container trains.

In terms of active track testing for the prototype train, trials were first conducted on the East Coast route and for this reason the set was 'officially' taken into Eastern Region stock with 'E' prefixes given to running numbers. The early 1973 trials were not without their problems. Some difficulties were experienced with the power units and turbocharger, but Paxman representatives were on hand to look after these faults. Another problem involved excessive wear of the power cars' disc brakes, about 30% more than calculations had predicted. Adjustments to all these areas were made before main-line high-speed testing commenced.

During the course of test running it was agreed to develop a three-phase train supply, rather than use the originally fitted 800-1,000V ac system; to enable on-train trials, one power car was modified to supply three-phase output, while at the same time authorisation was given for the building of a three-phase train supply test vehicle, which became the generator van (see Chapter 3).

Some of the early and very important high-speed tests were to prove that the train, travelling at a full 125mph, could stop within the same distance as a loco-hauled train travelling at 100mph. On test the HSDT decelerated from 125mph to a dead stop on both wet and dry rails in 1,930yd, compared with 2,220yd for a comparable loco-hauled formation. The HSDT's braking therefore exceeded the design specification, which gave room for any effects of brake blowdown induced by the anti-wheelslip device.

In terms of the passenger vehicles, bogie hunt was experienced during early main-line runs, but this was soon rectified by tweaking the suspension. A more serious problem was a smell from the brake pads, which during a fierce brake application became very hot and gave off a burning smell that was sucked into the train by the air-conditioning system and gave passengers cause for concern. Although this problem was largely rectified by closing the air-conditioning vents when a brake application was made, the problem remained, as when the train stopped the vents reopened and the smell entered the vehicle. Although numerous different designs of brake pad compound were tested, the problem was perpetuated on production sets and is still experienced even today.

The trials on the ECML were conducted under the control of the Director of Mechanical & Electrical Engineering (DM&EE) from Derby in conjunction with BR Research. The set was outbased at Leeds Neville Hill and operated mainly over the northern section of the route. The set moved from Derby to Neville Hill in January 1973 and a month later was moved to Darlington for staff training before hopefully being introduced on a Leeds-Newcastle duty, a slimmed down plan of a 1972 scheme to use the new train on a Leeds-Edinburgh daily service. However, ASLEF went into further dispute

Above:
With BR very supportive of the Stockton & Darlington 150 celebrations in 1975, the prototype set was used on 27 September 1975 to operate a Royal Train taking HRH the Duke of Edinburgh to Eaglescliffe for an event in Preston Park. The fully formed set is seen at Stockton. *Ian Carr*

with the BRB over rates of pay for high-speed drivers, and the Leeds-Newcastle service was abandoned. However, while working from Darlington, a number of high-speed test runs were conducted, with the blessing of ASLEF, mainly over the racing stretch of the ECML north of York. During the course of these tests, three high-speed records were achieved. In June 1973 a short five-vehicle set was formed up for performance testing. On 6 June a top speed of 133mph was attained, at that time the highest speed ever reached on rails in the UK. One week later, on 10 June, the train broke its own previous record and the world speed record for diesel traction, 133mph set by the Germans on 23 June 1939, when it reached 141mph and maintained that speed for just over a mile between Thirsk and Tollerton (17-18 miles north of York). The following day the record fell again when the set hit a maximum of 143mph.

Although many test runs were carried out on the ECML, proving the train in every way, the one thing that the BRB wanted more than anything was to gauge the passenger reaction, but this was not possible until industrial action ceased. After many tests between York and Newcastle, the set was eventually returned to Derby where further extensive static and some dynamic tests were carried out.

On 2 August 1973 the train carried some of its first non-railway passengers when a press demonstration run was operated between King's Cross and Darlington. Passengers included the Rt Hon Richard Marsh, Chairman of the BRB, MPs, press from all over the world, union officials and rail industry guests. In both directions the train was put through its paces, hitting 125mph on the racing section north of York. The trip went very well and the high-speed project received the stamp of approval from all those on board.

By early 1974, with production trains under construction for use on the Western Region out of Paddington, it was decided to transfer the prototype set to Old Oak Common. Soon after, ASLEF and the BRB formulated a manning agreement for high-speed trains and the prototype was used for staff training on the WR in preparation for the delivery of the production sets. The story surrounding the production HST sets is covered in subsequent chapters.

Drinks

Aperitifs
miniature bottles

Martini Vermouth	24p
Dubonnet	41p
Sherry	39p

Spirits
miniature bottles

Whisky, Gin, Rum	✻52p
Vodka	✻52p
Brandy VSOP	46p
Cognac	43p

✻Large measure

Wines
¼ bottle

Red	71p
White	71p
Rosé	71p

A selection of Chocolates, Cigars and Cigarettes is available at usual prices.

Weights and Measures Act 1963.

Whisky, Gin, Rum and Vodka are offered pre-packed in a securely closed container.

All prices include VAT.

Beers

Bass and Worthington	20p
Double Diamond	20p
McEwans Export	20p
Guinness	20p
Mackeson Stout	20p
Whitbreads Pale Ale and Brown Ale	19p
Light and Brown Ales	18p
British Lager	20p
Danish Lager	21p
Cider	large can 21p
Shandy	large can 17p
Newcastle Brown Ale	large can 32p
Younger's Tartan Bitter	large can 30p
McEwans Export	large can 32p

On draught *per ½ pint*

Whitbread Tankard	16p
Heineken Lager	17p

Minerals and Cordials

Mineral Waters	small can 14p
Ginger Beer	bottle 15p
Pepsi Cola	can 15p
Fruit Juices	can 14p
Fruit Squashes	glass 12p
Lime Juice Cordial	glass 12p

Your guide to High Speed catering

Seat service
Buffet bar
Restaurant car

Travellers-Fare

MAIN MEALS FRESHLY COOKED TO ORDER

The choice is yours!

We offer you each item individually priced so that you can order a meal to suit your own taste.

Starters
Soup	14p
Fruit Juices	14p

Main Dish
Bacon (2 rashers)	30p
Sausages (2)	26p
Fried Egg	12p
Steak and Kidney Pie	20p
Pork Chop	65p
Pizza	35p
Ham Salad	77p

Vegetables
Peas	15p
Baked Beans	15p
Tomatoes (each)	9p
Chips	15p
Mixed Salad	22p

Sweets
Fruit Pie (hot or cold)	16p
Yogurt	12p
Cakes and Pastries	from 8p
Cream	portion 3p

Quick snacks and beverages

Toasted Sandwiches
Cheese and Tomato	26p
Ham and Tomato	30p
Bacon	35p
Beefburger	22p
Cheeseburger	33p
Eggburger	34p
Pickle	portion 6p

Sandwiches
Ham and Tomato	14p
Ham	12p
Cheese and Tomato	12p
Cheese	10p
Egg	9p

per ½ round

Sundries
Pork Pie	18p
Sausage Roll	10p
Cheese and Biscuit Snack Pack	12p
Biscuits	7p
Crisps	5p
Fruit Pie	16p
Fruit Cake	8p
Preserves and Honey	6p

Beverages
Tea	per cup 8p
Coffee – black	per cup 11p
Coffee – with cream	per cup 14p
Milk	per glass 8p

Seat Service
To help make your journey even more enjoyable, our staff will shortly be coming your way with a selection of drinks and cold snacks.

Buffet Bar
If you feel like something more substantial and more exciting, look for the tariff of toasted sandwiches, drinks and hot and cold snacks and main meals which are available in the Buffet Bar.

Restaurant Car
If you prefer to be pampered and waited on, the Restaurant Car is available for the service of full meals – Breakfast, Morning Coffee, Luncheon, Afternoon Tea and High Tea or Dinner. The Chief Steward will call you to the Restaurant Car at the appropriate times.

During its period at Derby in May 1974, when a major 100,000-mile overhaul was carried out, it was decided that the original locomotive and coach classification of the HSDT would be dropped and the set officially reclassified as a multiple-unit, allocated the numeric TOPS identity 252 and set No 001, therefore becoming No 252001. At the same time the trailer coaches were renumbered from hauled stock to a new HSDT 4xxxx series, and the power cars were reclassified from 41xxx to 43xxx. Details of the renumbering are shown in the Appendices. Also in early 1974 two of the original prototype vehicles, TF No 11001 and TS No 12001, were taken out of the set, returned to Derby and stripped before being transferred to BREL Wolverton and rebuilt as Royal Train vehicles Nos 2903 and 2904 respectively (see Chapter 4).

While undergoing its classified overhaul, the bogies below power car No 43001 were modified with damping and suspension of the design to be installed under the production power cars; from then on the two power cars could be recognised by looking at the bogies. The fitting of the 3-phase alternator to one power car was also made at this time.

Set No 252001 was transferred to Old Oak Common from 4 December 1974 and immediately commenced driver and fitter training. This advanced quickly and after route clearance the set was allowed to enter passenger service from 5 May 1975. At first the set was slotted into existing loco-hauled schedules, operating to a maximum speed of 100mph. The first passenger services to be HSDT-operated were the 07.45 Bristol Parkway-Paddington, 10.15 Paddington-Weston-super-Mare, 13.48 Weston-super-Mare-Paddington and 16.45 Paddington-Bristol Temple Meads, before the set retired to St Philips Marsh depot overnight. This introduction was an outstanding success; the reaction of the public was overwhelming

Above:
The menu as given out on the first HSDT timetabled passenger service on 5 May 1975, operated by Travellers-Fare, then the BR catering arm, and specially prepared for HST trains. The prices are somewhat interesting if compared with those for on-board services today — a special note should be made of the draught beer at just 16p for a half pint.

and a huge number of passengers changed their travel arrangements to take part in what has become a major episode of railway history. I was fortunate to be on one of those historic passenger runs on 5 May, and the impressions of the 10.15 Paddington departure are still quite vivid in my mind; after years of following and travelling behind diesel-hydraulic locomotives, a new era of rail travel was with us: quiet, clean and quite luxurious when compared with the then ageing fleet of vacuum-brake-fitted Mk1s on many WR services. No one at that time could possibly have foreseen what effect the HSDT would have on the UK rail system over the following 26 years.

On the Western Region, it was usual for power car 43000 to be at the Bristol end of formations and 43001 at the London end.

For the launch of the set on the Bristol Parkway-Paddington route a full breakfast service was offered to 1st Class travellers, with a potential of serving up to 120 meals on a single journey. At this time the two catering vehicles were coupled within the 1st and 2nd Class sections. A copy of the original menu card given out on the first day of public service is reproduced in the accompanying illustration (*left*).

In August 1975, when the UK rail industry was celebrating its 150th anniversary, the prototype HSDT was requested to take part in the cavalcade of locomotives and trains between Shildon and Heighington on 31 August. This it did, bringing up the rear of probably the most impressive line-up of locomotives ever seen in the world, led by the replica of *Locomotion*. Interestingly, Royal Mail produced a set of stamps to commemorate the 150th anniversary of rail transport, and the 12p stamp featured a painting of a production HST power car, showing the proposed yellow and black livery.

After several weeks of trouble-free running on the London-Bristol route, mainly working on weekdays with maintenance and testing carried out at weekends, on some occasions the set was taken out of service on weekdays and replaced by a loco-hauled set, but this was mainly for special testing or training. No 252001 worked to South Wales for the first time on 5 November 1975, when its diagram was altered to include the 09.00 Paddington-Swansea, 12.52 Swansea-Paddington, 16.45 Paddington-Bristol Temple Meads and 19.15 Bristol Temple Meads-Paddington, being stabled overnight at Old Oak Common.

No 252001 continued to operate on WR passenger services,

mainly on the Paddington-Bristol corridor, until October 1976, when it was taken out of service and returned to Derby, as by this time the production HSTs were coming on stream. After a period in store at the RTC, then Derby Carriage Works, the trailer vehicles

Above:
With its 2+7 formation, the sole member of Class 252 hurries through Corsham on 20 May 1975 with the 13.45 Bristol Temple Meads-Paddington. Note the three lights (two marker and one central headlight) on the front end. *John Cooper-Smith*

Left:
The climax of the Stockton & Darlington celebrations in August 1975 came over the August Bank Holiday weekend, when a cavalcade of traction operated and a display of steam, diesel and electric locomotives was held at the then BREL works at Shildon. One of the star attractions alongside its older brothers and sisters was the full prototype HSDT set, showing the world that at least at that time Britain's rail engineering still reigned supreme. No 252001 is seen in Shildon Works yard. *M. Hall*

found new leases of life; the two buffet cars entered departmental service at the RTC and were hugely rebuilt. As for the saloon stock, TF No 41000 also passed into departmental service, while Nos 41001 and 41002 were rebuilt by BREL Derby as production IC125 vehicles and are now in traffic as vehicles 41170 and 42357 respectively. TS cars Nos 42000/01/02 were also rebuilt as production TSs and are now numbers 42355/53/56.

The power cars were used for a number of further high-speed tests on the main line, especially the West Coast main line, involving the power cars of pre-series electric Advanced Passenger Trains (APTs). No 43000 (the original power car No 41001) became departmental No ADB975814 and No 43001 (the original 41002) became departmental No ADB975813. Eventually the former was handed over to the National Railway Museum at York in the summer of 1985, while the latter was retained at RTC Derby for some time and used as a dead load vehicle among other things. Eventually it was sold for scrap and broken up by Booth-Roe Metals in Rotherham in December 1990. The vehicle at the NRM has been displayed at the York site, stored at various locations and shown at a number of private locations.

A Poor Man's HST

The development of so-called high-speed running using two locomotives, one at either end of a rake of hauled passenger cars, took an interesting turn in 1971 when, as part of the Scottish Region's development of the prestige Edinburgh-Glasgow route, a new push-pull service was launched between the two cities formed of modern air-braked Mk2 coaches with a Class 27 at either end. The two locomotives operated together by means of multiple control blue star cables running through the coaches.

Reliability was a serious problem, but the ingenious use of a push-pull system created space for the Scottish Region to plan a more robust high-speed service using Class 47s and driving control vehicles at the remote end.

Many people deemed the push-pull Class 27 consist a 'poor man's HST', and in reality that is just what it was.

Above left:
The prototype HSDT set was taken out of passenger service on the Western Region in October 1976 and returned with its trailer vehicles to RTC Derby. The power cars were given classified overhauls at BREL Derby loco works and commenced a period of development running for BR Research and the Derby-based M&EE function, powering a number of test trains, some involving cab equipment, others the development of APT vehicles. Here, on 17 August 1978, power car No W43000 arrives at Derby with a single Mk2 coach. *J. A. Phillips*

Above right:
In the period immediately prior to their return to Derby from the Western Region, the prototype HSDT power cars were used for a number of development runs with Derby-based DM&EE and Research test cars. On 24 June 1976 power car No W43001 is seen at Swindon with DM&EE Mk2 Test Car 6 No ADB975290. *Brian Morrison*

Left:
Looking very tatty and not long before it was finally disposed of, Departmental No ADB975813 is seen in the yard at RTC Derby on 19 May 1988 just before a new design of obstacle deflector was fitted and tests carried out on the Old Dalby test track, where the power car was propelled into different obstructions, including a pile of animal bones to simulate hitting an animal on the line. *CJM*

3. The Production Trains and Deployment

Before delivery and operation of the prototype train, the BRB had gone public that a squadron build of High Speed Diesel Trains (HSDTs) would be introduced. The first area to benefit from their introduction at up to 125mph would be on the Western Region, covering routes from Paddington to Bristol and South Wales. At this stage, considering that much of the BRB's futuristic plans for high-speed rail travel in the UK was still with an electrically powered Advanced Passenger Train, it is quite surprising that in 1972 it was announced that the *proposed* fleet of HSDTs would be 161 sets, made up of:

27 sets for Western Region, Paddington-Bristol/Swansea route
42 sets for Eastern/Scottish Region, ECML operations
16 sets for Great Western, Paddington-Paignton/Plymouth/Penzance route
10 sets for Midland Region St Pancras-Sheffield/Nottingham route
36 sets for North East-South West Cross Country routes
30 sets for 'other routes' such as Trans-Pennine and Edinburgh-Glasgow

At the time of the announcement both the BRB and the Government quoted that between 30 and 40 sets would be built per year, seeing a total modernisation of the UK trunk rail routes in around five years. The above planned fleet catered for the 42 ECML sets to be 'displaced' in around six years by electric Advanced Passenger Trains, together with huge expansion to the electric railway and future APTs for many routes.

After the first authorisation was given for the 27 Western Region sets in September 1972, progressive orders were agreed by the Government until a final order for four extra ECML sets was sanctioned in January 1980, and 18 additional 'make-up' trailers, authorised the same year, became the final 'new' deliveries in mid-1982.

Sadly the BRB's desire and the original Government agreement for 161 trains was quickly reduced, with an eventual build programme of just 95 full train sets. At this point it is worth looking at each of the groups of the new build to understand their use and deployment. The then Department of Transport (DTp) gave the Production IC125 build authorisation in five separate 'agreements' following a 'special submission' for each by the BRB.

The five submission groups were:

1 WR Paddington-Bristol and South Wales
2 ER/ScR East Coast main line
3 WR Paddington-West of England
4 North East-South West Cross Country
5 ER/ScR East Coast main line, four additional sets

While the prototype train was under advanced construction, engineers at Derby were progressing the design of the production train. In the period after completion of the prototype's power cars and trailer vehicles, much was learned about their design and construction, and while the basic system was sound, a number of revisions would be needed for the mass production trains. The most significant change

Above:
Once the orders for the production HST power cars had been placed, BREL awarded the entire contract to its Crewe Works, where the main fabrication and assembly facility was turned over to power car production. In this view, looking down the two-line main fitting-out bay, 13 cars are under assembly. *BREL*

Below:
The very last power car ordered, No 43198, is seen in its skeleton form in the main construction bay on 6 April 1982, having just arrived from the fabrication area and prior to the bodyside skin being applied. *CJM*

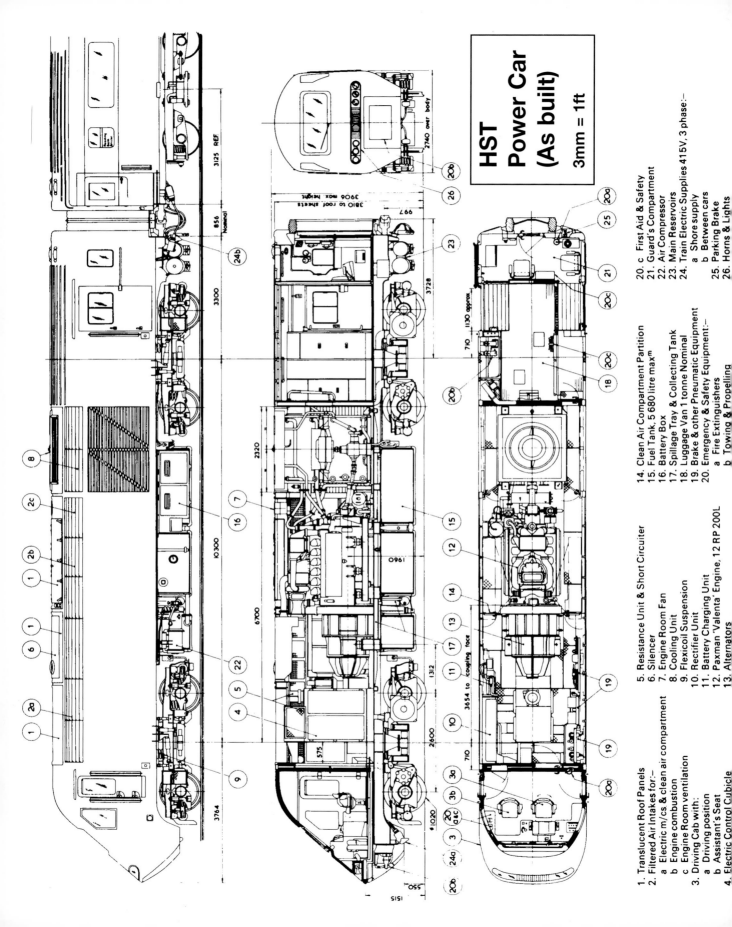

HST Power Car (As built)

3mm = 1ft

1. Translucent Roof Panels
2. Filtered Air Intakes for:-
   a Electric m/cs & clean air compartment
   b Engine combustion
   c Engine Room ventilation
3. Driving Cab with:
   a Driving position
   b Assistant's Seat
4. Electric Control Cubicle
5. Resistance Unit & Short Circuiter
6. Silencer
7. Engine Room Fan
8. Cooling Unit
9. Flexicoil Suspension
10. Rectifier Unit
11. Battery Charging Unit
12. Paxman 'Valenta' Engine, 12 RP 200L
13. Alternators
14. Clean Air Compartment Partition
15. Fuel Tank, 5 680 litre maxᵐ
16. Battery Box
17. Spillage Tray & Collecting Tank
18. Luggage Van 1 tonne Nominal
19. Brake & other Pneumatic Equipment
20. Emergency & Safety Equipment:-
    a Fire Extinguishers
    b Towing & Propelling
    c First Aid & Safety
21. Guard's Compartment
22. Air Compressor
23. Main Reservoirs
24. Train Electric Supplies 415V, 3 phase:-
    a Shore supply
    b Between cars
25. Parking Brake
26. Horns & Lights

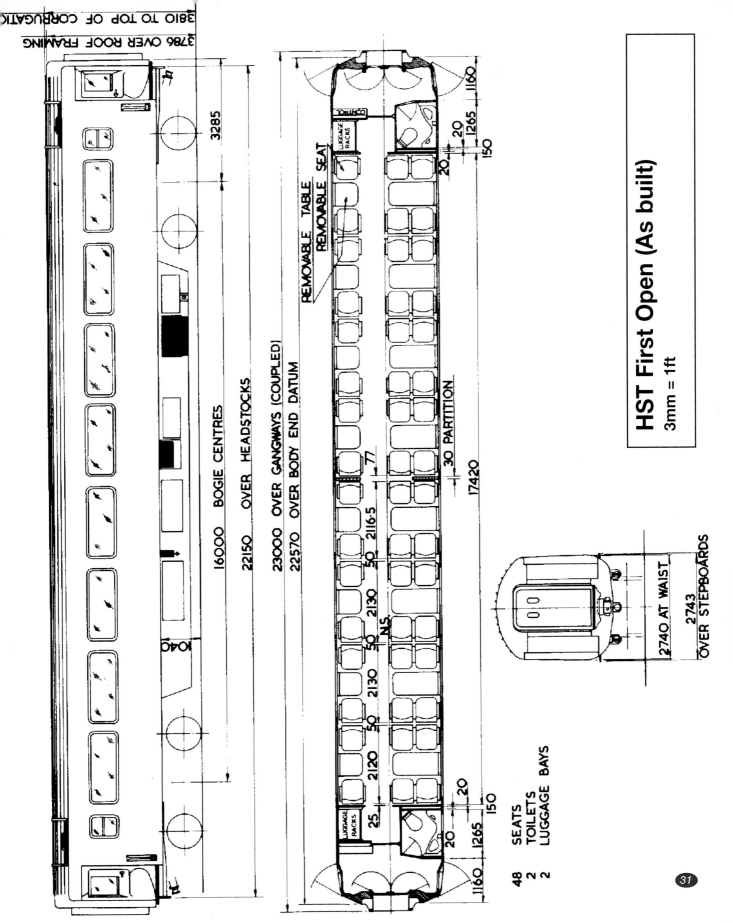

HST First Open (As built)

3mm = 1ft

48 SEATS
2 TOILETS
2 LUGGAGE BAYS

3786 OVER ROOF FRAMING
3810 TO TOP OF CORRUGATIC

3285

16000 BOGIE CENTRES
22150 OVER HEADSTOCKS
23000 OVER GANGWAYS (COUPLED)
22570 OVER BODY END DATUM

1040

REMOVABLE TABLE
REMOVABLE SEAT

LUGGAGE RACKS

TOILET

30 PARTITION

17420

2116·5
2130
2130
2120

50
N·S
50
50
25
77

20
1265
1160
150
20

2740 AT WAIST
2743 OVER STEPBOARDS

31

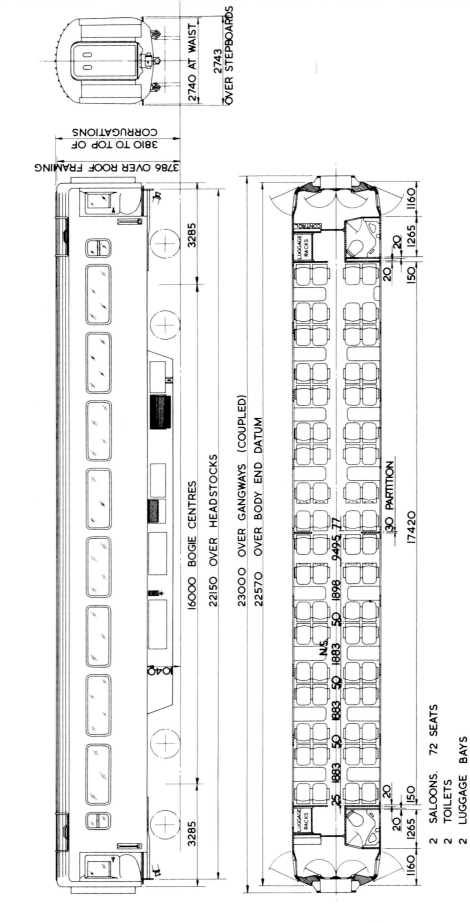

2740 AT WAIST
2743 OVER STEPBOARDS

3810 TO TOP OF CORRUGATIONS
3786 OVER ROOF FRAMING

3285
3285

16000 BOGIE CENTRES
22150 OVER HEADSTOCKS
23000 OVER GANGWAYS (COUPLED)
22570 OVER BODY END DATUM

1040

CONTROL
LUGGAGE RACKS
LUGGAGE RACKS

1160
1265
150
20
20

30 PARTITION
17420

949.5
77
1898
50
1883
N.S.
50
1883
50
1883
50
1883
25

20
1265
150
20
20

1160

HST Trailer Second Open (As built)
3mm = 1ft

2 SALOONS. 72 SEATS
2 TOILETS
2 LUGGAGE BAYS

32

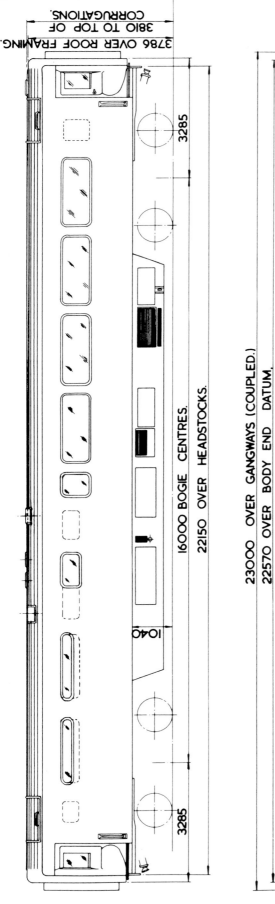

HST Trailer Restaurant
Second Buffet (As built)
3mm = 1ft

1 SALOON 35 SEATS.
1 STAFF COMPT.
1 KITCHEN. 1 SERVICE AREA.

3786 OVER ROOF FRAMING.
3810 TO TOP OF CORRUGATIONS.

3285

3285

16000 BOGIE CENTRES.

22150 OVER HEADSTOCKS.

1040

23000 OVER GANGWAYS (COUPLED.)

22570 OVER BODY END DATUM.

CONTROL

LUGGAGE

WASTE DISPOSAL UNIT

20
20
1265
1160
150

N.S.

8700 SALOON.

CUPBOARD

STAFF COMPT.

LOCKERS

BAIN MARIE

OVEN

REFRIG UNDER

FRYER GRIDDLE

KITCHEN

STILLS UNIT

SINK

1010
20
30
80

3382

CUPBOARD

DRAWER

CUPBOARD

KEG BEER CUPBOARD

SINKS

SERVICE AREA

BOTTLE COOLING SHELVES

GLASS FRONT REFRIG.

STORAGE

4198

SHELF

CUPBOARD UNDER SHELF

170

2575

EMERGENCY DOOR

EMERGENCY DOOR

SHELF

SHELF

33

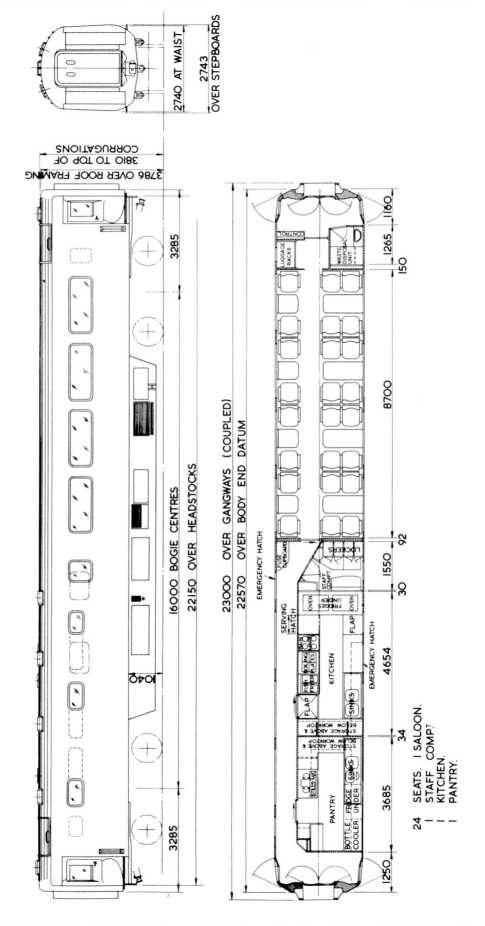

**HST Trailer Restaurant
Unclassified Kitchen (As built)**
3mm = 1ft

2740 AT WAIST
2743 OVER STEPBOARDS

3786 OVER ROOF FRAMING
3810 TO TOP OF CORRUGATIONS

3285
16000 BOGIE CENTRES
22150 OVER HEADSTOCKS
3285
1040

23000 OVER GANGWAYS (COUPLED)
22570 OVER BODY END DATUM
EMERGENCY HATCH

1160
1265
150

8700

92
1550
30
4654
34
3685
1250

CONTROL
LUGGAGE RACKS
WASTE DISPOSAL UNIT
LOCKERS
FUSE CUPBOARD
STAFF COMPT.
OVEN
FRIDGES UNDER
OVEN
SERVING HATCH
BAIN MARIE
BOILING PLATES
FISH FRYER
KITCHEN
FLAP
FLAP
EMERGENCY HATCH
SINKS
FLAP
STORAGE ABOVE & BELOW WORKTOP
STORAGE ABOVE & BELOW WORKTOP
SINKS
STILLS W.H.
PANTRY
BOTTLE COOLER
FRIDGE UNDER
SINKS

24 SEATS. 1 SALOON.
 1 STAFF COMPT.
 1 KITCHEN.
 1 PANTRY.

34

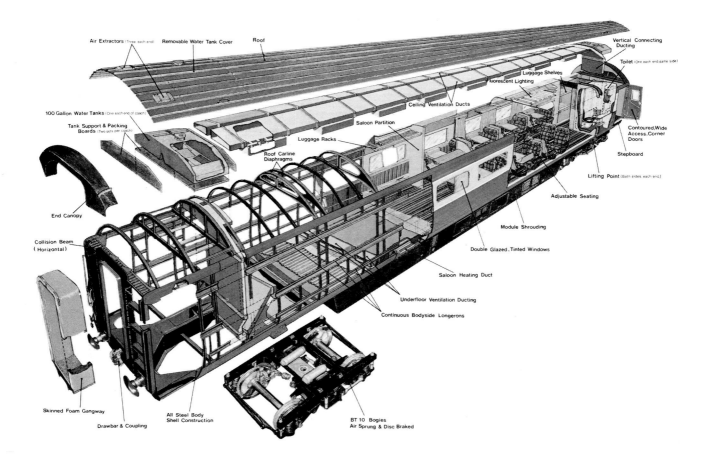

Air Extractors (Three each end) · Removable Water Tank Cover · Roof · Vertical Connecting Ducting · Toilet (One each end,same side) · Luggage Shelves · Fluorescent Lighting · Ceiling Ventilation Ducts · Contoured,Wide Access,Corner Doors · 100 Gallon Water Tanks (One each end of coach) · Saloon Partition · Stepboard · Tank Support & Packing Boards (Two sets per coach) · Luggage Racks · Lifting Point (Both sides, each end) · Roof Carline Diaphragms · Adjustable Seating · End Canopy · Module Shrouding · Collision Beam (Horizontal) · Double Glazed, Tinted Windows · Saloon Heating Duct · Underfloor Ventilation Ducting · Continuous Bodyside Longerons · Skinned Foam Gangway · All Steel Body Shell Construction · Drawbar & Coupling · BT 10 Bogies Air Sprung & Disc Braked

would be in the design of the power cars, where, following the industrial action by the driver's union ASLEF, it was agreed that a two-position driving cab would be featured on subsequent vehicles and that cab-side windows would be incorporated.

The exterior design of the vehicle was refined by industrial designer Kenneth Grange, who devised what became an icon of the 20th century. The HST power car's streamlined appearance has made it almost timeless, while generating the appearance of speed, efficiency and, above all, grandeur. While retaining the raked-back end, the vehicle was largely different. Gone were the buffers and marker lights in the lower windscreen panel — the new styling was far more streamlined, with all nose-end connections hidden under a hinged lower body panel. Coupling from the 'sharp' end was now to be by a removable bar coupling. Head/marker and tail lights were now housed in two clusters, one on either side just above the base of the body by the side of the ribbed horn grille. The horns were repositioned from the roof line to reduce in-cab noise.

The redesign of the driving cab, by placing the secondman's or second driver's seat adjacent to the driver on the right-hand side of the cab, required a large rectangular window, thus providing both seats with a good view of the line ahead. The provision of side non-opening windows in the main cab area gave a major improvement in light distribution and reduced the claustrophobic atmosphere of the prototype vehicle. However, on a negative point, it eliminated the installation of instrumentation on the cab side walls. On the prototype no cab air-conditioning was installed, although requested by drivers. On the redesigned production cars, with some 30% more glass, the extra heat generated by solar gain dictated the installation of air-conditioning from the drawing-board.

The Grange-redesigned front end was very smooth and elegant with the removal of the buffing equipment. The new design saw a central hinged door, which pivoted upwards to reveal a retractable coupling 'eye' on to which a lightweight coupling bar was attached, which then connected via a hinged joint to a split-end that hooked over a standard draw-hook, being retained in position by a pin. Air pipes (main reservoir and brake pipe) and a 415V train supply socket were also housed under the front plate.

A re-designed bogie, given the classification BP16, was also used; although incorporating many features of the prototype design, the production version was a more robust structure and had revisions to the damping to improve ride.

The interior of the production power car followed largely that of the prototype vehicle (details are given in Chapter 2), although the driving area was redesigned as mentioned above. The radiator (cooler) group was slightly repositioned towards the power unit and the recessed floor on the prototype was replaced with a flat and far safer area. The movement of the radiator unit allowed an extra 12in for the guard's van office and luggage area. By the time the production vehicles were on the drawing-board any plans to have a slab end driving position had gone, and this area was also included in the van space. By this time a decision had been taken that the production trains would be used in semi-permanently formed 'sets', and there were

Left, centre & bottom:
Three views showing the original livery and equipment layout for HST Mk3 passenger vehicles. The top view shows FO No W41020 from the single-seat side, the middle illustration is of TSO No W42027, while the bottom picture is of original-design TRUB No W40337 shown from the seating end. All three views give a clear illustration of the equipment frame layout between the bogies, which is largely different on the refreshment vehicle to cater for the different needs of this coach design. *All CJM*

Upper right:
The cab modules of the HST power cars were formed as a separate section, fully manufactured with front valance and side skirt before being split down for fitting on to the protruding section of the main underframe. This view shows an almost complete cab section in terms of its fibreglass construction, awaiting early fitting out. *BREL*

Lower right:
Concurrent with the power car construction at Crewe, the trailer vehicles were being assembled on a multi-line facility at Derby Litchurch Lane, where upwards of 40 vehicles were under construction at the same time. In unpainted condition, six vehicles are seen awaiting their turn through the paint shop prior to detail fitting out. The fibreglass sections of the coaches are easily recognisable, being finished in white. *CJM*

no plans to remove power cars from trailer sets. As will be discussed later, the guard's accommodation at the inner end of the power car was to be very short-lived, as following intervention by the trade union a new design of passenger coach — the TGS — was introduced with a small guard's office and luggage area. The inclusion of full guard's facilities in HST power cars was made on Nos 43002-152, which were officially classified DMB; Nos 43153-198 were fitted with the luggage space but no guard's controls and were classified DM. The equipment was progressively removed from Nos 43002-152 after 1986. Vehicles fitted with guard's facilities had a side window between the luggage van door and vehicle end, as well as in the coach end. Following removal of the guard's facility these windows have been

progressively plated over, but even in 2001 a number still exist, especially on those operated by Virgin Trains.

Although on a letter of intent from September 1972, the first production IC125 order for 27 WR sets was actually signed by the BRB and BREL in April 1974. As with the prototype sets, the power cars would come from Crewe Works and the passenger stock from Derby Litchurch Lane. These sets, consisting of two power cars and seven trailers, were destined for the Western Region for use between Paddington and Bristol/Weston-super-Mare/Cardiff and Swansea. The passenger consist was originally planned as two FOs at the London end, a TRUK (able to provide a cooked food service for 1st Class passengers), a TSO, a TRSB (to provide a refreshment service for 2nd Class), and two further TSOs.

Before we look at the types of vehicle used in the production HST, a quick review of the construction is required. The fabrication of the HST trailer vehicles was based on a jig-assembly principle, consisting of a floor pan, sides, end and roof section, pre-formed from steel and married together in a vehicle-length welding jig. The coach design is such that all parts share a burden of the load — there is no separate underframe, the outside longitudinals forming the lower part of the body, with a corrugated steel floor fitting the space between the solebars. A light top frame supports a wooden floor.

The exterior panels of the coaches are of a stressed skin, which again shares load-bearing, the skin assembly being welded to the vehicle skeleton frame. Coach doors are fabricated in a mould using glass-reinforced polyester. At the vehicle ends a framework formed of steel beams and welded together assists in providing strength and rigidity. Traction and buffing forces are taken by castings in the centre of the drawbar into which the buck-eye couplers are attached.

The HST trailer coaches are basically loco-hauled Mk3s, with on-board power systems supplied by a three-phase train line supply, usually fed by one power car. Each coach has an air-conditioning unit powered directly from the three-phase. Train lighting uses a single phase of the train power line, rectified to 110V dc.

All vehicles are mounted on BT10 bogies, with secondary suspension provided by air springs. On the primary suspension (axle-bogie) the axleboxes are carried by arms pivoted at the inner end from the bogie frame with coil springs. The secondary suspension (bogie-body) uses air springs, which are fitted with a levelling device to maintain the correct height of the vehicle floor from track height whatever the internal load.

Each axle has individual disc brakes, and a linkage from the levelling device of the air suspension controls the brake pressure via a

load-proportional valve, ensuring that whatever the vehicle load, it will have sufficient brake pressure available without imposing undue speed retardation stress on other vehicles in the formation.

In common with the prototype train, the production FO and TSO vehicles were all based on a common structural design. The TS coaches seated 72 in the 2+2 configuration, and the seats were again laid out in bays of four around a fixed-position table, except in the middle of the coach where two rows of seats were located adjacent to the mid-vehicle screen facing the outer end. At one end of the coach, the fixed table was omitted to allow for disabled (wheelchair) access.

It is quite surprising that when the design for the production vehicles was finalised, hinged external doors were still used, one mounted at the end of each side by the corner post. By the time these vehicles were authorised various designs of sliding and folding plug doors were available, but these were not installed, and have not been retro-fitted. The door vestibules at each end fed a passenger circulating

area, with a toilet as on the prototype. The main passenger saloon was divided from the vestibule end by a sliding door controlled by pressure mats. Occupying saloon space opposite the toilet compartment was a luggage stack. Slight detail differences did exist between the prototype and production vehicles, including changes to the lighting and the installation of a glazed panel in the mid-length screen. Externally the most significant change was the omission of conventional side buffers, with all stresses being transmitted by the centre buck-eye coupling and rubbing plate. Another surprise omission was controlled emission toilets (CET), which rather than discharge waste on to the track store all toilet waste and used water for controlled disposal by suction emptying at a depot.

The production TF vehicles were again in keeping with the prototype, having 48 seats in the 2+1 configuration. All seats had a fixed table, a luggage stack was provided at the coach ends on the single-seat side, and toilets at each end were accessed from the vestibule on the two-seat side. To provide easy access for disabled travellers, one of the tables at one end on the single-seat side was easily removable, while the seat backing on to the luggage stack could be unclipped and stowed in the rack area to provide space for a wheelchair.

During an early stage in construction it was announced that the production trains would be classified Class 253 for sets allocated to the Western Region and Class 254 for those allocated to the Eastern and Scottish Regions, mainly to identify different train formations and an original consideration for higher-power Eastern/Scottish sets. Power cars would be numbered in the 43xxx series, with trailer vehicles also following on from the prototype sets, in the 4xxxx series.

Construction of the first production train progressed slightly slower than planned, and the rather optimistic launch date of autumn 1974 slipped, mainly due to the miners' strike and general financial cutbacks. The first power car, No W43002, was completed at BREL Crewe Works during October 1975, having been shown off for the first time at the works Open Day on 20 September in a painted but untested state; at this time it had a wide black band around the top section of the body in place of the finally adopted blue, although the yellow base colour remained the same. Details of the livery are found in Chapter 11. The second power car (No W43003) was soon finished, but then underwent a major period of on-works testing as well as 'light power car' runs in and around the Crewe/Chester area. In February 1976 both power cars were transferred to Derby, where they were married up with the Litchurch Lane-built passenger vehicles. A significant amount of sequence testing was then carried out to prove the integrity of the multiple operating system. Once static and local testing was complete, the fully marshalled set — formed of PC, TF, TF, TRUK, TS, TRSB, TS, TS, PC — was allocated to Leeds Neville Hill for type testing over the East Coast main line between Leeds and Newcastle.

The first production train to be transferred to the Western Region was the pioneer set No 253001 in April 1976, and this was soon joined by other fully commissioned sets, allowing a major training programme to get under way from both Old Oak Common and Bristol depots. By this time the prototype set was hard at work, showing the public what high-speed rail travel was all about. By August 1976 several production sets were fully commissioned with a handful authorised for passenger service, operating principally on the London-Bristol route at a top speed of 100mph, thus slotting in with the standard timetable.

Passengers did not have to wait long to be able to sample UK high-speed running at 125mph on selected sections of the Western Region main line, as testing, track infrastructure and staff training were

Upper right:
Following completion of assembly at BREL Crewe, each power car was given a main-line test; it was usually arranged to test two at a time coupled back-to-back, with the route between Crewe and Shrewsbury being a favourite testing run. On 15 April 1976 undercoat-liveried Nos 43015/013 are seen passing through Shrewsbury. Testing was usually carried out prior to painting, but to conform with operating regulations the running numbers were always applied in white on the light green bodysides. *I. Dewar*

Centre right:
If only one power car was to be tested, which happened occasionally in the early days of building, some unusual formations could be recorded. This photograph, taken on 5 August 1976, shows power car No 43025 hooked up to a Mk1 sleeper with 'Peak' Class 46 No 46025 at the rear near Willaston, close to Nantwich, between Shrewsbury and Crewe. *J. Winkle*

Below:
Prior to the delivery of many production power cars, a few active main-line tests with production Mk3 trailers were undertaken on the Western Region main line, powered by the prototype power cars. One such working, which involved bogie ride testing, is seen here passing Moreton Cutting near Didcot on 4 June 1976. *Alan Wells*

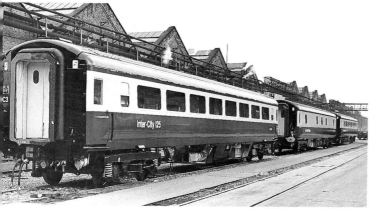

sufficiently advanced to allow 125mph timetabled operation from 4 October 1976. This date is very significant in terms of rail travel, not only in the UK but also throughout the world, for this was the first 125mph diesel-powered passenger service anywhere in the world. It came just 74 months after agreement to develop UK high-speed traction — a quite outstanding achievement when everything is taken into account.

From that date 11 trains each way on the Paddington-Swansea route and five each way on the Paddington-Bristol line were authorised for 125mph running. The fastest schedule covered the Paddington-Bristol Parkway section in just 73min, at an average speed of 92mph.

Top left:
With its emergency coupling arm attached, power car No 43018 stands in the yard at BREL Crewe on 11 April 1976 awaiting fitting of its front lamp screens, further testing and a visit to the paint shop before delivery to the Western Region. *C. N. Rayner*

Top right:
With the unique Class 47/6 No 47601 on the left, HST power car No 43006 stands by the Crewe Works traverser on 11 April 1976. The main work at Crewe throughout 1976 was the production of power cars to enable a timetabled introduction on the Paddington-Bristol/Cardiff route later that year. *C. N. Rayner*

Above left:
In company with a Mk3 sleeper vehicle for the Eastern Region, HST TSO passenger vehicle No 42316 stands in the works yard at Derby Litchurch Lane on 2 April 1982. This coach was delivered to the Western Region for Cross Country operations. Note that part of the underframe equipment is still to be fitted. *CJM*

Centre left:
A view of the Derby Litchurch Lane paint shop at the height of HST trailer car production. Once painted, a significant amount of fitting work was undertaken in the paint area before coaches went to the main construction bay. In many cases, due to late delivery of bogies, vehicles were almost completed while mounted on temporary or accommodation bogies. *CJM*

Lower left:
Although technically the first Western Region set, main-line test running for the original production set, No 253001, was undertaken on the Eastern Region. Based at Leeds Neville Hill, the set operated Leeds-York-Newcastle in March/April 1976. Seen departing from York on 22 March 1976, the set is formed of power cars Nos 43002/03 with six production TSOs coupled between. *M. T. Hemmings*

Right:
Once delivered to the Western Region, a major crew training period on the HSTs had to commence, with each driver having a three-week course on the new traction. During this period some very unusual formations were seen as deliveries from both Crewe and Derby were protracted. On 19 June 1977 a 2+1 formation with power cars 43002/04 and a TSO between them passes Southcote Junction on a Bristol-Old Oak Common via Westbury training run. The line in the foreground is the branch to the long-closed Reading Southern freight yard. *Les Bertram*

However, the full high-speed service was not introduced until October 1977. This was largely due to many technical challenges faced by the WR, as the first HSDT operator, compounded by production difficulties. Of the 27 sets delivered by October 1977, only 20 were rostered for daily use, with seven allocated for maintenance; this provided for an availability figure of just 74%.

Specimen WR Journey Time Savings with 125mph HST Running from 4 October 1976

Route	Loco-hauled Timing	HST Timing	Saving
Paddington-Reading	34min	26min	8min
Paddington-Bristol TM	1hr 47min	1hr 32min	15min
Paddington-Swansea	3hr 22min	2hr 55min	27min
Paddington-Bristol PW	1hr 35min	1hr 13min	22min
Paddington-Cardiff	2hr 16min	1hr 53min	23min
Paddington-Weston-s-Mare	2hr 26min	2hr 3min	23min

As mentioned above, when the original 27 WR sets were ordered the catering provision was perceived as requiring two vehicles, one for 1st and one for 2nd Class patronage. However, in the period surrounding the trains' delivery, these requirements changed, and at the time of delivery alterations to the original plan were being instigated. In terms of human need and financial return, the provision of two refreshment vehicles was obviously not required. Of the original 27 sets, 16 were delivered with both a TRUK and a TRSB, and of these the TRUKs saw *very* little service and only the very early operational sets saw two refreshment vehicles marshalled. The final four TRUKs were delivered to the Eastern Region for use in its first train deliveries, with the remaining seven vehicles of the original order, Nos 40521-27, being cancelled. The catering requirement on the WR was then fulfilled by 10 TRUBs (40300-09) and 18 TRSBs (40001-17). The other original TRSBs, Nos 40018-27, were also transferred to the East Coast.

Prior to the introduction of the HSTs on the WR, another major hurdle had to be overcome — that of driver training. The original HST drivers received basic training, but now that squadron introduction was to be made a defined training course was needed; this was based on three weeks per driver, agreed with ASLEF several years before, and consisted of a diesel conversion course from existing traction. In reality the HST was deemed a new traction type, with drivers having to come to terms with much new equipment, a new driving technique and a far more important role in on-line fault rectification. The fleet driver training was carried out by a team of 30 senior traction inspectors working from Old Oak Common, Bristol and Cardiff. The 15-day course consisted of half classroom/theory work and half practical driving.

The next area to receive HSTs was the East Coast main line. After the relatively easy investment submission by the BRB to the DTp for the 27 Western Region sets, some complacency reigned within the BR Board, which was quite stunned when the original submission for 42 eight-trailer sets was reduced by the DTp accountants to just 32. The grounds for this reduction was the belief that *only* the longer-distance 'fast' services on the ECML would give the necessary financial return on the £31 million investment for higher-speed trains. Although the Eastern Region was disappointed by the revised fleet size, as long as the ER 'racehorses' — the Class 55 'Deltic' 3,300hp locomotives — were to be available, an integrated HST/loco-hauled service could operate. On 24 April 1975 Mr W. O. Reynolds OBE, General Manager of the Eastern Region, told the media that the reduced fleet ordered would *only* be able to cover 'principal services', and that the King's Cross-York, Lincolnshire and Humberside routes would have to continue with 'old' locomotives and hauled stock for several years until investment was forthcoming. One huge problem, which could not be foreseen at the time of the DTp funding, was that when the HSTs were introduced, ECML passengers would wait for travel on a 'new' train, even preferring to stand, while the handful of remaining loco-hauled services would have spare capacity.

The production of the agreed second phase of HST building followed the first through the Crewe/Derby workshops, with 27 sets officially allocated to the Eastern Region, their numbers prefixed by the letter 'E', and five, Nos 254016-020 (43086-095), allocated to Scotland at Edinburgh Craigentinny, carrying the prefix letters 'SC'. The 27 ER/ScR sets were formed (from the London end) of PC, TF, TF, TRUK, TRSB, TS, TS, TS, TS, PC.

The first HST set to go to the Eastern Region, numbered 254001, arrived at Heaton depot, Newcastle, in August 1977, followed by a formal dedication and hand-over at York on 7 September. Right up until construction it had been planned to upgrade the Paxman power units on the ER/ScR Class 254s to 2,500hp, thus providing a total train output of 5,000hp for the slightly longer East Coast sets. However, technical problems with such a modification, compounded by the desire to maintain the *entire* fleet as 'standard', saw the upgrade cancelled.

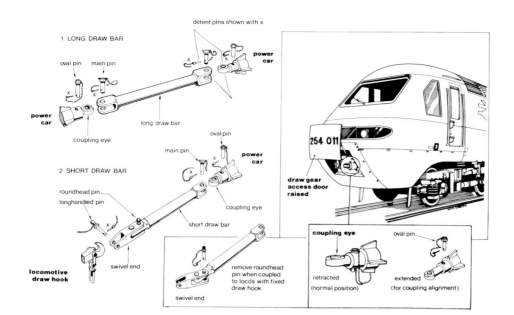

Left:
The emergency coupling components, showing the method of assembly of the bar coupler for the attachment of either two power cars nose-to-nose, or a power car to a locomotive fitted with a normal coupling hook.

Below right:
Although all staff involved in the operation of HSTs go through the emergency coupling procedures as part of their training, frequently when a loco is required to be attached to a power car it becomes a major operation, with the attaching loco having to be positioned exactly in the correct place to allow the emergency coupler to attach. This was the view at Doncaster on 7 September 1980 when a set led by power car No 43093 failed and had to be assisted south by Class 47 No 47292. *Derek Porter*

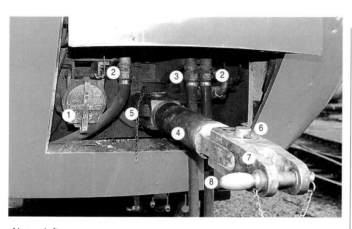

Above left:
An HST power car showing the emergency front connection door open. **1** Three-phase train supply jumper; **2** Main reservoir pipe; **3** Brake pipe; **4** Emergency bar coupler; **5** Power car 'eye' head; **6** Swivel end; **7** Cut-out for loco hook; **8** Long-handled locking pin. *CJM*

The HST introduction on the East Coast was very problematic. Under the original plan it was decided to introduce a mixed HST and 'Deltic'-powered high-speed service. The first HST schedules were due to be launched in May 1978 on the King's Cross-Newcastle/Edinburgh route, followed by full deployment a year later in May 1979. These initial plans were thwarted by late deliveries of stock from BREL, mainly due to late supply of component parts from outside the rail industry. Therefore the Eastern/Scottish HST launch was a phased-in introduction as trains became available in the May 1978-May 1979 period; at the start of this period just eight sets were available.

All 32 trains were on stream by early 1979, and a high-profile launch of the new high-speed Anglo-Scottish service was planned for May. Again the ER and ScR were denied the glory of launching their 'new railway', this time by an accident. While work was being carried out inside Penmanshiel Tunnel on 13 March 1979 as part of the ECML upgrade, a section of the tunnel roof collapsed, sadly killing two civil engineers. The collapse was major and effectively severed the East Coast main line between Berwick and Dunbar. Initially the BRB started to plan an HST-operated service between London and Newcastle/Berwick, with a conventional service between Edinburgh and Dunbar, a bus service linking Dunbar and Berwick. Indeed, this was organised on a short-term basis. However, the BRB, in conjunction with local authorities and the Scottish Office, agreed to construct a temporary line around the blockage while remedial action was taken; this was formalised in record time and opened on 20 August 1979 with a ceremonial run of a through HST between Edinburgh and London.

On their introduction on the ECML, HST performance was good. From May 1979, for example, the 10.00 King's Cross-Edinburgh 'Flying Scotsman' became the fastest train connection with Edinburgh in just 4hr 37min, with one intermediate stop at Newcastle — an end-to-end average of 85.12mph. From the same period Leeds/Bradford joined the HST network, as did Aberdeen with two services per day.

During the build of these ECML sets, power car No 43081, delivered in February 1978 was the 8,000th loco built at Crewe.

Above left:
After the game of trying to find out how to attach the Class 47 to the power car, No 47292, painted in standard BR blue livery, awaits departure from one of the through freight lines at Doncaster heading for Bounds Green. *Derek Porter*

Above right:
Pulling out of the eastern end of Sonning Cutting and heading towards Twyford on the up main line, set No 253009, with power car No 43018 leading, forms the 10.50 Bristol Temple Meads-Paddington on 4 March 1980. *CJM*

Centre right:
With a passing speed in excess of 200mph it is always pleasing to capture two HST sets side by side, and even better when the correct staggered position is achieved. On 4 July 1983 this was the view at Sutton on Trent near Retford with power car No 43071 coming towards the camera leading a double refreshment car set on the 11.00 Edinburgh-King's Cross passing the 14.10 King's Cross-Newcastle with power car No 43076 at the rear. *CJM*

Lower right:
As part of the modernisation on the Western Region's West of England route to allow HSTs to operate at their maximum potential, several major resignalling schemes were introduced, including the Exeter area, where semaphore signalling was replaced with colour lights. One location to lose its 'proper' signals was Aller Junction, west of Newton Abbot, where on 15 June 1981 set No 253014, led by power car No 43029, heads west with the 10.25 Paddington-Plymouth. *CJM*

The third tranche of HSTs ordered was again for the Western Region, this time to upgrade and modernise the West of England route to Paignton, Plymouth and Penzance, travelling from/to London by both the usual Berks & Hants route via Westbury, and via Bristol. The announcement that the Western Region had persuaded the BRB to submit an investment proposal to the DTp for HSTs on the West of England route was surprising, as the only operation at more than 100/110mph for trains using the Berks & Hants route would be between Paddington and Reading, although trains using the traditional route via Bristol would benefit a little more with high-speed running for most of the route. However, the Western Region put forward a very convincing business case for deploying HST sets over both routes; it was foreseen that 1970s development of the motorway network between London and Exeter (M4/M5 corridor), compounded by upgrading of the road network west of Exeter to Plymouth, plus the launch of direct, low-cost air services from Cornwall, Plymouth and Exeter to London, were all likely to seriously erode rail travel unless an upgraded high-speed rail option was introduced.

It should be recorded that although the HST option was put to the BRB for the West of England route, other ways of route/train improvement were also considered. The most interesting option was the use of Class 50s, one at either end of a rake of semi-permanently coupled Mk2 air-conditioned coaches, fitted with through multiple (orange square) wiring for the locomotives. However, the cost of such an operation was considered high: the fuel consumption of a pair of 50s flat out all the way from London to Penzance, offering very little improvement on previous schedules due to longer acceleration/deceleration times, would have cost more than funding an HST fleet, and even though speeds would be sub-125, the high speed and enhanced image would be beneficial to winning patronage.

dual-type main-line fleet. It is also interesting that the West of England submission makes direct reference to the fact that, if agreed, cascading would allow the Eastern Region route from Liverpool Street to Norwich to benefit from the spare Mk2 stock and assist in the long-term modernisation of that section of the Inter-City network.

The 14-train-set West of England submission from the BRB to the DTp was agreed in May 1977, with a gradual deployment on Berks & Hants services from October 1979. A full West of England HST timetable was introduced from May 1980, when 12 sets had been delivered. On the West of England route the timetable was not impressively upgraded, with the London-Plymouth gain being restricted to around 20min. From October 1979 the Penzance-Paddington 'Cornish Riviera' covered the Paddington-Plymouth leg in just 3hr 13min. From delivery of the full Paddington-Penzance HST service in October 1980, the fastest ever service between the two points was launched, achieved by the 'Golden Hind' in exactly 5 hours.

The full upgrading of the West of England main line took several years to complete, and it was not until 1985 that the two prestige London-Penzance trains, the 'Golden Hind' and 'Cornish Riviera', covered the Paddington-Exeter section in 120min. The WR West of England HST investment also covered major depot alterations, with Plymouth Laira being upgraded for HST stock and a major new facility constructed at Long Rock, Penzance.

The fourth fleet of HSTs to go for DTp submission was perhaps the most controversial, as these were not for one specific operating region but for a passenger corridor, that of the North East-South West route, which of course later became the InterCity Cross Country network. This NE-SW corridor, principally linking such places as Edinburgh, Newcastle, York, Leeds and Derby with Bristol and the West of England via Birmingham, had in the past been under the domain of different regional operating authorities, mainly the Scottish, Eastern, Midland and Western Regional Boards, although historically the route could be said to have started life with the Midland Railway Derby-Bristol main line. Under BR management it was largely forgotten, until 1972, when the BRB set up an inter-regional team to develop the lucrative inter-regional passenger business through a central hub of Birmingham New Street, which was to act as the major passenger interchange point for travellers from the North West or North East wishing to travel to the West Country, or even intermediate stations on the London route.

As part of the submission for the West of England HST fleet, it was agreed that the Berks & Hants route would receive resignalling and track improvements; semaphore signals would be replaced with colour lights, and speed restrictions lifted to allow 100-110mph running for much of the route. The resignalling would include new signal centres at Westbury and Exeter, with the elimination of all mechanical signalling east of Liskeard. Another advantage of the West of England submission was that the WR would be operating a predominantly HST railway for main-line services and could thus integrate the Paddington-Swansea/Bristol/Paignton/Plymouth/Penzance routes as one operational pool, thus achieving some 20% saving over working a

With hugely improved connections and careful timetabling at Birmingham New Street, the Cross Country network was born. Soon passenger growth was increasing by margins that could not have been foreseen, and quickly new routes were added covering the Southern England to points such as Poole, Bournemouth, Portsmouth and even Brighton, travelling south from Birmingham via Oxford. By the mid-1970s Birmingham had become the hub for interchange between North East-South West and North West-South East travel.

With this high growth, major benefits could be seen from using new stock on these services. At one time electrification of the main routes was considered. However, with no real prospect of electrification at route extremities, the HST diesel option was the most sensible to develop, and would also give a standard quality of service for passengers using the NE-SW services at its extremities where they would interface with the Scottish/Eastern and Western Regions.

Although the investment submission could *not* demonstrate much post-100mph running over the Midlands sections — the new core route of the Cross Country network — performance benefits could be obtained with faster acceleration/deceleration as well as the ability to attain 100-125mph performance north of York and to exploit marginal increases on other sections.

After much deliberation the BRB formulated an investment case for 36 train sets, for delivery in two phases. The first would cover services from Edinburgh/Newcastle via York, Leeds or Doncaster to Derby and Birmingham for onward running to Cardiff, Bristol, Plymouth and Cornwall. The second phase of delivery would cover the North West, Glasgow, Liverpool and Manchester to Birmingham and such South East/South West points as Poole, Bournemouth, Portsmouth and Brighton, as well as furthering the coverage to Bristol, Plymouth and Cornwall.

The first of these two submissions to the Government went to the DTp in the spring of 1978 and was for 18 sets, formed of PC, TF, TRSB, TS, TS, TS, TS, TS, PC, and these were approved in June 1978 and followed the WR West of England sets through the build programme. A number of technical problems were at this time plaguing the HST fleet and the delivery of sets was delayed. The introduction, planned for the winter 1981 timetable, had to be shelved, and only a partial launch was possible in November 1981. All 18 sets were, however, delivered and commissioned for a full service from May 1982. The first deployment on the Cross Country network was from October 1981, with two sets used on a Leeds-Bristol and Leeds-Plymouth daily return. The Edinburgh-Plymouth service was transferred to HST operation in November. By May the following year, further Cross Country HSTs were introduced.

The second tranche of 18 proposed Cross Country sets for phase two of the service was sadly never authorised. The submission was put together by the BRB, but by this time the growth of passenger travel was falling, mainly due to the country's financial recession, compounded by revised legislation on nationalised spending. The Cross Country corridor therefore had to make do with a mix of HSTs and loco-hauled formations.

The final submission for HSTs came from the Eastern/Scottish Region, which, following the introduction of the original HST service, had seen passenger growth beyond any expectations; overcrowding became commonplace and frankly passengers were being turned away! Also, the ER board wanted to add Teesside to the HST map, develop the Hull corridor and add Sheffield as a destination via the ECML route to compete with or even replace the time-honoured St Pancras route. A submission from the ER Board to the BRB's investment committee for seven additional ECML sets was accepted and made into a Government/DTp proposal for submission in August 1979. After deliberation the DTp came back and offered sanction for investment in just two train sets. An outcry from the BRB quickly followed, which became very public throughout the national media. The Government was forced into a rethink and eventually agreed to the funding of four sets in January 1980.

Although authorisation was given for the four trains, the BRB was still very unhappy that its sound business-led proposal had basically been rejected by the Government. It was thought that any further such submissions could be faced with the same uncertainty, and within a few months the BRB made the announcement that after just 95 HST train sets had been built, the project would be terminated. This came as a huge shock to many, but in reality the rail industry had to act in a responsible manner. Since the first investment propositions had been made, huge changes had taken place; the UK was now in recession, finance was difficult to obtain, long-distance travel trends were changing, and Inter-City passenger journeys were dropping. The peak year had been 1979 with just over 9.5 million loaded train miles; by 1981 this had dropped to 8.7 million.

After the 1977 Labour transport policy document, which required the Inter-City passenger carrying railway to 'pay its way', the rail industry had serious problems with financial housekeeping. The full-fare 1st Class business market was at a very low ebb and general ticket sales were falling; much was attributed to low-cost coach travel over short to medium distances and low-cost 'turn up and go' air travel for longer distances. BR's Inter-City management tried to win back growth by lowering fares, a policy that did not wholly work. Sadly it was sanctioned by the BRB and agreed by Government that a 10% cut in train miles would be introduced between mid-1981 and October 1982. These cuts affected all routes and of course required a smaller train fleet.

The Changing Market

By virtue of its operating area, the Western Region was more seriously affected by the recession than the Eastern/Scottish Regions or the actually expanding Cross Country mainly leisure travel operation. Several factors contributed to the WR's problems: the first and potentially the most damaging was the M4/M5 motorway, which was taking massive traffic from rail. It was not only the businessman in his car, but also the leisure traveller who turned to road, and cheap, comfortable and fast coaches were now frequently available between London and Bristol/Bath, Newport/Cardiff and even as far west as Exeter and Torbay. In general, travel times were only slightly longer and the cost was considerably less, which attracted the customer base for the route.

From 1980 the decrease in Western Region passenger numbers allowed re-diagramming of HST sets; by now the Paddington-Bristol/South Wales and Paddington-West of England sets operated as one common fleet, with two complete trains reallocated to the Eastern Region to assist its ongoing train shortage. With the downturn in passenger numbers, the WR was also looking at revamping its entire service to operate at a slightly reduced level with less stock. This was achieved by withdrawing lightly used services, drastically reducing terminus turn-round times, especially at country locations, and improving availability by changing the maintenance operation. This rationalisation was implemented in both the May and September 1982 timetable changes and saved five HSTs.

The one major route that had not so far benefited from the introduction of HSTs was the Midland main line from St Pancras to Nottingham and Sheffield. This relatively short, self-contained railway had been included in the original HST modernisation plan, but the abandonment of the train build project after 95 sets saw the Midland route left outside the new high-speed network. Various demands were made at times by local authorities along the line for modernisation of 'their' route, including the powerful Sheffield City Council. A number of possible options were considered for the line, including the use of Class 47s on push-pull passenger rakes, but none offered any financial return over and above deploying conventional locomotives and stock on the route. As previously mentioned, at one time the Eastern Region, in its bid for additional sets, was planning to introduce a London King's Cross-Sheffield via Retford service, which would have been fine to provide a service to Sheffield, but major conurbations such as Leicester, Nottingham and Derby would have been left out in the cold. The position seemed to have reached stalemate within the business-led, financial-return railway. However, the position changed drastically after the formation of separately accountable business sectors to operate the rail industry in 1981.

The 1981 changes to InterCity saw Cyril Bleasdale appointed as its Sector or Business Director. He was now responsible for the HST fleets' deployment, and within weeks of taking up his new role he announced that the Midland main line would benefit from HST operation.

The five spare sets generated by the Western Region were the key factor in this change. However, they were not sufficient to operate a full St Pancras-Nottingham/Sheffield service, and the route either had to use the HSTs on core services (about 15 London departures per day) and retain older loco-hauled stock on other trains, or a further pool of HSTs had to be found. After much shuffling of HST assets, five further sets were found, three from the Cross Country fleet by tightening up rosters and two from the East Coast main line, made available by improving deployment and a marginal reduction in services.

The service improvements possible on the Midland main line were furthered by the completion of the West Hampstead area resignalling, covering 62 miles of railway between St Pancras and Irchester, Northamptonshire. On this route four long sections of 100mph operation were authorised as well as the removal of most mechanical signalling.

HST introduction of the Midland main line was slow. Deployment from the end of 1982 and early 1983 was not possible due to the tail-end of the Bedford-St Pancras 'Bed-Pan' electrification work, and it was not until May 1983 that a full HST service was introduced out of St Pancras, but it rapidly changed the service and attracted new custom.

At the time of the transfer of the Western Region and Cross Country sets to Midland duties, a problem with stock formations emerged. All 10 sets were 2+7 formation, whereas the passenger levels on the Midland required 2+8. This was compounded by the fact that the former Cross Country sets had only one 1st Class vehicle, and a minimum of two would be needed as the St Pancras route catered for a growing business market. The problem was overcome by the authorisation and construction of 19 additional trailer vehicles, which were used to re-form all the Midland sets to 2+8, and at the same time to re-form the East Coast sets with just one refreshment vehicle by the abolition of the remaining TRUKs.

After the early 1980s the basic allocation/deployment of the HST fleet remained fairly constant. One of the most significant changes came in May 1986 when the Western Region re-formed 10 of its allocation with an additional TS, thus forming 2+8 sets for the main business services. These extra vehicles came from maintenance spares, but as some were 1st Class, internal refitting was required to Standard Class levels. A major problem in re-forming these sets with an additional vehicle was the need for extended covered depot accommodation, and this was provided at Laira and Old Oak Common but not at Bristol St Philips Marsh. In 1987 a further two sets were able to be released from the East Coast, and these were taken over by the Cross Country operation to reduce the number of Mk2 loco-hauled sets in use. The redeployment was not long-lasting, however, as in May 1988 two of the Cross Country sets departed, one to the Western Region to provide cover for an expanded London-based operation to the Cotswolds, and the other to the Midland main line, to give that sector 11 train sets, enabling an improved timetable pattern.

A further development in the HST deployment story came in 1982, when, following pressure from the Highland authorities about the lack of InterCity development in their region and to the Highland capital, a trial run of a 2+9 formation (the extra vehicle was included to simulate a loaded 2+8 set) worked from Edinburgh Craigentinny to Inverness, carrying out restarting trials on the 1 in 60 gradient between Carr Bridge and Slochd. Minor problems were overcome and from mid-1984 a new 'Highland Chieftain' service was launched between King's Cross and Inverness.

On the WR, timetable development was possible from September 1983 when a Paddington-Carmarthen train was extended to Haverfordwest, an extension only made possible by means of a partnership between Western Region and Dyfed County Council, which agreed to underwrite any losses. The service was successful and was later extended to Milford Haven. Another West Wales development came in 1986 when HSTs took over from loco-hauled stock on the Fishguard Harbour boat trains. The WR Cotswold route was also developed in both the 1983 and 1984 timetables.

On the Eastern Region, passenger growth was significant and many marketing policies were put in place. One was the addition of the 'Executive' trading title to some prime business trains where a full Pullman-plus service was offered. The 'Executive' name had first been used in pre-HST days from 1973 with such trains as the 'Leeds Executive', 'Newcastle Executive' and 'Bradford Executive'. These premiere services all went over to HST operation in 1979 and were joined a couple of years later by the 'Hull Executive' and 'Cleveland Executive'. Further enhancements on the East Coast route came in May 1985 with the official redesignation of some sets as InterCity 'Pullman' to coincide with a relaunch of the 'Yorkshire Pullman' and 'Teesside Pullman' trains. The sets used on these were for a short while branded 'InterCity Pullman'. From May 1987 the Pullman name, but not the branding, was extended to the Midland main line's 'Master Cutler' service.

Following full electrification of the ECML a number of sets were transferred away to other routes. However, a small number were retained to form King's Cross-Aberdeen, Inverness, Hull and Bradford services. At one time a plan was considered to use the new Mk4 stock on these routes, re-formed with displaced power cars.

From their introduction, the HSTs' frontal indication was provided by two clusters of three lights on either side of the central horn grille at solebar height. Each cluster consisted of (from the outer edge) a headlight, tail light (red), and marker light (white). Originally, under normal running, the two front marker lights would be switched on together with one headlight (preferably the left-hand-side light in the direction of travel). However, from the late 1980s the Western Region decided that both headlights would be used, improving the visibility of an approaching train; this policy was later extended to all HST operators. The change required a minor modification to the wiring.

After privatisation, Midland Mainline embarked on a policy to replace the original lamp units with one of a new design, manufactured by Brush and incorporating the use of LEDs for the marker and tail lights.

HST Generator Car

Prior to the introduction of the main HST fleet, the Derby-based DM&EE converted Mk1 BG No 81448 into a mobile generator van, renumbered as ADB975325 in May 1973 and fitted with a stand-alone diesel and generator unit in one of the original van spaces. Authorisation for this vehicle was given for the development of three-phase train supply, rather that using 800-1,000V conventional supply.

The vehicle was predominantly used for test purposes but was occasionally employed on the Eastern Region in the mid-1970s when more electrically heated stock was in service than compatible locomotives.

Following a serious spate of HST power unit problems in the 1980s, many involving Western Region-allocated cars, No ADB975325 was transferred to Old Oak Common and used to provide a three-phase 415V supply to HST trailer stock if powered by a conventional loco.

After its days were finished in this role, the coach was stored, then eventually reinstated in 1999 for use as a generator car for charter and private stock. It has recently been sold to Riviera Trains and is now based at Crewe, renumbered to 6310 and repainted in mock Pullman umber and cream livery.

HST Compatibility

A problem that has always concerned railway operators about the HST fleet is its non-compatibility with other stock. Moving HSTs around as a set, with any number of trailers and a power car at both ends, is no problem. However, when non-standard movements are required, problems arise.

As mentioned earlier, the non-standard air-smoothed front ends caused designers major difficulties in devising a method for coupling to conventional stock in case of failure, and this was overcome by the emergency bar coupler.

Above:
Although originally only converted for the development of three-phase train supply prior to fitting on a train set, the ex-BG generator van No ADB975325 saw use on the Western Region during a power car shortage in the 1980s. The coach, painted in standard blue and grey livery, is seen at Reading as the rear vehicle of an IC125 set. Note the bodyside louvres and roof-mounted silencer group. *CJM*

Below:
At the non-generator end of the loco-hauled HST passenger set was a BG, which acted as a coupling adapter between the fixed buck-eye of the HST set and the conventional coupling of the loco. The generator set is seen approaching West Ealing on 8 August 1981, forming the 08.05 Worcester-Paddington powered by Class 47 No 47200. *CJM*

Shunting of vehicles within depots or workshops also gave rise to further problems as neither stock nor power cars could be hooked up to other locomotives or pilots except by means of a buck-eye coupling. To overcome most problems, depots tended to make up their own 'match' arrangements by using a spare coach with a buck-eye at one end and a standard hook for the loco at the other.

To make shunting easier at depots with a HST allocation, the InterCity engineer and the DM&EE developed a small but most effective lightweight drop-head buck-eye jaw, and fitted it to a small fleet of Class 08s; ten locomotives, Nos 08410/411/480/483/

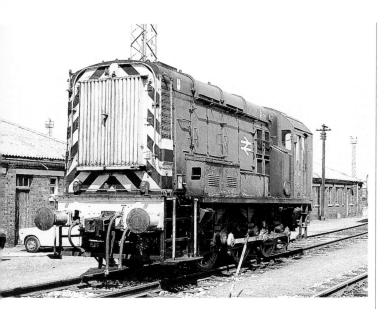

Above:
With its modified lightweight buck-eye coupling in the raised position, Old Oak Common-allocated No 08480 is seen at the depot on 14 June 1980. *CJM*

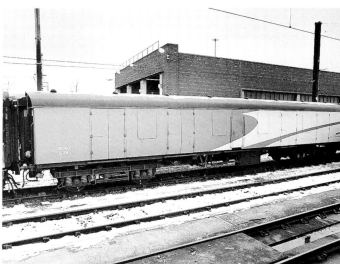

641/643/644/645/649/651, had been fitted by the end of 1980. By 1985 the modified fleet had grown to 14 locomotives with the addition of Nos 08748/785/874/881. In the period 1981-5 No 08663 was fitted for a short period.

For the movement of trailer cars around the network, a varied fleet of barrier or match coaches has been operated, being converted from either ex-passenger or van stock. In the 1970s/80s some very tatty vehicles were used, but by the 1990s a more robust fleet of barrier cars was in use, allocated in pairs to HST depots. Following privatisation, the lease companies now own the barrier cars, with some displaying their livery.

The barrier cars are also frequently used to attach a loco to the inner end of a power car for inter-depot transfers.

Barrier Cars in Traffic, March 2001

Number	Rebuilt from	Owner	Base
6330	Mk2a BFK 14084	Angel Trains	Laira
6334	Mk1 BG 81478	Porterbrook	Neville Hill
6336	Mk1 BG 81591	Angel Trains	Laira
6338	Mk1 BG 81581	Angel Trains	Laira
6340	Mk1 BCK 21251	Angel Trains	Laira
6344	Mk1 BG 81263	Angel Trains	Craigentinny
6346	Mk2 BSO 9422	Angel Trains	Craigentinny
6348	Mk1 BG 81233	Angel Trains	Laira
6392	Mk1 BG 81588	Porterbrook	Laira
6393	Mk1 BG 81609	Porterbrook	Laira
6394	Mk1 BG 80878	Porterbrook	Neville Hill
6395	Mk1 BG 81506	Porterbrook	Neville Hill
6396	Mk1 BG 81606	Porterbrook	Laira
6397	Mk1 BG 81600	Porterbrook	Neville Hill
6398	Mk1 BG 81471	Porterbrook	Neville Hill
6399	Mk1 BG 81367	Porterbrook	Neville Hill

Above:
With EWS/Res Class 47/7 No 47780 on the front, barrier car No 6338, rebuilt from BG No 81581, approaches Crewe on 17 February 1997 with power car No 43041 being transferred from Manchester Longsight depot to St Philips Marsh, Bristol, for maintenance. *CJM*

Upper left:

Over the years a number of ex-passenger and NPCCS vehicles have acted as barriers. Here ex-Mk2 TSO No 5395, renumbered 6347 and with its windows plated over and end door sealed up, is seen attached to power car No 43020 at Whiteball as it travels light from Bristol St Philips Marsh to Laira on 27 March 1997. CJM

Centre left:

After the passenger rolling stock was allocated to lease companies under privatisation, the barrier or match vehicles to enable conventional locomotives to attach to HST trailer stock were owned by Porterbrook or Angel Trains. Painted in Porterbrook's mauve and white livery, barrier No 6397 is seen at Leeds Neville Hill, now coded GSA. This vehicle was rebuilt from Mk1 BG No 81600. CJM

Above:

The first major accident to involve an HST took place on 18 August 1979 when the 13.00 King's Cross-Edinburgh derailed all vehicles at over 70mph as it passed through Northallerton with power cars Nos 43110/111 in charge. The accident was caused by the failure of one of the gearboxes on the leading power car, which eventually led the inner bogie to derail, taking the rest of the train with it. A total credit to the train's design was the fact that even at a relatively high speed all vehicles remained upright and in line. This is the view soon after the accident, looking towards the rear of the train. John Boyes

Serious HST Accidents

Considering the huge mileages accumulated by the HST fleet since its introduction, few serious accidents have befallen it, and until 1997 no passenger had been killed in an IC125 accident.

On 19 September of that year a fully loaded Great Western set approached Southall forming the 10.32 Swansea-Paddington and collided with a freight train crossing its path. The train, led by power car No 43173, impacted with the moving freight at over 80mph, which virtually destroyed the power car; it was subsequently withdrawn. The first passenger saloon, No 41050, was so seriously damaged that it was broken up on site, while in 2001 sister coach No 41049 remained in store awaiting disposal. Sadly this accident claimed the lives of seven people. Although this book is not a report of accidents, this tragedy was not in any way attributed to a problem with the HST train, but was caused by driver error. Power car No 43163 was at the rear.

Probably the most reported accident in recent times involving an HST took place on the approaches to Paddington at Ladbroke Grove on 5 October 1999 when a full set led by power car No 43011 forming the 06.03 Cheltenham-Paddington collided head-on with a Class 165 'Thames Turbo' departing from the capital. Such was the force of the impact, around 130mph and

Right:

A potentially very serious accident occurred near Tyne Yard on 1 August 1984 when the 07.30 Leeds-Edinburgh became derailed on defective trackwork while traversing the northbound local line; the train had been diverted from the main line due to engineering work. The accident saw part of the train fall down the embankment, but again the rigidity of the vehicle design saved any serious passenger injury. TSO No 42134 is illustrated, with the vehicle ahead down the embankment. Ian Carr

Left:
Following a depot collision, WR power car No 43049 from set 253024 is seen at Neville Hill in 1981; it was later repaired at Derby Works. The front end design of the HST power cars was such that impact damage usually allowed just sections of the front end to be replaced rather than the entire nose section. It is interesting to see that this example has lost its two buffer 'stubs' in its collision. *Derek Porter*

Below:
A sideswipe collision occurred at the north end of King Edward Bridge, Newcastle, on 30 November 1988 when due to driver error the 14.52 Aberdeen-King's Cross and 16.00 King's Cross-Aberdeen collided, resulting in vehicles 44027 and 42126 derailing. Recovery was carried out the following day. *Ian Carr*

ensuing fire that 31 people died (seven on the HST). The cause of this accident was again attributed to human error on behalf of the non-HST driver. No 43011 was destroyed, as were the two leading FOs, Nos 41042/060, with serious damage to the buffet car No 40213 and TSO No 42082.

Other Significant IC125 Accidents

Other significant accidents involving HSTs, excluding minor derailments and collisions, are:

18 August 1979	Northallerton	Derailment of entire train at 70mph due to a seized power car gearbox (Nos 43110/111)
1 August 1984	Tyne Yard	Train derailed on defective trackwork (Nos 43112/114)
30 November 1988	Newcastle (King Edward Bridge)	Sideswipe accident of two sets (No 43047)
7 December 1991	Severn Tunnel	HST hit by following 'Sprinter' during signal problems (Nos 43134/158)
25 March 1994	Newton Abbot	Train hit by following Class 158 (No 43071)
13 August 1994	Calton Tunnel (Edinburgh)	Train struck by runaway loco (No 43180)
8 September 1995	Maidenhead	Fuel tank fell off and caused major fire (No 43190)
11 November 1995	Paddington	Collision with Class 165, which had run signal (Nos 43018/138)
7 March 1997	Newton Abbot	Train derailed due to axle defect on coach (Nos 43130/170)

Right:
On 25 March 1994 the 07.20 Penzance-Glasgow was awaiting departure from Newton Abbot, with power car No 43071 at the rear, when the driver of the following 09.40 Paignton-Cardiff, formed of Class 158 No 158833, ran by the protecting signal at danger and collided with the train at around 20mph. Although no passengers were injured, the HST power car was seriously damaged and was repaired by Crewe Works. This view, taken just minutes after the accident, shows the two trains still wedged together. *CJM*

Above & left:
Perhaps Newton Abbot is not a good place for HST travel, for a further serious accident occurred close to the station on 7 March 1997 when the Great Western's 15.35 Paddington-Penzance almost totally derailed at it approached the station, resulting in one coach landing precariously on the parapet of a bridge. The cause of the accident was traced to the collapse of a wheel bearing on coach No 42078 (*left*), which caused the wheelset to come out of the bogie frame and derail. *Both CJM*

Above:
Although almost 200 HST power cars were built, very few spare cabs were assembled. During the mid-1990s several were built by DML Engineering of Devonport and installed on damaged vehicles, usually at Crewe Works. However, some accident-damaged cab sections have been retained as a possible supply of spare parts in the future. This cab top section from No 43158 is seen at ABB Derby Works in October 1994 when consideration was being given to the production of some replacement sections at Derby. *CJM*

Above:
Three days after the Southall crash, the remains of leading power car No 43173, with its side completely ripped away by the impact of the collision, is craned away. The body section was taken by road to Adtranz Crewe for the formal inquiry, after which a number of parts, including the power unit, were salvaged and reused. *Roland Kennington*

Centre left:
The Southall collision on 19 September 1997 was the first time an HST was involved in an accident that claimed lives, when the 10.32 Swansea-Paddington, led by power car No 43173, collided with a freight train crossing its path. The impact destroyed the power car and the first two passenger coaches. This is the view from the footbridge crossing Southall station the following day, with the wreckage of the train and the mangled remains of the freight train awaiting removal. The rear power car, which was not damaged, is No 43163. *Ken Brunt*

Lower left:
This quite amazing picture of power car No 43169 at Bristol Parkway on 7 April 1996 shows what can happen if deposits form in the exhaust system and catch fire. Thankfully little damage was done and fast-thinking train and station staff quickly evacuated the passengers and summoned the fire brigade. *B. W. Elliott*

Before we look at the changes made to passenger saloon interiors, we need to take a few minutes to look at the 'as delivered' vehicles. As previously mentioned, both the 1st and 2nd (later Standard) Class coaches were, with the exception of the later-ordered TGSs, built to a standard or common design and were easily adaptable to either interior style, the seats and trim being attached to floor and body rails.

Prior to the prototype train being built, a huge market research operation was undertaken to evaluate the public's aspirations for the future of passenger railway stock for longer-distance travel. Some of this was conducted at the instruction of the then BR design panel, with mainly 'land-based' passengers being questioned, while other research was undertaken travelling on Mk2 stock, where passengers could express their likes and dislikes much more easily. The results of this research showed the following (not in priority order):

- Comfortable seating
- Stylish or 'state-of-the-art' decor
- Full and effective air-conditioning
- Good general and detail lighting
- Low interior noise levels
- Low vibration levels
- Provision of food/drink service on board (at seat in 1st Class)
- Clean interior
- Clean and functional toilets

Above right:
A production HST 1st Class interior, showing the original layout with orange seat moquette, white nylon headrests, orange and black carpet and dull orange table-tops. *CJM*

Right:
The interior of a refreshment vehicle, showing the original style of layout. Note that two proper cash registers are included, which were quickly dispensed with in favour of plastic cups to hold money, and the fitting of two beer pumps, one dispensing Tankard beer and the other Heineken lager. *CJM*

Many of the above were of course already incorporated in the final versions of the Mk2 build, but designers and operators tried to pay as much attention as possible to these needs.

Prototype Train Vehicles

A full description of all the prototype train's passenger vehicles is given in Chapter 2. The four original First Open (FO) coaches were numbered 11000-03 and the Second Open (TSO) numbered 12000-03, and before the prototype train entered full passenger service two of the vehicles, FO No 11001 and TSO No 12001, were taken out of development running and transferred to the Royal Train fleet (see 'Royal Train conversions' below).

After its short operating life on the Western Region, mainly working between Paddington and Bristol and Weston-super-Mare and the occasional trip to Swansea, the prototype set was withdrawn from service following the introduction of the first of the production sets. Basically at this point the train had served its purpose and technically the vehicles were almost scrap! However,

such is the UK rail industry that this was unlikely to happen. After a period at the Railway Technical Centre, Derby, the prototype vehicles were split up; some of the trailer cars operated within other test trains for equipment development work, while some took part in static test programmes at Derby. The two refreshment cars were soon to see further use. The original TRSB, No 10000, which became No 40000 under renumbering, was taken over by the Derby-based BR Research Division, where in 1986 it was massively rebuilt and renumbered to RDB975984. The vehicle was identified as 'Lab 15' and named *Argus*, being used as a high-speed instrumentation and recording vehicle. Internally the original kitchen/buffet was removed and a staff accommodation area, laboratory bay with state-of-the-art multi-channel recording equipment and a small generator cabin built. During its years operating with the Research Division the vehicle saw a number of internal and structural changes depending on the test programmes being undertaken.

On privatisation of the rail industry in the mid-1990s the coach was

Above left:
The prototype TRSB No 10000, renumbered to 40000, was taken over by the Derby-based BR Research Division after its useful passenger life was over, and in 1986 it was massively rebuilt and renumbered RDB975984. The coach was then identified as 'Lab 15' and named *Argus*, being used as a high-speed instrumentation and recording vehicle. Internally the original kitchen/buffet was removed and a staff accommodation area, laboratory and state-of-the-art multi-channel recording system plus a small generator cabin built. *Argus* is seen in the BR Research yard on 16 September 1997. *CJM*

Left:
The original TRUB No 10100, later 40500, was rebuilt in 1986 as BR Research vehicle No RDB977089 or 'Lab 21' and used for various Derby-based tests. Painted in Research livery, the coach is seen in the RTC yard in 1989. It was eventually gutted of instrumentation and sold to Booth-Roe, Rotherham, for scrap in February 1993. *CJM*

Above right:
Quite considerable rebuilding was needed to bring the prototype Class 252 trailer vehicles into line with Class 253/254 standards. The original No 11002, later renumbered to 41001, is seen in Derby Litchurch Lane Works on 2 April 1982 being rebuilt to production TF No 41170. It will be seen that the original buffer beam has been rebuilt without side buffers, a fixed buck-eye coupling and revised piping and body connections. *CJM*

transferred to Derby-based Serco/Railtest, which continue to operate the coach in much the same role. Today it is identified as Test Car 4 and classified QXA.

The second of the prototype train set refreshment vehicles, No 10100, renumbered to 40500, also passed to the Research Division at the RTC, where it was again hugely rebuilt in 1986, this time as RDB977089 or Lab 21 for use as a high-speed brake and suspension test and development vehicle. Much of this work was involved with Mk4 vehicle and bogie design and testing. After this role had been completed, it was used as the instrumentation coach for a number of other static test projects at Derby as well as dynamic testing of rolling-stock on the main line. The coach was eventually stripped of all equipment under the rationalisation policy of the Research operation and stored. Devoid of its bogies, it was eventually sold to and broken up by Booth-Roe, Rotherham, in February 1993.

The pioneer Mk3 passenger vehicle, No 11000, later renumbered 41000, also passed to departmental work at the RTC Derby, working for the DM&EE, where it was renumbered ADB975814, or Test Car 10. It was given a huge rebuild for its DM&EE duties, with large instrumentation racks and a lab built towards the centre of the structure, a generator bay at one end for power supplies, and staff accommodation at the other. The vehicle was modified in the Engineering Development Unit of the RTC and repainted in dark blue and red test train livery. It was used in a number of test formations of high-speed stock, including being formed with Mk4 development vehicle No 12201 in February 1989 for tests over the northern section of the East Coast main line, powered by Class 43s Nos 43051/116 and TGS No 44019. After the vehicle's useful life was over at Derby, the technical equipment was removed and the coach offered for sale. It is now preserved by Peak Rail at Matlock.

The remaining five of the prototype train's trailers, FOs Nos 41001/2 (originally 11002/3) and three TSOs, Nos 42000/01/02 (originally 12000/02/03), were all rebuilt at BREL Derby Litchurch Lane as 'production' HST vehicles, modified as FOs and renumbered as follows:

41001 (11002) rebuilt to 41170
41002 (11003) rebuilt to 41174
42000 (12000) rebuilt to 41172
42001 (12002) rebuilt to 41171
42002 (12003) rebuilt to 41173

This rebuilding work saw the bodies taken back to raw shells, with a number of modifications made to bring them up to the then standard. The conversion work was carried out under a new lot number, 30967 of 1982, and included the removal of end buffing gear, strengthening of the body base, and alterations to wiring, doors and end vestibule. Surprisingly, while the interior decor was fully upgraded, the mid-coach dividers and roof panels were not changed, thus these 'production' vehicles had no glazed mid-length draught screen and had one in three roof light gondolas missing. Today, with privatisation rebuilding, it is more difficult to identify these vehicles. Another recognition factor is the exterior window surrounds, which on the prototype were set in rubber and self-coloured, whereas on 'true'

Right:
The authorisation for the conversion of 12 spare TRUKs to loco-hauled RFM vehicles was a major help to the InterCity business on the West Coast main line. Two vehicles were authorised first, followed by another 18. No 10201, the original 40520, is seen in the Engineering Development Unit yard at the RTC Derby; this coach and No 10200 spent several months working off the EDU after conversion at Litchurch Lane Works. *CJM*

production vehicles the windows had aluminium surrounds. Due to an imbalance in the number of 1st and 2nd (Standard) Class vehicles, it was decided to rebuild Nos 41171-74 again in the mid-1990s as TSOs, renumbering being as follows:

FO 41171 modified to TSO 42353
FO 41172 modified to TSO 42355
FO 41173 modified to TSO 42356
FO 41174 modified to TSO 42357

These vehicles now operate for Virgin and First Great Western from Laira, Plymouth.

Production Train Vehicles

The production IC125 vehicles largely followed the prototypes in interior design and comforts. When introduced, all FOs accommodated 48 in the 2+1 seating configuration and toilets were located at each end of the vehicles, with a full-height luggage stack at both ends inside the saloon sliding door. The seat style was the same as on the prototype set, with upgraded removable covers for easy cleaning. The moquette used was, however, orange fleck for 1st Class, a colour that was matched by the colour of the table-top surface, which was finished in Formica laminate. The seat frames were finished in beige and the armrests in black, with silver ashtrays in the left-hand side armrests at the end; these were made from aluminium and had top openers with hinged interiors for ease of emptying. White nylon-covered headrests were provided, which were adjustable in the vertical plain, sliding on elasticated runners. All seats were slightly reclinable by the depression of a handle adjacent to the seat cushion and the manual movement of the seat by the passenger's body. Each seat bay had a square-section grab handle to assist passengers walking along the train. The interior decor was predominantly cream, mainly using melamine surfaces for easy cleaning. Reading lights with open bulbs and individual switches were located in the underside of the luggage rack, which towards the inner face was formed of a wide grille enabling passengers to see if items of luggage had been left on the shelf. Straight hanging curtains were provided by all windows, which could be drawn if required. Carpets were fitted throughout and had an orange and dark blue stripe running widthwise down the vehicle, thus helping to give an impression of extra width. Main coach lighting was achieved by a bank of fluorescent lights, hidden behind opaque gondolas running widthwise above the centre aisle of the coach. The lighting was controlled by on-train staff, with an end-of-vehicle switch

enabling half lights to be selected for night running. The vestibule areas were finished in hi-glow yellow, with a brush mat floor. The toilet compartment was finished in white, with a black toilet seat.

For the 2nd (later Standard) Class traveller, in 'as-built' condition the TSO vehicles accommodated 72 in the 2+2 style, with most seats grouped around tables. The seating moquette in 2nd was a mix of light and dark turquoise, as this was deemed to be more resistant to wear and staining than the colour used on the prototype (orange). Table-tops were finished with a similarly coloured laminate surface and a brushed aluminium surround. Individual armrests were provided for each seat, formed from a black rubber-based hard-wearing compound; as in 1st Class, ashtrays were located in the armrest ends. No adjustable headrests, reading lights or window curtains were provided in 2nd Class vehicles, but the standard style of square grab handle was provided on the seat backs. Above-seat luggage racks were provided along the length of the coach on both sides, while full-height luggage stacks were located at both ends. Additional luggage stowage space was available between the seat backs. Roof lighting and the end vestibules were the same as in 1st Class.

Although a more detailed description of the buffet car layout is given in the catering section, for completeness here the vehicles were constructed to 1st and 2nd Class standards. The TRSB was set out in 2+2 2nd Class style including seat design, trim and equipment, while the unclassified TRUK vehicle was given the 1st Class interior, with the exception of reading lights, as insufficient train line power could

be provided. The changing buffet car scene, which led to several extra designs being introduced, saw TRBSs being given 2nd Class interiors, while TRBs, TRUBs, TRBFs and TRFMs all used the 1st Class layout and trim.

After the changes in internal layout of the refreshment fleet were finalised, which resulted in each of the formed HST sets having just one buffet/kitchen car, the TRUK fleet became spare. As has been previously mentioned, some were rebuilt for Royal Train use, while others were stored for a prolonged period at various East Coast depots and at Derby. The BRB strove to find a new use for these expensive assets; rebuilding to saloons was always a possibility, but would have been costly, and as the vehicles were built as refreshment cars this was their preferred use. The answer came with a major conversion project for a new modular catering scheme for the West Coast route, whereby 12 cars were rebuilt at BREL Derby Litchurch Lane into loco-hauled catering cars of type Restaurant First Modular (RFM), as the first tranche of a fleet of 58 vehicles; others were converted from existing loco-hauled Mk3b FOs and Mk3a RFBs.

The loco-hauled rebuild was quite a major operation, with the entire vehicle being gutted internally and electrically and rebuilt; only the original frame was reused, and even this had some window spaces changed for its new role. The first two converted vehicles, Nos 10200/01, spent some time working from the RTC Derby to satisfy the engineers and operators of their technical and structural suitability. One of the most significant changes was the provision of standard buck-eye couplers and buffers as well as conventional ETS.

Right:
The first Mk3 to sport the 'new' InterCity or APT livery of light and dark grey offset by a red and white mid-height body band was Departmental vehicle No RDB977089, the original TRUK 10100 (40500) from the prototype train. This was repainted at Derby Litchurch Lane following a major market research campaign and transferred to Marylebone on 13 April 1983 for inspection by senior BRB members. The coach is seen inside the paint shop at Litchurch Lane. *BREL*

Lower right:
To demonstrate the proposed internal fittings of the Class 442 'Wessex Electric' sets for Network SouthEast, which were basically an EMU version of an HST, stored TRUK No 40516 was refitted internally with Class 442 seating, while externally it was repainted in full NSE livery. It is seen in the yard at Derby Litchurch Lane. *CJM*

The conversion programme commenced in 1984, with all vehicles in traffic in around 16 months. The vehicles rebuilt were:

40502 modified to 10204
40503 modified to 10205
40504 modified to 10202
40506 modified to 10203
40507 modified to 10206
40508 modified to 10209
40509 modified to 10210
40510 modified to 10211
40516 modified to 10207
40517 modified to 10208
40519 modified to 10200
40520 modified to 10201

Today these vehicles are all operated by Virgin Trains West Coast, with the exception of No 10203, which is allocated to Anglia Railways on the Liverpool Street-Norwich route. Although originally converted to seat 24 1st Class passengers in the 2+1 style, some slight revisions have been made and seating now varies between 18 and 24. All have one toilet compartment.

A very interesting development involved vehicle No 40516, which in the autumn of 1986 was rebuilt internally at Derby Litchurch Lane with seating in Standard, First Open and First Compartment style for use in the Mk3-based Class 442 'Wessex Electric' units, then under advanced design. To finish off the display vehicle, it was repainted in full Network SouthEast livery. After refinement of the design had been made, the interior was removed and the coach formed part of the Mk3a RFB rebuild contract, emerging as car No 10207.

One of the other TRUKs, No 40513, was the subject of an interesting conversion project. With the authorisation of the InterCity business director of the day, the coach was rebuilt as a lounge car and reclassified Trailer Lounge Unclassified Kitchen (TLUK). The rebuilding work, which included the total upgrading of the passenger area to a boardroom or lounge, included many cosmetic changes to the normal interior, including net curtains, wood veneer and wall-mounted pictures. The kitchen was retained but upgraded, while staff accommodation and storage lockers were fitted.

The plan was to be able to offer a private saloon to a corporate or business customer, which could be coupled within the consist of any HST service, usually at one end behind a power car. The coach would be locked off from the rest of the train to provide excellent private hospitality facilities. The TLUK, or 'Executive' saloon as InterCity usually called it, was normally kept at Bounds Green, London, and apart from an official launch between Leeds and King's Cross, saw

very little lounge car use. On privatisation, it was allocated to the portfolio of Porterbrook Leasing, which by the time of its take-over found the vehicle stored and in need of major classified overhaul at Derby Litchurch Lane Works, where it remained in mid 2001. Reports have been received that it is to be sold to Irish Rail.

When the need arose for extra HST First Opens, an unusual choice was made to fully rebuild two of the stored TRUKs, Nos 40505 and 40511. The change of these vehicles from refreshment cars to full passenger saloons was a major undertaking, with windows having to be changed on both sides of the body to conform with the passenger layout, as well as major structural changes to install a toilet compartment at the former kitchen end. Rebuilding work was carried out at Derby Litchurch Lane, with the bodies and underframes being rebuilt as FOs Nos 41179 and 41180. Both are now operated by First Great Western from Laira depot.

The above rebuilds leave just one TRUK remaining, No 40501, which has been out of service for many years. It is owned by Porterbrook Leasing and in early 2001 was stored with a bleak future at Derby Litchurch Lane Works, reportedly destined for long-term store at Cotswold Rail near Moreton-in-Marsh as part of a 'reserve' fleet.

Enter the TGS

Soon after the first production HSDTs were in service on the Western Region, a string of complaints was received from guards about the rough ride and excessive noise levels of their travelling position at the

Left:
The authorisation of funding to construct a fleet of Trailer Guards Standard (TGS) vehicles for the HST fleet was a major achievement for the trade union movement, moving the guard from the noisy environment of the power car into the passenger area. To allow large items of luggage to be transported, a double opening door was provided. Vehicle No 44001 is illustrated. *CJM*

seat, table and electric food cooker were provided. A door on one side of a dividing wall led into a side corridor and into the luggage cage, which was accessed by a standard outward-opening door on each side, plus an additional opening section to assist in loading/unloading larger items. The guard's 'signal to start' equipment was located by each of these doors.

To construct these vehicles a revision of Derby Litchurch Lane's standard bodyside jig was required to remove one large window position from each side, move the position of the smaller window and revise the door opening design.

Once the TGS vehicles were available, one was inserted in each set at the 2nd Class end adjacent to the power car, with the guard's/luggage end coupled to the power car; each vehicle replaced a TS, which was later reused to strengthen other sets.

The First Refurbishment Programme

In terms of internal decor, the HST fleet retained its 'as delivered' internal layout and decor until 1983, when, following formation of the railway business sectors, the InterCity function deemed that the front-line workhorses were looking *very* tired. Considering that some of the vehicles had emerged back in 1976, this was not surprising; normal wear and tear compounded by the higher aspirations of the travelling public of the 1980s indicated that a major overhaul and facelift were due.

The InterCity business carried out considerable research into external and interior styles in early 1983, and in March/April BR Research Division vehicle No RDB977089, the original prototype TRUK No 10100 (later 40500), was externally repainted in a new InterCity livery based on the then Advanced Passenger Train (APT) colours. It also had new moquette applied to various seats to demonstrate the possibilities of an internal upgrade. After basic acceptance at Derby, the vehicle was hauled to Marylebone on 13 April for inspection by senior members of the BRB, including the Chairman. Also brought to London in the same consist was the one-off InterCity lounge car, No 40513, which at that time was still painted in the original blue grey livery.

Following the trial repaint, authorisation for the new identity was granted with very few significant changes. Externally the colours were two-tone grey, offset by a red and white waist-height band; 1st Class vehicles were given a deep yellow stripe at cant-rail height, with refreshment vehicles having a red band. On the bodyside the InterCity 125 legend was carried in black on the lower body panel at one end.

A major upgrade to the passenger environment was called for in the overhaul programme, which commenced in August 1983. The seats in the 2nd (or by then Standard) Class vehicles were all given a red moquette, offset by an orange and grey fleck. Table-tops were finished in textured off-white with aluminium edges. Carpets also followed the red/orange/grey theme, with a chevron pattern in the aisle area. Wall panels were finished in warm cream, with the coach end panels finished with red angled bands. Brushed aluminium square seat-back grab handles were retained. Roof lighting was upgraded with the solid opaque defusers being replaced by slatted gondolas, improving the interior aesthetics.

In 1st Class a dusk pink seat moquette was used with winged

inner end of the power car. The problem was taken to the trade union and a period of dialogue between the BRB and the guards' union, the National Union of Railwaymen (NUR), resulted in a significant change to the IC125 fleet.

A fleet of 102 Trailer Seconds with a guard's office and luggage van was ordered, sufficient to insert one in each set, plus five maintenance spares. Construction of the new vehicles, classified Trailer Guards Second (TGS), was carried out at BREL Derby Litchurch Lane between 1980 and 1982. One coach, No 44000, was built at first in 1980 under lot number 30953, and served as a design prototype. It was quickly followed by a production run of 90 vehicles (Nos 44001-090) built under lot 30949 between 1980 and 1982. Two subsequent orders were placed in 1982 for four, then seven, vehicles, giving a fleet of 102.

Internally the TGS was a standard vehicle, with 15ft 6in at one end used for a guard's office and luggage van. From the non-luggage end, the coach was laid out in the traditional TS style with a toilet accessed from the vestibule area. That half of the coach was exactly the same as a standard TS, with four bays of four seats around tables on either side of the central aisle. Adjacent to the central divide were two airline seats on either side of the aisle facing the toilet end. The other half of the coach, from the centre, had on each side two bays of four seats with tables, followed by three rows of airline-style seats facing the centre of the coach. On one side, adjacent to the guard's access door, only a single seat was provided, improving access to the non-passenger area.

The guard's area was separated from the passenger saloon by a manual sliding door, which went directly into the office area, where a

Above:
Power car No 43098 *Tyne and Wear Metropolitan County*, painted in the first revised InterCity livery with yellow and black as the predominant colour, changing into standard InterCity colours at the inner end, leads a blue-and-grey-liveried passenger rake past Duffield on 10 July 1986 with the 15.00 Sheffield-St Pancras. *CJM*

Above right:
With a full rake of InterCity stock, complete with power cars in the yellow/black livery, the appearance was very smart. On 8 July 1986, No 43006 leads a full, then standard, InterCity rake through Midgham on the Berks & Hants main line with the 10.50 Paddington-Penzance. *CJM*

Centre right:
As part of the major revamping of the InterCity HST business, the Pullman title was revived in the mid-1980s, with a handful of vehicles repainted and branded with the Pullman name. TRUK No 40511, then from the East Coast fleet, is seen at Ilford carrying the 'InterCity Pullman Restaurant' branding. This vehicle was eventually taken out of service when full Kitchen cars were withdrawn and rebuilt as TS No 41180; it is now operated by First Great Western. *Brian Morrison*

Lower right:
Launched in 1987, the 'Swallow' logo and '*INTERCITY*' name applied to the side of power cars was devised by design consultancy Newell & Sorrell and was probably the most pleasing of the liveries under the BR banner. InterCity 'Swallow'-liveried power car No 43178 pulls out of Kennaway Tunnel and approaches Dawlish on 12 January 1993 with the 08.47 Penzance-Paddington. *CJM*

headrests, which completely changed the appearance of the accommodation. New floor carpets were fitted and the end wall panels were covered in a carpet-style tufted veneer, shaded in dark grey and deep maroon. Lighting was upgraded as in Standard Class. The below-window-height dado panels were applied with a seat-colour moquette, while new dusk pink pleated curtains were provided. Tables were refitted with a textured off-white surface and the standard aluminium surround.

The internal refurbishing also extended to the refreshment vehicles. Those with 2+1 seating had the 1st Class styling and those with 2+2 seating the Standard Class interior. The upgrading of the catering facility is detailed in Chapter 12.

During this internal refit programme, which took some six years to complete and was undertaken by Derby Litchurch Lane Works, it was decided not to change significantly the internal layouts of the vehicles,

although this was an option considered at the design stage, with many people believing that some form of break would be an improvement within the tube-like appearance of the almost 70ft-long passenger saloon. However, to keep costs down this suggestion was declined. The most significant change was the adoption of airline-style seats in some Standard Class vehicles, increasing passenger numbers. This was done

following discussions with rail user groups, who considered that lone passengers, especially women, would prefer to travel with just one person adjacent. However, this is something of a myth, as when passengers board an HST it is the seats grouped around tables that are occupied first. The revision to the seat layout was applied to all Second (Standard) Class carriages.

To launch the HST upgrade programme, two passenger rakes and five power cars were redecorated in the then new IC colours; power cars Nos 43125/126 and 43129/130 were allocated to the launch trains, and No 43151 was spare. Nos 43125/126 were released to normal traffic from Plymouth Laira, operating with blue/grey stock from mid-September 1983, then worked as set No 253028 with the first fully upgraded passenger rake for a media filming run over the picturesque Copy Pit route over the weekend of 24/25 September. After this, the two trains, quickly joined by other vehicles and power cars, entered traffic on the Western Region. Not long afterwards the first Eastern Region set emerged in the new identity; however, the new 'Executive' colours were quickly seen on the ECML with the emergence of lounge car No 40513 from September, which was used on the Leeds/York/Newcastle-London route.

As part of the 1983 refurbishment, on-train telephones were installed for the first time, using VHF radio BT 'System 4' equipment, utilising a fixed ground link based on the motorway network. A telephone was located in one of the 1st Class vehicles at one end in place of one of the luggage stacks. The equipment's operation was poor at times, with a reduced signal or none at all in many areas.

As with mobile phone technology, development of cellular communication equipment rapidly expanded and soon, in a two-year rolling programme from 1986, BT/Cellnet-based phones with exceptional transmission quality were installed on the entire HST fleet. WR sets were the first to be equipped, followed by East Coast, Midland main line and Cross Country. In each case the telephone number was that of the vehicle, but incoming calls could not be received.

In addition to providing passenger telephones, in one First Class vehicle and the buffet car a staff phone was provided in the buffet car and conductor's office.

Today, with the massive increase in personal mobile phones, some consideration will be given to removing phones from sets during the next refurbishment phase. Although not part of further refurbishment, the 1983 InterCity livery, soon gave way to the InterCity Swallow colours - detailed in the livery chapter.

Above left:
Repainting into the InterCity 'Swallow' livery was a comparatively quick process and, to the credit of InterCity, mixed-livery formations were not frequently recorded. On 29 March 1996 No 43195 *British Red Cross 125th Birthday 1995* pulls away from Aberdeen at Nigg Bay with the 09.10 Aberdeen-Plymouth. The smoky power car on the rear is No 43121. *CJM*

Centre left:
A 2nd or Standard Class interior of a 1983-refurbished HST TSO, showing the 2+2 seating in red moquette. The coach illustrated has been set out for 'Silver Standard' service, with tablecloths and paper headrests. This service level was implemented by the Western Region for full-fare Standard Class travellers. *CJM*

Leftt:
The 1980s-refurbished 1st Class used dusk pink as the standard seat colour, which gave a very pleasing ambience to the coaches. The four-seat 1st Class bay illustrated shows a Pullman layout as used on the 'Golden Hind' service between Penzance and Paddington. *CJM*

The Privatisation Era

The biggest change to the HST passenger fleet in terms of interior decor and fittings came in the post-privatisation period from the mid-1990s, when the fleet became the property of two lease companies, Porterbrook and Angel Trains, and was operated by Great Western/First Great Western, Midland Mainline, Great North Eastern Railway and Virgin Trains. As soon as the privatisation process was complete all of these operators quickly developed their own aspirations for interior upgrades and external livery, and without exception these have considerably enhanced the passenger environment and largely changed the appearance of the stock. In each case the 1st Class 2+1 seating and 2nd/Standard 2+2 seating has been retained. We will review by operator the changes made.

The **Great Western** franchise was first awarded to a management buy-out team, which traded as Great Western Trains and chose a traditional Great Western green colour for its power cars and passenger stock, offset by a wide ivory or off-white lower section, on to which a Great Western 'Merlin' logo was applied. On power cars a large 'Merlin' transfer was applied midway along the upper green panel. The green and white of this scheme was very smart, suited the body style, and was well accepted by passengers.

Internally the image was totally different from anything previous seen, with a deep blue moquette being adopted for 1st Class seats, offset by large, soft, cream headrests and dark blue window curtains, blue and deep red carpets and a dark grey marble-effect wall covering at the vehicle ends. The vestibules were finished in ivory offset by green, and the toilets ivory and white, also offset by the green house colour. Passenger tables were totally remanufactured with a mock walnut top surface and a dark grey surround. New-style information and menu display mounts were added below the window at the inner end of each table. In Standard Class the original-style seats were retained but re-covered in a deep turquoise shaded moquette, the tables were upgraded with an ivory surface and turquoise surround, and carpets were in grey and blue fleck. A change from the previous BR layout was an alteration to the vehicles' mid-length screens, which were modified to almost full seat width, being solid towards the vehicle outer walls and full-height glazed towards the centre. The coach ends and the solid sections of the mid-vehicle screens were finished in a grey marble-effect laminate rather than soft textile. The internal refit was carried out by Railcare Wolverton. To conform with the Disabilities Act, one disabled person's toilet was inserted in each set, at the buffet car end of the adjoining Coach E, where a Transitec rotary-door toilet module and a wide bi-section sliding door were fitted into the now reduced-size passenger saloon.

After the Great Western franchise was purchased fully by First Group, some revision was made to the exterior livery, with the green and ivory of the original identity being retained, but now offset by a gold band midway up the body and a swathe of progressively widening narrow green bands applied lengthwise on the ivory-coloured lower body panel, providing a very pleasing appearance. The 'Merlin' logo was sadly lost with the revised identity, replaced by a First Group 'F' with the name 'Great Western'. On power cars, the 'Merlin' logo disappeared and a First Group 'F' and the word 'First' were applied on the upper panel.

Internally a redesign of the 1st Class headrest was made with the ivory-coloured cushion replaced by a blue winged headrest.

On **Midland Mainline** a new and very striking image was adopted for the National Express Group-owned franchise. The external livery is a mid-turquoise upper body, with a grey lower panel, offset by three bright orange bands at waist height. The new company logo of a stag is applied on the bodyside. On power cars the same livery is used with a large 'Midland Mainline' legend and animal logo. Yellow warning

Above:
Sporting the first version of Great Western green and ivory livery, a colour scheme adopted by the management buy-out under privatisation, a full reliveried set led by power car No 43018 passes Crowcombe Heathfield on the West Somerset Railway forming a return charter to Peterborough on 22 March 1997. This was the first time an HST set had worked over the entire length of the WSR. *CJM*

Below:
Showing the very pleasing First Great Western livery, based on the original GW scheme but with additional bodyside branding and the First Group 'F' on the side, No 43175 passes round the tight curve at Langstone Rock near Dawlish Warren on 4 March 2000 with the 06.42 Penzance-Paddington. *CJM*

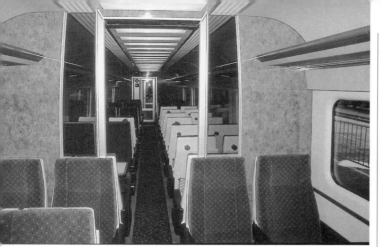

Above right:
Great Western's 1st Class was a major improvement on the previous interior, with dark blue moquette for the seating, dark red carpet and deep blue curtains. Table-tops were finished in mock walnut, but cannot be seen in this view, which shows a Pullman seating layout with white tablecloths. *CJM*

Centre left:
TSO No 42029 at Dawlish shows off the First Great Western colours, using traditional GW green on the upper body panels and an ivory and green band on the lower, offset in the middle by a gold stripe with the 'F' logo and 'Great Western' name. FGW has retained silver window frames and sensible coach-side letters adjacent to the doors. Its carriage numbering is alas very small and applied on the very base of the body on the dark green band, being almost illegible if dirty. *CJM*

Above:
The Midland Mainline turquoise, orange and grey colour has taken a little getting used to by many observers, but does suit the sleek body lines of the HST. On 22 May 1997 No 43049 *Neville Hill* departs from Derby with the 10.00 St Pancras-Sheffield. *CJM*

Above:
Midland Mainline decided that its repaints into corporate livery would also include the window surrounds, which hitherto had been in silver. In terms of decals MML has applied a very useful sign by passenger doors indicating where seat numbers are located in the coach, seen directly to the left of the door at window-base height. Vehicle numbering is in the traditional location and quite readable. TSO No 42140 is illustrated at Leicester. *CJM*

ends were retained. Compared with the exterior livery, the internal styling of the Midland Mainline sets is quite tame. In 1st Class the basic 2+1 layout was retained, now with dark green/grey and orange fleck moquette. The original-style tables were retained. The carpets are finished in dark green fleck. The above-seat luggage racks and curtain pelmet rails are finished in green velour, while deep turquoise curtains are used. The end vestibules were repainted in light cream with green keylines. To enable Midland Mainline to upgrade its catering and offer two levels of 1st Class service (First/Premier), a movable deep turquoise curtain arrangement is incorporated in all 1st Class carriages, enabling bays to be curtained off from the rest of the vehicle.

In Standard Class dark green, grey and orange was adopted as the seating colour with vertical stripes, which looks very drab when viewed without passengers and far less pleasing than other operators' schemes. The carpets are finished in dark grey fleck, with cream-coloured green-keylined vestibules. In an attempt to satisfy passenger concerns about security of luggage, new mid-length two-tier steel luggage stacks were installed in place of one seating bay. The Midland Mainline upgrade programme, undertaken by Adtranz Derby Litchurch Lane Works, also included a major upgrade to the public address system, with an 'advance bell' warning tone and a much improved variable output.

Midland Mainline retained the original-style mid-vehicle draught screen, which is now covered in a green velour.

The **Great North Eastern Railway** upgrade to its fleet of nine HSTs is by far the most impressive. Designed by Vignelli Associates, externally GNER adopted an all-over dark blue colour scheme, offset by a mid-height red/orange band, on which the company name and class of travel is applied. In the middle of each vehicle is a superb coat of arms, specially designed for the Sea Containers-owned company. On some sets these are cast in gunmetal, while the majority are high-quality transfers. Internally the upgrade is quite staggering. In 1st Class a mid-brown seat moquette has been used, with much of the interior trim finished in mock-walnut. A new 'art deco'-style central light gondola is fitted, which lifts the entire aesthetic appearance of the vehicle to one of quality. At the coach ends a novel but useful red/green indicator light has been provided to show if a toilet is engaged or vacant. Above-seat luggage racks of the original style are retained, but now finished in GNER blue, while the brown seating colour is applied to the roof

panel from the luggage racks to the light units. Cream curtains are fitted. The vestibule ends are finished in cream, and seating has been retained in the traditional 2+1 style.

In Standard Class a brown interior colour is used with seats finished in a brown and dark blue fleck, using the original design of seat. Tables are of the original style, but now finished with a wood-effect veneer surface. The end wall panels are also finished in a wood-effect laminate, while the walls, above-seat racks and ceiling are finished in off-white. The rebranding and upgrade of the GNER sets, carried out at Railcare, Wolverton, cost £6 million.

Probably the most impressive of the privatised identities is that of **Virgin Trains**. Externally its sets are painted in Virgin red, offset by dark grey ends and white full-length stripes on the lower bodyside.

Internally the traditional seating layouts have been retained, 2+1 in 1st, or Club Class as it has now become, and 2+2 in Standard Class. In 1st (Club) shades of green have been adopted as the prime colours; the original-style seats have been retained, but re-covered in a new dark grey/green-based moquette incorporating lighter grey irregular shapes and a yellow fleck. Winged headrests are fitted, having a separate, shaped in-fill cushion and antimacassar. Carpets based on grey, green and a yellow fleck are installed, with the section under the seats and tables being of a plain grey for ease of cleaning. Mid-grey dado panels below window height with mid-green pleated curtains, matching pelmet and luggage rack underside make for a pleasing interior.

Reading lights have been retained in the underside of the luggage rack, and on the first few refurbishments the original square open-bulb style unit was retained, after which a more pleasing spotlight was installed. Standard mid-coach dividers have been retained, as has the conventional lighting.

In Standard Class the 2+2 seats have been re-covered in the same moquette as in the 1st (Club) area. New carpets of a similar style to that in 1st Class have been installed, and tables of a slightly revised design, with ivory-coloured tops and aluminium edges, have been fitted, shaped to assist passengers in reaching the window seats. During the course of the refurbishment work, undertaken at Eastleigh Works, new mid-vehicle luggage stacks were fitted in all Standard Class vehicles following a request from passengers who were not happy that their luggage was stowed at the vehicle ends. The new metal racks took the place of one seating bay.

As will be seen from the numeric tables, a small number of coaches have been rebuilt from 1st to 2nd, or 2nd to 1st, over the years. This has been done to assist in vehicle type demand and is a relatively easy operation. Due to an insufficient number of TSOs for the 1986 summer service on the WR, TGSs Nos 44082/092/095/096 were rebuilt by Derby Works as standard TSOs and numbered 42342-45. To cater for a further imbalance of FOs to TSOs in November 2000, FO No 41082 was modified to Standard Class seating and renumbered to 42363.

Right:
By far the most impressive of the privatised liveries is that of Virgin Trains, which uses red as the main colour, tastefully offset by white body bands. A typical Virgin 2+7 formation, led by power car No 43102, with No 43084 at the rear, approaches Aller Divergence, west of Newton Abbot, on 11 September 2000 with the 07.10 Edinburgh-Plymouth service. *CJM*

Below:
The different appearance of the standard HST passenger coach design when painted in the various private owner colours is quite surprising. Very striking in its Virgin Trains red is TF No 41159 at Carlisle. VT decided to retain the yellow 1st Class cant-rail band above the passenger doors on its repaints. *CJM*

Below:
Virgin's 1st Class uses a pleasing selection of green colours, and tables of a revised design making it easier to gain access to inner seats. Green pleated curtains offset by grey rack and side panels give an air of quality and elegance. *CJM*

Above & below:
The Eastleigh Works Virgin Trains interior refurbishment has principally seen new moquette, laminates, carpets and tables, cleaning up the older interior. During the course of the refurbishment work, in answer to customer requests, mid-vehicle luggage stacks were added in place of one seating bay. *Both CJM*

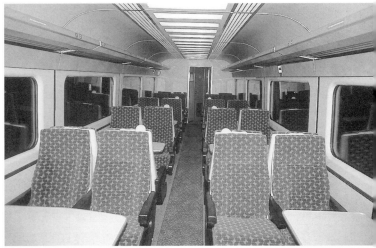

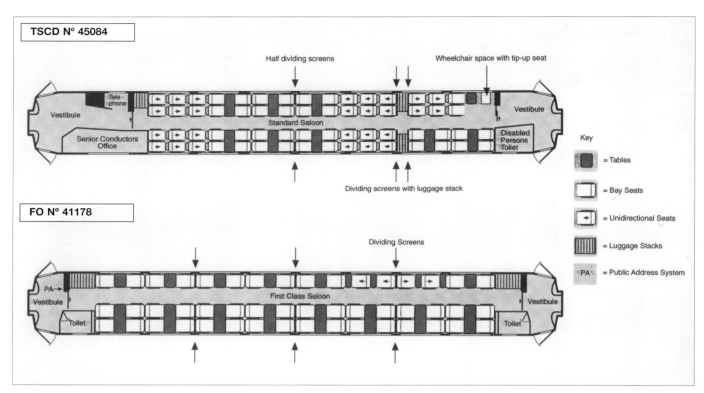

TSCD Nº 45084

Half dividing screens

Wheelchair space with tip-up seat

Telephone

Vestibule

Standard Saloon

Vestibule

Senior Conductors Office

Disabled Persons Toilet

Dividing screens with luggage stack

FO Nº 41178

Dividing Screens

PA→

Vestibule

First Class Saloon

Vestibule

Toilet

Toilet

Key

= Tables

= Bay Seats

= Unidirectional Seats

= Luggage Stacks

PA = Public Address System

In the autumn of 2000, when the rail industry was recovering from the effects of the Hatfield rail crash, poor weather, especially flooding, caused huge operating problems for the industry. One effect of this was water ingress into wheel axle assemblies, especially on Virgin Trains and First Great Western examples. While this problem was being dealt with, to avoid total cancellation of services VT re-formed many HST sets with anything from three to the booked seven passenger vehicles, resulting in some very interesting formations.

InterCity 'Market Test Vehicles' FO 41178 and TSCD 45084

Towards the end of 1992 the InterCity business sector formulated plans for the trial refurbishment of the HST fleet, to be encompassed in the work undertaken during the next programmed overhaul/refurbishment scheme, then due to commence in 1995. There was neither the funding nor the desire to rebuild an entire train at this stage, and it was therefore agreed to produce two Market Test Vehicles for active operation.

It was becoming increasingly noticeable that the interiors and services provided for passengers on European high-speed trains were considerably better than in the UK, and this major project was aimed at reversing that trend. In terms of passenger information, much more was required to satisfy the traveller, who wanted real-time information displays, detailing the actual time, route of service and calling points. A more advanced method of seat reservation was seen as advantageous, with an electronic system replacing bits of paper clipped to seat backs. It was also foreseen that some form of reservation updating must be possible even after a train had departed its station of origin; with advances in train-to-shore communication, this would enable passengers to make last-minute reservations.

Through market research passengers had also put forward to the InterCity business that improved toilets were a major requirement of long-distance travel, and that the guard or conductor should be more conveniently located towards the centre of the train, thus better able to provide a visual presence and a source of passenger assistance.

With the above in mind, it was decided to convert two Market Test Vehicles, with rebuilding undertaken at the Engineering Development Unit (EDU) of the Derby RTC, under the control of the InterCity engineering director. The two coaches selected for rebuilding were TS No 42011, which at the time was stored with serious fire damage and required a large injection of finance for repair, and TGS No 44084. The work was carried out between January and April 1993 and inspected on 8 April by then IC business director Chris Green.

TS No 42011 was rebuilt as an FO and renumbered 41178. Seating was provided for 48, in the conventional 2+1 1st Class style, but to include four airline-style single seats an amendment was made at one

end: the second and third bays on the single-seat side were revised, the two seats in bay two facing the 'outer' end of the coach with fixed half-size tables, while the seats in bay three faced the centre of the coach, again with fixed but small tables. For a long time draughts had been a constant source of complaints from passengers, and this was addressed by the retention of the mid-length glazed screen, which was supplemented by two additional glazed screens breaking up the two saloons in the quarter and three-quarter positions. The above-seat luggage racks were now fitted with an electronic edge display showing seat reservation details. These were programmable by an on-train device before the commencement of each journey, and could be updated by the train's conductor using a hand-held controller. On the Market Test Vehicles the system could not be updated by an external global positioning system, but it was planned that advances in communications would enable this on production vehicles; it is interesting to note, though, that by the spring of 2001 no HST operator had introduced electronic at-seat reservations. However, Virgin Trains, with its new Class 220 and 221 'Voyager' stock, has included such a system from new, and it is expected that some HST operators will now carry out a retro-fit programme.

The electronic passenger information displays were located at the coach ends above the saloon-vestibule door and consisted of a two-line 18-character red dot matrix display supplied by Facon. On the right was the actual time, taken from the global positioning satellite (GPS) receiver, while on the left were two display lines showing pre-programmed information such as the train's title, route and stopping

Left:
The two Market Test Vehicles, TSCD No 45084 and TF No 41178, stand outside the Engineering Development Unit at the RTC Derby on 19 April 1993. *CJM*

stations. The train's position and next stopping point were calculated from the GPS system. If this system had been introduced for squadron use, the display would have been able to show a central control generated message.

Passenger entertainment was considered a major requirement for upgraded train interiors, and CD and radio jack systems were installed; these could, if desired, be played over the train's public address system, but usually would be directed to individual jack sockets by each seat, with the passenger having selection over four channels of CD music and two radio channels (BBC Radio 4 and Classic FM). Personal headphones could be purchased from the train's buffet or customers could use their own equipment.

Saloon lighting was a major challenge for the designers. The InterCity Board wanted to upgrade the then standard plastic gondola arrangement, but a suitable design was hard to source. In fact, when the Market Test Vehicles were shown off to the press at Derby on 19 April 1993, the original gondola diffusers were still in use, but these were changed before the vehicle entered passenger service. In saloon 41178, individual directional lights were also provided in the base of the above-seat luggage rack, individually switched by the passenger.

One of the most impressive upgrades to the vehicle was the reworking of the original seat by updating and softening its form, while improving the ergonomics by providing extra foam support in the lumbar region. The retention of the seat frame and back boards was possible, with a new cushion and swab assembly covered in a new and very smart moquette. The design and assembly of the revised seat was carried out by ABB Interiors, and for the average passenger the seat was 'new' and gave the overall impression of quality. For vehicle No 41178 two bays of seats were of the upgraded design and the rest were of the original style with revised moquette; some bays had further revised headrests to gauge public opinion. The seats were finished in various shades of dark maroon, dusk pink and deep purple. Carpets were also of a new weave incorporating several tones of grey and red.

The toilets at both ends of the coach were fully refurbished with the use of light-coloured easy-to-clean surfaces. The standard layout

of equipment was retained. The end vestibule areas lost the stark bright yellow, with a more welcoming magnolia finish; revised-style litter-bins were also fitted.

The most heavily rebuilt vehicle of the market research pair was the original TGS, No 44084, which was converted to Trailer Standard Conductor Disabled (TSCD) No 45084. The original guard's/luggage doors were replaced with conventional passenger doors, leading into a full-width vestibule. Taking up the same space as the original guard's/luggage accommodation, a new open-plan guard's office was housed on one side, with a side corridor leading into the passenger saloon via an automated sliding door. The guard's office was set out with a high-quality seat incorporating a headrest at a table, with, on an angled panel, a cellular telephone, telephone handsets to the catering car and driver, and switch controls for lights and separate office heating. A fax machine was also provided, working on the cellular system. The office was equipped with a locker, wardrobe, emergency brake handle, a second tip-up seat and a rubbish bin. The guard's office had a glazed door and a separate window to enable passengers to see the conductor. On the corridor side of the coach, opposite the new office, was an emergency equipment cupboard as well as a public BT telephone. The new design enabled the vehicle to be formed mid-train rather than at a set end. If the design had been furthered, the coach would have been marshalled at the catering end of the refreshment vehicle.

Inside the passenger saloon, a luggage stack was provided on both sides adjacent to the office area, with seats set out in the 2+2 style. Three rows of airline seats facing the centre of the vehicle were provided, followed by three bays of four sets around fixed tables. A further three rows of airline seats were then installed, again facing towards the centre of the vehicle, before full-height luggage stacks were provided on both sides. On the toilet side, towards the No 2 end, two more bays of seats were located, while on the non-toilet side further airline seats were provided, with the end seat of a tip-up design to enable a wheelchair to be parked.

The toilet on this vehicle was considerably rebuilt and incorporated a large pneumatic sliding door and equipment positioned to enable use by disabled or wheelchair passengers. The sliding door leading into the passenger saloon was also designed to allow a wheelchair to pass through, and was of a two-section sliding type.

Seating in the Standard Class vehicle was fully upgraded and incorporated various seat refinements. The principal colour was deep rose, offset by mid-grey. New-design grab handles were provided on the seat backs, which were easier to hold on to than the original metal squares. A revised UK system of seat numbering was incorporated, with numbers centrally placed on seat backs and pulled away from the facing/back dual numbers. As in the 1st Class vehicle, electronic seat reservation equipment and a GPS-controlled passenger information display was fitted at the vehicle ends.

The two Market Test Vehicles were evaluated at the EDU before transfer to Leeds Neville Hill for a technical audit, after which the pair were taken to St Pancras for staff training in mid-April 1993, before being inserted in the 'Master Cutler' Pullman service from 17 May for use between Sheffield and St Pancras. From August they were transferred to Plymouth Laira and used in the Cross Country 'Cornishman' service, before being transferred to the Great Western's 'Golden Hind' Pullman service.

Although the pair served as a major source of information for the InterCity business, the next round of refurbishment to some 1,392 vehicles in the period 1995-2000 did not really happen in the way then foreseen. Privatisation loomed, and after the IC125 fleet was split between two owners and a number of operators, each with its own considerations for refurbishment and facelift, very few of the futuristic designs of the Market Test Vehicles came to fruition. The one that was perhaps the biggest loss was the rebuilding of the TGS vehicles into mid-train guard's/conductor's offices, thus making the on-train staff more apparent to travellers.

After their period of demonstration use, the two vehicles were stored. Eventually No 41178 was taken over by Angel Train Contracts and rebuilt as a TSO, being renumbered 42362 and now operated by First Great Western. The prototype TSCD No 45084 was, after a long period in store, rebuilt at Adtranz Derby as a standard TSO and numbered 42360; again this vehicle is now owned by Angel and operated by First Great Western.

Central Door Locking

Today it seems quite surprising that for many years the HST stock was in passenger service at speeds of up to 125mph with passengers able to lean out of a coach door window and open the door, as no locking of any type was installed, apart from a dead-lock for stabling security. Readers might also be surprised to learn that during the design of the prototype train, an early form of central door locking was planned, which, at above 7mph, would have locked and prevented the doors from opening. However, in the quest for speedy delivery and the inclusion of proven technology, central or speed locking was abandoned during the construction of the first two prototype vehicles.

Following a major public outcry at the large number of people who fell from moving trains either by deliberately opening doors or by doors allegedly opening for no reason, an electronic central door locking (CDL) system was authorised for the IC125 fleet in June 1993, with a supply and fit contract awarded to ABB. The first three vehicles to be fitted were Nos 42005/016/017 in November 1993, to enable testing and staff training. To permit a train to enter IC Great Western operation in spring 1994, vehicles Nos 40205, 41011/012, 42015 and 44002/005 were also modified in January of that year.

The CDL system is very simple but very effective. It operates by an electro-pneumatic bolt, housed in a modified vestibule door surround, dropping when activated into a catch in a modified door panel above the opening window.

Above:
Central door locking equipment: **1** Door lock bolt unit on door; **2** Emergency door release valve; **3** Door unlocked light; **4** Conductor's door control panel, with a panel available and power light at the top, two door release buttons on the second row, a door closed indicator on the left of the third row and a door lock button on the right. On the bottom row is a buzzer and a key switch to energise the panel. CJM

The installation of the equipment was quite a major operation with changes needed to the vehicle's electrical and pneumatic systems, requiring the provision of a new train-length jumper to allow control of the equipment from any part of the train. In the vestibule, most of the door surround area was replaced and a new control cabinet provided, one in each vestibule, covering left and right side operation. The control equipment consisting of a key switch to activate the panel, two door unlock buttons, which had to be pressed simultaneously, a door lock button and a buzzer button to give the 'train ready to start' signal to the driver. A separate cabinet housing a telephone gave conductor-driver communication as well as public address. Externally, a square orange door obstruction light was installed by each door, which, when illuminated, indicated that the doors were unlocked.

The installation of the equipment, while contracted to ABB, was carried out at a number of sites to expedite installation, including ABB Crewe and Derby, DML at Devonport Dockyard and Hunslet Barclay, Kilmarnock. The project was completed in the spring of 1995.

After the installation of CDL it was officially prohibited for a train to be in service with the equipment either not working or isolated; if an en route failure happens, the train must to be taken out of service at the next station.

Concerns Over Emergency Egress

Following the Ladbroke Grove collision on 5 October 1999 between an FGW HST and a Thames Trains Class 165, which claimed 31 lives, serious concern was levelled at both train operators on the methods of egress from modern trains, especially those fitted with central door locking.

FGW led the field with a complete review of emergency passenger detrainment strategy, on-board signage and methods of emergency

Above:
How the window breaks if the emergency hammer is used on the two panels of glass. In an emergency a passenger should use the hammer carried in every coach to break the two glass panels in a corner or close to the edge. After the glass shatters it should be possible for the window to be pushed out. *CJM*

Below:
Recently a novel trial method of breaking coach windows has been developed by Safescape (Alert Safety Technologies), whereby a box, attached to the inside of the window, has a button that, when depressed, causes an electric charge to fire a 'bullet' through the glass panels, which can then easily be pushed out. A standard emergency hammer is seen above the new button. *CJM*

passenger egress. From mid-2000 the company began placing 'safety cards' on trains detailing the position of emergency equipment and what to do in case of a serious problem.

The four least damaged vehicles from the Ladbroke Grove crash, TSOs Nos 42073, 42074, 42361 and TGS No 44024, were, after repair by Adtranz, taken out of FGW's operational fleet and stored on the West Somerset Railway at Minehead, as it was considered inappropriate to return the vehicles to passenger service at that time.

At Minehead, the coaches were used by FGW, and Her Majesty's Railway Inspectorate (HMRI), to develop new methods of improving internal signage, lighting and other egress features that *might* then be fitted in the future.

Development reached the passenger testing stage on 27/28 November 2000, when several 'emergency egress exercises' were staged with more than 100 non-railway passengers to gauge effectiveness. TSOs Nos 42073/074 were used for the tests, with No 42073 filled with smoke to simulate a fire; the 'passengers' then had to use the on-board facilities to obtain as quick a release as possible, including manual release of the central door locking.

One of the most serious complaints made after recent accidents has been the darkness inside vehicles if incidents occur at night or if the vehicle fills with smoke. This was addressed by fitting 'snap lights' to the bulkhead at each end of the test coaches, these being chemical lights that, when activated by pulling a handle, give two hours of light. The idea was that the lights could be passed around the coach to

Below:
A test using 'snap lights' to provide interior illumination of vehicles involved in accidents was tested at Minehead in December 2000. However, the first passenger to take the 'light' made a quick exit from the coach and left his fellow passengers in the dark. This is how the unused chemical-based 'snap light' box would look if it was installed. *CJM*

provide illumination, but during the Minehead trial the first passenger to get hold of a 'snap light' kept hold of it, getting off and leaving the rest of the passengers in the dark — a rethink is therefore needed in this area.

Some tests were carried out using aircraft-style floor-level 'exit lights', which would illuminate during an accident and would probably be the most effective form of emergency lighting to guide passengers to the exit, even in part-smoke-filled vehicles. For those with sight problems a form of tactile labelling was fitted to seat ends.

Demonstration was also given of the method that should be adopted if passengers are required to detrain in an emergency by breaking coach windows. Although concern was shown by the Ladbroke enquiry into the hammers supplied on FGW stock, which were alleged to have broken, FGW has found no faults with the green grip-handled hammers presently fitted. It was demonstrated that by hitting a window hard in a corner both inner and outer glass panels can be broken easily, with the shattered glass pushed out from the inside.

A new and novel piece of equipment was also demonstrated, made by Alert Safety Technologies, consisting of a 4in-square box attached to the inside of a window near a corner, with a button (covered by anti-tamper glass) that, when depressed, 'fired' a bullet-like bolt through both panels of glass, immediately shattering both screens and allowing the window to be quickly pushed out. The company has also developed a thin skin, which, if applied to a window, will stop shattering of the screen into thousands of fragments of broken glass and allow it to be pushed out more quickly as one sheet.

New Safety Features

During the 1990s the subject of Automatic Train Protection (ATP) was one that frequently made headline news in the national media each time any sort of accident occurred on the UK rail network involving passenger trains either travelling too fast or passing signals at danger. When built, the HST fleet was not equipped with any such system, but following considerable pressure in the mid/late 1980s, especially after the Clapham Junction and Purley collisions, two trial systems were sanctioned on 6 March 1989, one for the NSE Chiltern route from Marylebone, where new Class 165 stock would be ATP-fitted for use with a new SSI signalling system, and the other on the Great Western main line from Paddington to Bristol via Bath and Box.

The Western Region system, to be supplied by ACEC of Charleroi, Belgium, later part of GEC-Alsthom, required the entire fleet of Western Region IC125 power cars to be ATP-fitted. Route fitting was carried out in 1991-2 with on-train installation falling a little behind. The system, when fully commissioned, operated well, stopping a train by emergency brake application if it attempted to pass a red signal, or warning the driver and, if no action was taken, applying the brakes if speed exceeded the line limit or the train was travelling towards a speed restriction or red signal too fast to stop.

In terms of on-train equipment new cab speedometers and control boxes were needed, as well as electrical frames in the engine compartment and underside pick-up aerials.

By the latter half of the 1990s, while the track equipment and most on-train systems were still being fitted, much of the development work had been completed. From this time it was not uncommon to find either the system switched off or defective. However, the ATP story in terms of the Great Western main line was brought home with a vengeance after the Southall collision, where an HST was driven past a red signal and into the path of a crossing freight train. During the inquiry it was revealed that both the ATP and the automatic warning system on the HST were isolated. After this the GW management agreed that all ATP systems would be returned to full operation and trains not allowed into traffic with the equipment isolated. The use of ATP on HST-operated routes was brought home again after the

October 1999 Ladbroke Grove accident, where, if the equipment had been fitted to the Thames Trains Class 165, the accident would not have occurred.

When the HSTs were first constructed, a standard driver's safety device (DSD) was installed, operated by a foot treadle that had to be kept depressed when the master switch was in a directional position. With the onset of single-manning, a driver's vigilance system was fitted from the late 1980s, whereby unless selected controls are operated in the intervening period an alarm sounds every minute, which has to be acknowledged by release and reapplication of the DSD treadle; if no reset is made within 2sec an emergency brake application is made. An emergency brake application is also made if the master switch is moved while the train is in motion.

Another recent safety feature installed on HST power cars is the Driver's Reminder Appliance (DRA). This is a cab-desk-mounted push switch, which a driver should depress when his train is held at a red signal. Depressing the button cuts off traction power from the power controller and shows a red light. When the signal is cleared, the button face is pulled out, the light goes out and traction power is restored.

Track Protection Warning System (TPWS) is also now being installed, which will apply train brakes if a train approaches a red signal too quickly to stop, or attempts to pass a red aspect.

Royal Train Conversions

To provide two new Royal Train saloons to be launched in the Queen's Silver Jubilee year, 1977, it was decided in 1975-6 to rebuild two of the original prototype HSDT vehicles for Royal use, and replace two LMS 12-wheel saloons of 1941 vintage. Suitable vehicles had been sought for some time for an updated Royal Train, as it was seen that air braking, electric heating and air-conditioning were needed. Various options were studied and eventually it was agreed to take over two of the prototype HSDT cars that were technically spare

Above:
The interior of the Queen's lounge inside The Queen's Saloon, No 2903, rebuilt from prototype HSDT FO No 11001. By studying the ceiling lighting, ventilation and side roof panels one can see the origins of this vehicle. *BR*

to operating needs. To reduce problems with the formation of the remaining prototype train, one 1st Class vehicle, No 11001, and one 2nd Class, No 12001, were selected. Both were first returned to BREL Derby Litchurch Lane where they were stripped of all interior fittings and most technical equipment, before being transferred to the Royal Train division at BREL Wolverton Works. Here the pair were totally rebuilt. Vehicle No 11001 was modified under the 1977 lot number 30886 to become the new Queen's Saloon numbered 2903, while the 2nd Class coach No 12001 was rebuilt as the Duke of Edinburgh's saloon and renumbered 2904.

Saloon 2903 (11001): Although for its new role the vehicle was based on the HSDT body shell, internally this coach is more like a palace on wheels. At one end, on one side, a single-leaf outward-opening door was removed and replaced by a double inward-opening pair of doors that would give a 'more dignified' status to Royal arrivals and departures; this modification required major structural changes to the rigidity of the coach. The other three normal doors were retained. Inside, the vehicle is laid out as a lounge, bedroom and bathroom for the Queen, plus a combined bedroom/bathroom for the Queen's private dresser. The interior decor of the vehicle was left up to the Royal Household, with the Queen playing a major role in design and selection of materials. The coach was officially handed over to the Queen as planned during Jubilee Year, when she was given the keys by the BRB Chairman in an official ceremony. A plaque marking this is carried in the double-door vestibule.

2903 technical details

Design code:	AT5G
Diagram No:	AT5250A
Lot No:	30886/77
Maximum speed:	100mph
Bogies:	BT10
Brakes:	Air
Heat:	Electric, index 9X
Toilets:	1 (CET)
Weight:	36 tonnes

Below:
Rebuilt by Wolverton Works from prototype HSDT vehicle No 12001, The Duke of Edinburgh's saloon, No 2904, is seen at Glasgow Central. This coach retains its original window configuration at the near end, but a revised layout is seen at the far end. *CJM*

Saloon 2904 (12001): The second vehicle converted for the 1977 Royal Train upgrade was for the Duke of Edinburgh. This coach retained its standard four outward-opening doors, with some revisions to window positions on both sides. Internally the coach was laid out with a combined lounge/dining room, bedroom/shower room, kitchen area and a small bedroom/bathroom for the Duke's valet. The kitchen bay was incorporated into this vehicle to enable it to operate without the full Royal catering vehicles if needed. In normal operation, saloon 2904 is coupled to 2903 and for ceremonial events the Duke would usually use the Queen's double doorway.

2904 technical details

Design code:	AT5G
Diagram No:	AT5260A
Lot No:	30887/77
Maximum speed:	100mph
Bogies:	BT10
Brakes:	Air
Heat:	Electric, index 15X
Toilets:	1 (CET)
Weight:	36 tonnes

In addition to the two former prototype HSDT vehicles passing to Royal Train use, four of the production TRUK vehicles have found their way into Royal operation, mainly as part of the 1988 modernisation of the Royal fleet. In the late 1980s most of this overspecified fleet of HST refreshment vehicles were stored, and the chance was seized to obtain more modern stock to upgrade the Royal fleet as part of a £7.5 million Government investment. The vehicles were converted between 1988 and 1990.

2916 (40512): This was the first of the four to enter Royal stock, being rebuilt at BREL Wolverton to lot No 31059 in 1988 as vehicle No 2916. Its new use was not far removed from its original role, as it was modified to a Royal Kitchen/Dining car for Her Majesty to entertain up to 14 guests sitting around a central table. The kitchen equipment was upgraded from HST days. This vehicle remains operational today and is usually deployed when the full Royal formation is used.

2916 technical details	
Design code:	AT5G
Diagram No:	AT5370A
Lot No:	31059/88
Maximum speed:	100mph
Bogies:	BT10
Brakes:	Air
Heat:	Electric, index 13X
Seating:	14
Toilets:	0
Weight:	43 tonnes

2918 (40515) and 2919 (40518): These two vehicles were taken over for Royal Train use in 1989, and rebuilt by Wolverton Works under lot Nos 31083/89 and 31085/89. They were intended to improve the Royal Household accommodation on the active train. The original catering equipment was removed and day/night travelling accommodation, storage space and luggage stores fitted. Sadly, both these coaches were part of a batch of Royal coaches that were officially 'stored' in the late 1990s as surplus to operating needs and are currently decommissioned at Wolverton Works. They could be returned easily to front-line operation.

	2918 technical details	2919 technical details
Design code:	AT5G	AT5G
Diagram No:	AT5380A	AT5400A
Lot No:	31083/89	31085/89
Maximum speed:	100mph	100mph
Bogies:	BT10	BT10
Brakes:	Air	Air
Heat:	Electric, index 10X	Electric, index 10X
Toilets:	0	0
Weight:	41 tonnes	41 tonnes

Right:
Not looking much like an HST vehicle is Royal Train car No 2919, which started life as TRUK No 40518. This was the former kitchen end of the vehicle, which now has a much revised window arrangement. The end of the coach now sports standard buffers, drop-head buck-eye couplings and a very much revised jumper arrangement enabling both standard train supply and three-phase supplies to be maintained. No 2919 is seen at Plymouth. *CJM*

2917 (40514): This was the most recent vehicle to enter the Royal fleet, being converted in 1990 at Wolverton Works under rebuild lot No 31084. Again this conversion was authorised to upgrade the Royal Household and train support staff accommodation by providing a state-of-the-art kitchen vehicle, with the classification of Kitchen/Dining car Royal Household being applied. The coach retains its full kitchen area, modified from HST days, and now has seating for 22 laid out in the 1st Class 2+1 style. This vehicle is still a part of the operational fleet and is usually used when the full Royal set is operating.

2917 technical details	
Design code:	AT5G
Diagram No:	AT5300A
Lot No:	31084/90
Maximum speed:	100mph
Bogies:	BT10
Brakes:	Air
Heat:	Electric, index 13X
Seating:	22
Toilets:	0
Weight:	43 tonnes

Above:
Major cosmetic changes were carried out to TRUK No 40515 for its Royal Train use. Again, the window arrangement was totally altered, as were the between-bogie equipment boxes and roof. No 2918 is seen at Worcester. *CJM*

Above:
Passing the site of the long-closed Challow station, and traversing the racing stretch of the Western Region main line between Didcot and Swindon, originally formed set No 253006, led by power car No 43012, travels at the line speed of 125mph with the 09.45 Paddington-Weston-super-Mare on 5 January 1980. *CJM*

Left:
Travelling over the up main line past Lower Basildon near Pangbourne, HST set No 253017, with power car No 43034 at the helm, storms towards Reading with a Swansea-Paddington express on 10 June 1978. *CJM*

Paving the Way

At an early stage in the planning for a high-speed railway of the future, be it powered by the electric Advanced Passenger Train (APT) or, as we have come to see, the High Speed Diesel Train (HSDT), it was realised that there was no use in developing a train that could travel at speeds of up to 125mph or above if the infrastructure could not cope with the added demands of higher-speed running. A huge amount of groundwork had therefore to be done by both the civil engineers and signal engineers to meet the needs of what was basically a new railway.

With the Western Region identified in 1971 as the first area that would see high-speed passenger train operation, preparation work started immediately. The first task was to establish which sections of the route would be suitable for enhanced speeds. In most cases the speed increase desired was from a 90-95mph base up to 125mph. A three-point plan was then drawn up to identify, first, which sections could *easily* be upgraded for 125mph running, second, which sections could be upgraded with an amount of engineering work, and third, which sections were suitable for speed enhancement but only to a sub-125mph level. Any level of speed increase over and above that already authorised placed huge amounts of extra stress on the running rails and trackbed, and any speed increases had to be achieved with a zero risk factor to trains.

To provide an operational return in the saving of minutes versus the cost of upgrading work, the sections of line to see speed increases would have to be as long as possible, without any low-speed gaps. As well as running at 125mph, valuable time savings could also be obtained from other speed increases, for example, from 60mph to 80 or 90mph on some of the more curved sections. The HSDTs, with their superior traction power and enhanced acceleration, would be able to get away from terminal stations and points of call far quicker, again saving minutes. Braking would also have to be much improved, with deceleration times reduced by around 20%, and again this would help to save valuable minutes and improve point-to-point timings.

In terms of the Western Region, the increase of road speeds up to 125mph was a daunting task for the civil engineers, and one of the first jobs was to undertake a complete reappraisal of the entire main-line network, the first time this had been done since Brunel built the route! From the first research, it could be seen that the Paddington-Bristol via Bath route was principally sound for speed upgrading, with the section from Wootton Bassett Junction (west of Swindon) to Stoke Gifford (Bristol Parkway) being very flat and very suitable for upgrading to high-speed operation.

Left:
Running off the 125mph section at Acton and starting to slow for Paddington, WR set No 253020 passes Acton Main Line on 1 June 1981 with the 09.40 Bristol Temple Meads-Paddington. Photography in this area is now virtually impossible with the erection of overhead power equipment for the Heathrow Express trains. On the far right are the two tracks leading to Acton Wells Junction and Willesden High Level. *CJM*

The first physical operation to be done on the WR was to arrange a programme to calculate the condition of the existing trackbed. This was achieved by boring 18-20in square holes, around 2ft deep, every 10 chains along the line; this was the first ever survey of this type undertaken on any UK railway. The results were not altogether encouraging; in several places the ballast below about 8in was found to be fully consolidated, with the subsoil providing only around 4-6in of ballast to hold the sleeper formation together — the current standard was 12in. Research showed that this was most likely to have been caused when the continuously welded rails were laid on the existing bed in the 1960s.

As high-speed running required the very highest standards of track condition, some form of major remedial work was needed. Several options were available, including a total dig-out and re-lay, and a programme of lifting the existing track and inserting 12in of new ballast; the latter sounded fine, but would cause serious problems with gauge clearance, especially in respect of bridges, tunnels and some stations. This option was also not favoured as it adversely affected drainage and destroyed the cess and edge formations. A third option was to remove the under-track formation using a ballast cleaning machine, removing 12in of old ballast, soil or whatever and inserting a new ballast level.

A major problem foreseen by the WR engineers was drainage; running at higher speeds would increasingly pound the track, and any water that was allowed to drain through the trackbed into the subsoil would form a 'wet patch' when the movement of the track and ballast stirred up the water and subsoil, forming a clay-like paste and causing possible subsidence. This problem had to be overcome, and in most locations bitumen was sprayed under the ballast to form a water-resistant screen; by angling this screen towards the cess, water would run from the track and drain away. In some areas, especially on a 9-mile section of the Swindon-Stoke Gifford route through Badminton Tunnel, special 'blanketing' of the sub-soil had to be carried out; this required digging out the formation to a depth of 24in and sealing the sub-soil level before re-laying the ballast and track.

In the main, most of the Western Region route upgrades for 125mph running were undertaken in planned overnight and weekend engineering possessions. However, the extent of the remodelling on the Swindon-Bristol Parkway route via Badminton was such that the BRB agreed to total route closure of the Wootton Bassett-Westerleigh Junction section between May and October 1975. The work undertaken in this five-month period would have required three years of weekend possessions!

During the course of the WR's major route upgrade programme, no firm date was established for the introduction of HST stock, so no firm deadline date for the work existed. However, progress was such that by early 1976 autumn completion of both infrastructure and train deliveries was running parallel.

The WR's authorisation for full 125mph operation was first granted for the 20-mile section between MP43 (Pangbourne) and MP63 (Challow) in late 1975. This was followed in early spring 1976 by the 20-mile section between MP12 (Hayes) and MP32 (Twyford) on the fast lines, and a few weeks later the 7-mile section between MP87 (Wootton Bassett) and MP94 (Hullavington) was upgraded. In

October 1976 the route onward from Hullavington to Bristol Parkway was authorised for 125mph running. The route west from Wootton Bassett to Box was not upgraded until May 1978. Before authorisation for 125mph running could be given for the section west of Didcot, two-aspect signalling had to be replaced by three aspects, thus increasing braking distances.

The WR, in addition to major route upgrading to allow prolonged 125mph operation, had five 90mph-restricted 'black spots' to deal with for increased speeds. These were at Twyford, where the curves of the main lines were straightened out and platforms and bridges altered; Tilehurst, where alterations were made to the track alignment; Pangbourne, where the alignment was changed and the main-line platforms abolished; Chippenham, where there were major structural changes and realignment of station tracks; and Thingley Junction, where major realignment was carried out to permit the Westbury line junction to be retained in a revised position and the main line route canted for post-90mph running.

The WR's quest to improve high-speed performance on the main London-Bristol route did not finish with the introduction of HST sets. Further major refinements were made in the immediate London area to allow full 125mph running from just 4 miles from Paddington, near Acton Main Line. The 125mph speed was then sanctioned as far as Reading, where a maximum of 80mph was imposed, then 125mph running continued to Swindon, where the top speed on the through non-platform lines was 100mph, while on the main line to Bristol via Bath 125mph running extending only to Box. On the route via Badminton the line speed to Bristol Parkway was largely 125, and west thereof 100mph was the maximum speed with a number of restrictions.

When the IC125 fleet was authorised for use on the West of England route, many people thought that trains would soon be traversing the beautiful Berks & Hants route at such speeds. Sadly, they were very wrong, as the route did not lend itself for any high-speed operation; even with quite significant engineering works and the abolition of mechanical signalling, the top speed is still only 110mph, and that is for only a short distance. The obvious gains in using HSTs on this route came from improved passenger perception of the train, faster acceleration from stations and the ability to achieve the maximum speed on the 36 miles between Reading and the capital.

As part of the preparation work for HST operations on the Western Region, it was foreseen that programmed maintenance requirements would increase with higher-speed running. To cater for these — which would normally take place at night or at weekends — crossings were laid at frequent intervals and many sections of the route were signalled for bi-directional running. This would also allow fast-running HSTs to pass slower passenger or freight trains travelling in the same direction.

As part of the signalling upgrade to allow 125mph running for the greatest distance, a new 'flashing yellow' signal aspect was developed; this pre-warned drivers that a diverging route had been set and would clear on approach. The first use of this was at Didcot in 1979. Following this trial installation and agreement by the authorities, flashing yellow aspects have been introduced at a large number of locations throughout the country.

The second core route for HST introduction — the East Coast main line — required less major upgrading to allow full-speed operation; principally the route had been authorised for 100mph running for some time, using Class 55 'Deltic' locomotives and Mk2s. Much early-1970s modernisation and resignalling allowed much of the 100mph railway to be increased to 125mph without any further major engineering operations. Eight route 'black spots' were highlighted in the initial phase, where improvements for high-speed running were required. These were at Hatfield, where easing of the curves on the main lines allowed a top speed of 105mph; Offord, where realignment allowed a rise in speed from 70 to 110mph; Peterborough, where rebuilding of the station area allowed a massive speed increase from just 25mph to 105mph for non-stop non-platform-line trains; Grantham, where realignment allowed a top speed of 100mph; Doncaster, where upgrading of pointwork, signalling and a slight realignment permitted a top speed of 100mph on the non-platform through lines; Selby, where (before the introduction of the Selby Diversion) track improvements allowed a modest speed increase from 45-50mph to 80mph; Durham, where a top speed of 75mph was made possible by realignment and resignalling; and Newton Hall, where a new alignment was built, but only with a maximum speed of 85mph.

While 125mph is the ruling top speed of the East Coast route, a number of lower restrictions are imposed, due to curvature, signalling and station approach layouts. The most significant upgrade on the

Above:
Some of the most significant work to remodel the ECML for HST operation was at Peterborough, where massive engineering work enabled the through line speed to be increased to 105mph. Departing from the platform line, power car No 43046 leads the 14.50 King's Cross-Leeds on 12 October 1984. *CJM*

Right:
The building of the Selby Diversion from north of Doncaster to south of York had the biggest effect on the ECML and the development of the high-speed network. On 6 July 1983, when trains still travelled by way of Selby, power car No 43089 leads the 07.00 Edinburgh-King's Cross over the Selby swing bridge and through the station. *CJM*

ECML was of course the Selby Diversion, with an entirely new railway built from north of Doncaster to south of York, bypassing Selby completely and joining the Leeds-York route at Colton Junction where a high-speed (125mph) junction was provided.

Another significant development on the ER was, of course, almost total resignalling, with new power boxes at King's Cross, Peterborough and Doncaster. It is interesting to read the East Coast route modernisation plan of 24 April 1975, where it talks about a new flyover at Newark, removing the flat crossing of the ECML by the

Nottingham-Lincoln line, a project that after 26 years has still not been implemented. However, the 1975 East Coast upgrade still cost over £60 million.

On the Midland main line route, where 125mph running was not possible, little infrastructure change was required for the introduction of HSTs. The same also applied to the Cross Country operation, where the trains' use of 'other people's railways', the East Coast main line, West Coast routes in the north and the Western Region in the west, benefited from the upgrades previously carried out.

6. The Power Cars in Detail

Each power car of an HST formation produces crankshaft power of 2,250hp. This 'power' is then converted into electrical energy to drive the train and supply on-board auxiliaries, both for the power car and the passenger coaches. The 12-cylinder Paxman 'Valenta' unit, formed with two banks of six cylinders in a 'V' formation, and the electrical alternator group, supplied by Brush, form a single unit.

The electric alternator is a brushless unit, and the current generated in the stationary windings is collected via fixed connections instead of brushes in contact with slip-rings on the shaft, as on a conventional generator. Four rotors are mounted on the shaft, two of which are electromagnets, which, as they turn, generate current for traction and auxiliary services. These outputs are of three-phase alternating current (ac); however, the traction supply is converted (rectified) to direct current (dc) before passing to the traction motors.

The electromagnets require a dc excitation supply, and this is provided by the other two rotors on the shaft, which turn between the poles of the fixed electromagnet field. The current generated by their windings is ac, but this is rectified by diodes.

The engine/alternator group is mounted in the power car body, with the alternator towards the cab end. A flexible rubber bulkhead separates the engine from the generator area, forming a 'clean air' compartment for the electrical equipment.

Outside air enters through filters behind a row of grilles on both sides of the roof. The intakes in the engine bay ventilate the area and supply air through ducting to the turbocharger, which drives air into the cylinders at a pressure of up to 24psi in the fraction of a second that the air inlet valves are open. A mist spray of fuel, mixed with the pressured air, forms an explosive mixture that drives the pistons down. Within a diesel engine, the air and fuel mixture is 'fired' by the heat generated by the compression caused by the rising piston. The turbocharger, powered by exhaust gases, compresses the incoming air, raising its temperature but reducing its density. This action would reduce its effectiveness, so as the air passes from the turbocharger to the cylinders it goes through an inter-cooler, where the heat is passed to circulating water.

The main diesel fuel is atomised into the cylinders by pressure pumps or injectors controlled by a sliding toothed rack, and unless the turbocharger is delivering the proper air supply, the movement of the fuel rack is limited and the engine will not give its full power.

Following the piston's power stroke, the burned gases are exhausted via the turbocharger and silencer to escape to the atmosphere via roof vents. During early running of HSTs on the Western Region, it was found that the exhaust from the train's rear power car blackened the power car roof and stained the cab window. To overcome this, a curved roof plate was mounted slightly above the original roofline, extending from the exhaust vents to the cab; as air rushed through this gap it provided a 'barrier' against the exhaust and pushed it upwards and clear.

Below:
A broadside view of standard power car No 43097 painted in revised Virgin Trains livery at Carlisle. *CJM*

Right:
A refurbished Paxman 'Valenta' 12RP200L power unit stands in Neville Hill depot awaiting installation to a power car. At the far end is the alternator group.
CJM

The Paxman power unit has both a primary and secondary cooling system; one cools the cylinder jacket and the other the lubricating oil, inter-cooler and hydraulic fan drive. Cooling air for the radiator is drawn in via the large side grilles in the main body and expelled via grilles in the roof. The actual radiator fan is engine-driven via a hydraulic system.

Some 1,050 gallons of diesel fuel are carried in a between-bogie tank, which gives an IC125 a range of around 1,500 miles, depending on the route worked and the load. This is sufficient to cover the average daily roster of around 1,000 miles and the longest Virgin CrossCountry daily mileage of 1,200.

Unlike other diesels, which use their generator to turn the diesel engine for starting, the alternator of an IC125 cannot be used in this way, so a separate starter motor is provided. When the cab-mounted 'start' button is depressed, a motor-driven oil priming pump starts to build up oil pressure; when this is reached, the fuel pump motor starts and an engine starter motor is energised at low power, while a relay moves a pinion forward to engage with a toothed ring on the engine flywheel. When engaged, the motor is transferred to full power and the engine rotates to its firing speed. As the engine reaches 175-200rpm the starter motor is de-energised by a centrifugal switch and drops away. The oil pump continues running until pressure reaches 25-30psi, when the power car's engine-driven pump takes over.

If the engine fails to start correctly within 15sec of the start button being depressed, the sequence stops, with a 20sec time-out before a restart can commence.

In the driving cab, the main driving controls are a master switch for selecting 'off', 'reverse', 'engine only' (neutral) or 'forward', and a power controller with an 'off' and five notch (power) positions. With the power controller 'off' and the master switch in 'engine only', the engine rotates at its pre-set idling speed of 750rpm. At notch 1, idle speed continues but the traction contactors close and current flows to the traction motors. The idling speed is increased to 1,000rpm in the power car from which the train supply is being provided at notch 1. To provide for additional power, the power controller notches give a pre-set engine rpm increase as follows:

Notch 1: 750rpm (1,000rpm if train supply is provided)
Notch 2: 1,000rpm
Notch 3: 1,145rpm
Notch 4: 1,350rpm
Notch 5: 1,500rpm

In each power notch, the pre-set engine speed is maintained by a governor, although the train speed varies; the load on the power unit is constant in any power position, maintained by the governor, and does not vary with track speed. The engine governor has two operations — it oversees the level of fuel supplied to the cylinders, and adjusts the alternator excitation so that the power output of the alternator is constant, at the value requested.

At slow speeds the traction motors require a high current, but as the speed rises the current drops. To prevent the engine from overloading, or to prevent power being under-utilised, alternator volts *must* increase as the train speed increases and decrease as the speed drops, so that the product of voltage v current (electrical power) is equivalent to the engine horsepower of the power demand notch. This is controlled by electronics overseeing the supply to the traction alternator exciter.

The control governor is designed to provide the various engine speeds by operating four solenoids that are powered in differing combinations. The power units at both ends of an HST are controlled together by the driver in one cab, and electrical command signals from the power controller are transmitted to the governor of the 'other' power car via four wires within the 36-way train-length control jumper.

Each power car has four traction motors, two mounted on each bogie; these are each geared to an axle and are suspended in the bogie frame. As the motors are not axle-mounted, a flexible drive system is used. A pinion in the gear-case is supported at one end on the axle and hung from the bogie frame by a rubber-bushed link at the other.

Surprisingly, when the HST fleet was built two types of traction motor were used. Cars Nos 43002-123/153-198 were fitted with four Brush TMH68-46 traction motors, while Nos 43124-152, technically built for the West of England sets, were fitted with GEC G417AZ

units, a scaled-down version of the type first used on the Class 87 locomotives. The traction motors are connected across the traction alternator in series-parallel. At maximum speed (125mph) the voltage across each motor is approximately 1,250V, giving a large enough margin over the back electromotive force for the unit to operate throughout its speed range without field weakening. The decision to use different traction motors for part of the standard fleet arose from BR's wish to dual-source all major components to avoid being exploited by any one supplier. Serious problems befell the GEC motors, resulting in a major upgrade project. At one time BR was planning to use GEC traction motors on subsequent HST builds, but this plan was dropped. Angel Trains are known to be considering re-fitting all FGW power cars with Brush traction motors when these become available due to cascading.

Traction motor cooling air is provided by four traction motor

blowers, two at each end.

Wheelslip with high-power locomotives or power cars can be a major problem, and on the HST power cars wheelslip is detected by a relay system. When an axle slips, its motor accelerates and the voltage across it increases when compared with the other on the same bogie. The difference in voltage causes current to flow via a relay coil, whose contacts close, sending a signal to the load regulator to reduce power, at the same time changing the driver's wheelslip warning lamp from blue to red.

If an axle locks or slides along the rail when the brakes are applied its speed retardation effect is considerably reduced and wheel face damage will occur. Wheelslide detection comes into action when the power controller is at 'off' and the train is coasting; axle speeds are measured directly by pulses from probes on a motor armature shaft on the trailer car axleboxes. If an axle is seen to be decelerating faster

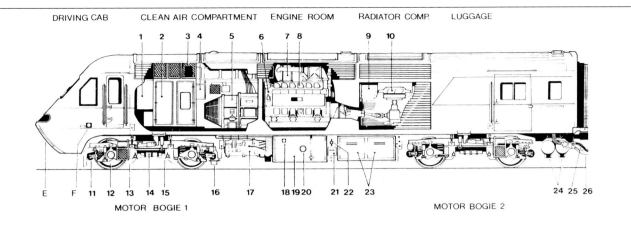

DRIVING CAB   CLEAN AIR COMPARTMENT   ENGINE ROOM   RADIATOR COMP.   LUGGAGE

MOTOR BOGIE 1   MOTOR BOGIE 2

1.	Rectifier and traction motor blower (No.1 bogie)	16.	AWS receiver
2.	Control cubicle	17.	Air compressor
3.	Short circuiter	18.	Fuel filter
4.	Battery charger	19.	Fuel tank
5.	Main and auxiliary alternators	20.	Fuel gauge
6.	Engine governor	21.	Shed lighting switch (other side)
7.	Turbo-charger	22.	Battery isolating switch (both sides)
8.	Paxman 'Valenta' diesel engine, 12RP 200L (2250 bhp)	23.	Batteries
9.	Cooling group (primary and secondary system radiators)	24.	Main air reservoirs
10.	Engine driven cooling fan	25.	Brake pipe/main reservoir pipe hoses
11.	Disc brake cylinder	26.	Train supply jumper cables (415V AC)
12.	Wheel disc	E	Emergency coupling access panel
13.	Tractor motor (one of four)	F	Fire pull handle
14.	Tread Brake		
15.	Parking brake release wheel		

than others of the same group, a signal is sent to a brake cylinder blowdown valve, which slightly reduces brake pressure until adhesion is regained.

Except for the starter motor, oil priming pump and fuel pump, all auxiliary machines are operated by three-phase motors powered from the auxiliary alternator. The exceptions have dc motors, which are operated from the battery before the engine fires up. An electronic automatic voltage regulator controls the output of the auxiliary generator from 207.5V at engine idling to 415V at full engine speed.

Battery power at 110V dc is provided by underslung cells; battery charging operates from the 415V three-phase system, and is controlled automatically by thyristors. Lighting in the power car is at 110V dc, but the nose-mounted headlamps are supplied from the auxiliary alternator via a transformer.

Battery chargers in both power cars are powered from the three-phase line and operate when the supply is switched on from either vehicle of a train consist. Only one power car provides supply, normally the rear vehicle, so that if that fails the driver is able to switch to the alternator at the lead end without stopping the train. The cab air-conditioning units are powered by the three-phase supply.

All HST axles are fitted with air-operated disc brakes, with power cars having a tread brake to skim the wheels and thus improve adhesion. The air brake system is electronically controlled: a small magnet unit attached to the driver's brake controller passes over a series of reed switches, which generate coded messages that represent the 'notch' at which the brake controller is set. These codes are then transmitted over three train wires in the main jumper and converted electronically into voltages controlling operation of electro-pneumatic

valves allowing air to enter or be released from a control reservoir.

A brake distributor valve for each bogie of the power car, and one for each trailer vehicle, allows air into and out of the brake cylinders as the train pipe pressure changes. Pressure in the control reservoir is continuously monitored and converted into an electrical signal. When equal to the demand, the control reservoir pressure is maintained. This means that the train pipe and brake cylinder pressures, which are dependent on the control reservoir pressure, are also maintained at a constant level.

Unlike other locomotives, there is no independent or 'straight' air brake on an HST power car, its braking being controlled in conjunction with the train. Each power car is fitted with a parking brake, applying pressure to the wheel by the tread brake block. This brake is applied by spring and released by air pressure. Manual 'wind-off' handles enable the brakes to be released by hand if a power car is shunted and no air is available.

Power car bogies have a fixed centre transom, sideways movement being allowed for by flexing of the four vertical coil springs of the Flexicoil secondary suspension system. These springs also twist when the bogies curve. The springs sit on the bogie side frames and are housed in pockets at the end of cross-stretchers on the underframe. Traction as well as braking forces from each bogie are transmitted through a kingpin pushing down from a cross-stretcher into a seat within the bogie transom. Primary suspension is by coil springs between the bogie frame and arms on the axleboxes. Hydraulic dampers prevent undue movement in the suspension system causing 'hunting'.

As mentioned in an earlier chapter, when built there was accommodation for the guard within the luggage area at the rear of the

power car; originally this had a capacity of 1.5 tonnes, but this has now been increased to 2.5 tonnes.

Coupling between power cars and passenger stock is by means of buck-eyes. Train-length control cable connections are made by multi-pin jumpers.

Power Car Re-engining

In 1983, the UK had one of its hottest summers for many years, and while this was enjoyed by many, the rail industry, especially the high-speed train operators, were thrown into chaos, caused by a spate of overheating problems with 'Valenta' power units.

On power units such as the Paxman 'Valenta' some 60% of generated power has to be dissipated as heat; some is expelled via the roof exhaust, while much is disposed of through the engine, achieved by circulating water around the engine then via the radiator or cooler group. Calculations show that the radiator of an HST power car sheds some 1,250hp of energy at full speed.

The main element of the cooling system is a sufficient supply of coolant water, maintained at the correct temperature, a protective device being coupled to the cooling system to ensure that water temperature does not rise too high above 95ºC. If it does, the engine shuts down and the driver gets an HWT (high water temperature) light on his desk. If insufficient coolant is present, the engine also shuts down.

The 1983 summer problems saw engines shutting down due to HWT, but these were compounded by a series of cracks inside the engine allowing the coolant water to leak out. At first it was considered that the problems were caused by a sudden spate of serious engine cracks in the Paxman power units. This problem hit BR at a very bad time, coming on top of the GEC traction motor problems on the West of England sets and led to GEC (which was also the parent company of Paxman), falling out of favour with BR and BR eventually seeking litigation, which resulted in a £7million compensation payment from GEC covering loss of earnings.

Both BR and Paxman were originally convinced that the problems were power unit-based. However, a major research undertaking by both BR and Paxman eventually found that the power unit was not the main cause; the cooler group was not keeping engine coolant liquid at its correct temperature, and this was causing engine cracking to increase. Further research found that the HWT protective devices were either poorly set or did not work at all, and thus the engines were not being looked after. Apart from repairs to the HWT system, blockages of the radiator group were also found. Inside the system the pipe-jointing compound was melting in the higher than usual temperatures, then, as the engine cooled, the compound hardened,

Right:
The view from the front, with Virgin Trains traction inspector John Thompson controlling power car No 43079 on the West Coast main line at exactly 95mph. *CJM*

Below right:
The cab layout of an HST power car not fitted with Automatic Train Protection, DRA or TPWS. **1** Electric train supply dimmer switch; **2** De-icer/mister switch; **3** Desk light switch; **4** Tail light switch; **5** Tail light switch; **6** Marker light switch; **7** Headlight switch; **8** Engine compartment light switch; **9** Cab light switch; **10** Emergency brake plunger; **11** Brake controller; **12** AWS indicator; **13** Inspection light socket (a fan is now fitted on some VT power cars in this position); **14** Brake test switch; **15** Main reservoir gauge; **16** Brake cylinder pressure gauge; **17** Brake pipe gauge; **18** Windscreen wiper valve; **19** Cab air-conditioning switch; **20** Electric train supply 'off' button; **21** Electric train supply 'on' button; **22** Electric train supply indicator; **23** Parking brake indicator; **24** Parking brake 'off' button; **25** Parking brake 'apply' button; **26** Brake overcharge button; **27** Fire alarm test button; **28** AWS in/out indicator; **29** General fault indicator; **30** AWS/DSD alarm; **31** Call alarm; **32** Reading lights; **33** Ashtray; **34** Speedometer; **35** Wheelslip indicator; **36** Engine stopped indicator; **37** Main alternator amp meter; **38** Engine start button; **39** Engine stop button; **40** Driver/conductor buzzer button; **41** Clock; **42** Power controller; **43** Master switch with key socket in centre (forward, engine only, reverse, off); **44** AWS reset button; **45** Horn valve. The cab illustrated is that of No 43116. *CJM*

resetting and blocking panels and pipeways. Rectification saw units removed and overhauled by the suppliers.

A second problem was the blocking of the exterior radiator fins by general dirt and contamination, stuck to the radiator by oil mist. This problem was largely overcome by new cleaning methods.

Returning to the engine cracking, this was proving a major problem to resolve. The cast aluminium exhaust manifolds were showing extensive cracking, which, although reduced by the modification to the cooler system, was still causing major concern. Paxman, in conjunction with BR, set up detailed monitoring of several power units in 1985 to try and understand more about the problem. Paxman

was keen to replace the cast aluminium manifold with a cast-iron unit, which showed less likelihood to crack. BR, however, was happy to continue with the aluminium unit as failure rates were reducing to around two per month.

Disaster returned to the HST fleet in 1986 with a huge increase in engine failures due to cracks. Paxman was at its wits' end — no obvious cause could be seen for the problem, and to reduce the effects on passenger services, a large batch of replacement cast-iron exhaust blocks were ordered.

Just when a blank was being drawn on the problem, WR engineers found that the increase in cracking started at the same time as a revised anti-freeze was introduced, which included a new chemical designed to protect the interiors of engines by causing a form of chemical corrosion to form a skin. This chemical caused an allergic reaction to some elements of the aluminium alloy and caused cracks at a rate between three and four times quicker than before. To try and improve the miles per casualty figure in July 1986, some power cars were temporarily derated to 2,000hp.

All the problems that BR encountered with the Paxman engines, even though most were actually a direct result of BR's own poor maintenance and deficiencies, saw the rail industry explore a policy of re-engining the HST fleet.

Mirrlees had, during the early 1980s, developed a small 2,400hp unit — the 12MB190 — which would fit into a Class 43 power car with few structural modifications. Although slightly heavier than the Paxman units, BR agreed to refit a batch of four power cars with the new engines for trials, and have one engine spare. Before installation for main-line running one engine was tested at Derby, and in May 1986 was trial-fitted into power car No 43091 at Derby Locomotive Works to sort out the final design of the body support mounts. The four vehicles selected for trial fitting were Nos-43167-170, the work being carried out by BREL Derby, following a DM&EE 300-hour bench test in mid-1986. The first car modified was No 43167 at the end of 1986, which entered service from Bristol St Philips Marsh on 31 January 1987. Nos 43168-170 were modified in early 1987. When this trial re-equipment was undertaken, the plan was for 'around' 140 to be refitted, but time proved that this was not to be.

In 1988, with the changing face of the rail industry emerging and separate businesses being formed, compounded by InterCity losing Government subsidy, the requirement was for a lean and efficient operation, based on major cost reduction. As part of this the previously considered Mirrlees re-engining was dropped, and in May 1988 BR went out to tender for an HST re-equipment programme that, if agreed, would cover 147 vehicles.

After first-round submissions, four companies were invited to make a formal bid: Paxman (UK), Mirrlees (UK), MTU (Germany) and Pielstick (France). The bids were required to include a maintenance deal and cover for the vehicle to be delivered to a workshop in an operational state, and to be returned by rail fully operational.

In 1987 Paxman commenced development of the successor to the 'Valenta', given the alphanumeric title 12VP185, and the engine first operated in August 1991. BR showed considerable interest in this engine development, and after prolonged discussions and with

Upper right:
An HST number panel showing the running number 43028 below the shed sticker 'MA' for Longsight (which is wrong for an HST). Below is the technical detail plate, which shows Class 43, a total weight of 70 tonnes, a brake force of 35 tonnes, the electric train heat (supply) index (not applicable on HST power cars), an 'RA' (route availability) of 5, and the maximum permitted speed of 125mph. The square box in the middle is a glazed-fronted fire pull handle, which when operated sets off the engine room fire extinguishing system. *CJM*

Below:
Production HST speed/horsepower curve.

Lower right:
Traction/brake horsepower required by two HST power cars to reach 80, 100 and 125mph on level track with various train weights.

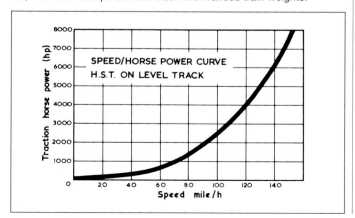

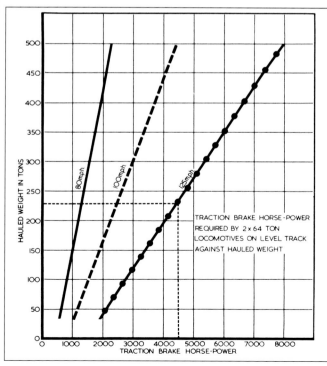

Right:
Simplified HST electrical system.

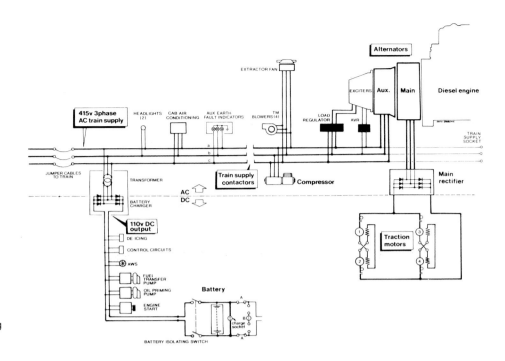

Below left:
The new generation of Paxman HST power unit, the Paxman 12VP185, which has been purchased by the main HST operators in small numbers. It has proved to be highly successful and many would like to see a further squadron re-engineering contract authorised. *GEC Diesels*

Below right:
Plymouth Laira depot was given the job of installing the first of the VP185 engines, fitted here to power car No 43170. With a special lifting frame the blue-painted prime mover is seen being carefully hoisted over the bodyside in the heavy repair section of the depot. *GEC Diesels*

changes in the rail industry, an agreement was signed in May 1993 for trial installation. However, prior to being fitted into a power car a Type Test of the engine was carried out at Derby between December 1993 and February 1994. The test engine was set to deliver 3,500hp and underwent 3,000 running cycle simulations of the on-off nature of rail traction units. These tests proved highly successful and a trial installation into vehicle No 43170 was carried out at Plymouth Laira in the summer of 1994. The engine and power car were also fitted with a DEMON (Diesel Engine MONitoring) system, where through a Vodaphone link the condition and performance of the engine could be monitored at the RTC Derby and by Paxman in Colchester. No 43170 returned to front-line service in September 1994.

After nine months of virtually trouble-free running, No 43170 was the subject of a special event at Paddington on 13 June 1995 when it was named *Edward Paxman*. The high-profile gathering also witnessed the signing of a contract for Paxman to supply a further eight 12VP185 engines to the UK rail industry, which by now was beginning the process of privatisation. Delivery commenced in August 1995 and the engines were installed in cars 43047/059/074/075/167/168/169/177 as well as 43170. As will be seen, this included all the trial re-engined Mirrlees locomotives. Apart from one, No. 43167, all were operated by FGW and MML. No. 43167 is with GNER and to avoid costly spares being maintained by the company, No. 43167 was re-engined in aummer 2001 with a standard 'Valenta', the VP185 going to FGW.

Left:
As late as 1980, prototype power car No ADB975813 visited BREL Derby Locomotive Works for classified attention to its bogies and running gear prior to being used for further main-line tests. In the background two production power cars undergo attention. *John Chalcraft*

Below:
Today one of the principal depots that carries out classified attention to HST power cars is Laira in Plymouth, where a two-road section of the shed is dedicated to such repairs for operators First Great Western, which manages the depot, and Virgin Trains, which hires in maintenance under contract. Five power cars are seen under repair in this view: nearest the camera on the left is No 43158 having a replacement power unit installed, while on the right No 43189 receives power unit and exhaust attention. This area at Laira can take up to eight power cars at one time. *CJM*

During the construction phase of the HST sets, it was agreed that purpose-built maintenance facilities would be required to carry out service and planned overhauls. Unlike the trains that they replaced, where the locomotives and stock were maintained separately, the HSTs would receive all levels of attention, except major overhauls, as a fixed train set.

Once the entire HST fleet was in service, it was allocated to and maintained by seven principal depots:

Bounds Green (North London) — BN
Craigentinny (Edinburgh) — EC
Heaton (Newcastle) — HT
Neville Hill (Leeds) — NL
Laira (Plymouth) — LA
Old Oak Common (West London) — OO
St Philips Marsh (Bristol) — PM

In addition, a large number of other depots and terminals were equipped to carry out routine maintenance, such as Long Rock (Penzance), Landore (Swansea), Etches Park (Derby), Longsight (Manchester), Polmadie (Glasgow) and Clay Hills (Aberdeen). If required, fuelling could be undertaken at any depot.

Under the original BR maintenance policy, vehicles were maintained on their line of route, with one exception: sets that finished their working day on the Midland main line at St Pancras were tripped via the North London line to Bounds Green.

Under the present privatised railway, HST allocation is at Craigentinny (GNER), Neville Hill (Midland Mainline and Virgin), Laira (First Great Western and Virgin), and St Philips Marsh (First Great Western). In addition, facilities exist at most of the depots that dealt with the trains in the 1970s. Old Oak Common ceased HST maintenance in mid-2001 after the new Class 180 DMUs for First Great Western were introduced.

Every HST formation is given a service examination with replenishment of consumables each working day; this includes fuel, water and oil, and is normally carried out with the train fully marshalled, it being returned to service in just a few hours. To facilitate this, new fuel/inspection points were assembled at most depots that could undertake fuel and exam operations of the power cars at each end of a formation simultaneously.

However, different levels of maintenance are followed, classified from A through to F, based progressively on the number of hours and miles operated, with each level of examination progressively more thorough, until a major or works exam of level F or G is reached. This sees the power car or passenger vehicles stripped down and a major overhaul carried out, taking several weeks to complete. For example, a power car undergoing a G exam at Neville Hill in 2000 would be programmed out of service for around 20 working days, and would see a full body repaint and all internal components removed and replaced on an exchange basis, including bogies and possibly the power unit, depending on the hours operated by the prime mover since its last replacement.

Right:
Between construction and February 1988, HST power cars received classified attention at BREL Derby Locomotive Works, alongside locomotives of Classes 20, 24, 25, 45 and 46, with usually around six power cars in the works at any one time. This view, looking along the main repair bay, shows two power cars and five 'Peak' locomotives receiving attention. The power car on the left is No 43037 and the one in the centre of the shop No 43036, both from Western Region set No 253018. *BREL*

From their construction in the 1970s until February 1988, power cars received major or classified overhauls at BREL Derby Loco Works, the final vehicle to receive classified attention being No 43118. After early 1988 a new maintenance regime based on component exchange was introduced, with selective regional depots taking on the role of major or Level 5 facilities. In terms of HST power cars these exams were then undertaken at Laira, Neville Hill and a very few at Stratford DRS. On the Western Region, the depot at St Philips Marsh, Bristol, was used, part of what became known in the railway industry as The Bristol Traction Group, which also saw some power cars and trailer stock maintained at Bristol Bath Road and Landore, Swansea.

During the 1970s and 1980s some HST power car collision damage was repaired by BREL Doncaster, especially when damage was confined to front-end and side panelling.

Coaching stock vehicles were likewise maintained at BREL Derby Litchurch Lane until early 1988, since when the allocated depot has been responsible for all levels of maintenance. The Level 5 depot at Ilford and some of the other major engineering sites also took part in some passenger vehicle overhauls in the 1980s.

With today's privatised railway, the maintenance operation has considerably changed; no major workshops carry out programmed overhauls, with all levels of repair (except collision) undertaken by the depots listed above.

In addition, Neville Hill also undertakes selected work on GNER power cars. In recent times since privatisation, some of the major private workshops have also been awarded large refurbishment contracts when such work fell outside the remit of allocated depots; this was funded by the 1990s-formed rolling-stock lease owners. Works associated with these refurbishments are Alstom Eastleigh (Virgin trailer stock), Railcare Wolverton (GNER and First Great Western trailer stock), and Adtranz Derby (Midland Mainline trailer stock). In mid-2001 half life overhauls ans re-wireing has commenced on FGW sets, with work sub-contracted to DML Plymouth and Laira.

Left:
Many depots that were to undertake servicing of HST rakes were refurbished or rebuilt to house fuelling aprons at suitable locations to enable fuelling and service exams to be undertaken while the power cars were attached to a full passenger rake. One location was Heaton, Newcastle, where ER set No 254002 is seen receiving attention in November 1977. *CJM*

Left:
Too many turntables went out with the steam era, which today are very much needed with a fleet of single-ended vehicles in order to permit operational flexibility, especially in areas where depot triangles do not exist. An HST turntable is incorporated into Leeds Neville Hill depot, on which power car No 43198 is seen on 10 February 1987. *CJM*

Above:
Laira depot in Plymouth underwent major reconstruction for the deployment of HST sets, with originally three and then four full-length inspection roads built in a new shed alongside the original locomotive facility. Two HST sets are seen inside the purpose-built depot on 19 January 1996: on the left is power car No 43154, while on the right is No 43078 *Shildon County Durham* off the westbound 'Cornishman' service. *CJM*

Above right:
HST trailer cars are frequently split from their sets at Laira and placed in what used to be the loco repair shed to receive classified or unscheduled attention. Here during the night of 19 January 1996, from left to right, are vehicles Nos 42356, 44020 and 44022 undergoing repairs. *CJM*

Centre right:
Painted in InterCity 'Swallow' livery, No 43055 *Sheffield Star* stands inside the HST inspection shed at Leeds Neville Hill on 3 January 1997. On the left is the first HST to be painted in Virgin colours, No 43063, being prepared for transfer to Edinburgh for the Virgin Trains CrossCountry franchise launch. *CJM*

Above:
Craigentinny depot, Edinburgh, was constructed for HST operations on the East Coast main line and has also played a major part in CrossCountry operations. Inside the repair bay on 25 February 1996, East Coast-operated No 43108 is seen split from its set awaiting lifting for bogie attention. *CJM*

Above:
Collision or damage repairs to HST trailer vehicles have historically been undertaken by Derby Litchurch Lane Works, and more recently the collision repair facility at Crewe. Refreshment vehicle No 40426 is seen under repair at Derby Litchurch Lane on 17 October 1994 following impact damage near Edinburgh. *CJM*

Above:
In immaculate condition, No 43185 *Great Western* stands outside the heavy repair factory at Laira on 2 February 1996. This power car had been repainted under the direction of then Area Fleet Engineer Geoff Hudson to take part in a special high-profile media event at Waterloo on 5 February when Great Western was officially handed over to the private sector as the first of the privatised rail operators. *CJM*

Above:
Major collision repairs to the HST power cars have in recent years been undertaken by Crewe Works under its various owners of ABB Transportation, ADtranz and now Bombardier. Following a collision with a runaway loco at Edinburgh in August 1994, No 43180 is seen at Crewe after a new cab had been fitted. *Darren Ford*

Above:
Power cars operated by Virgin Trains now receive their classified overhauls at Leeds Neville Hill, where usually one vehicle at a time undergoes major attention. Laira-allocated No 43197 *Railway Magazine Centenary 1897-1997* is seen in the painting bay in October 2000 when an F exam was being undertaken. *CJM*

8. The 'Surrogate DVT' Power Cars and Buffer-fitted TGS Stock

Following authorisation for the electrification of the East Coast main line from King's Cross to Edinburgh, as well as the 'branch' to Leeds/Bradford, a new fleet of InterCity 225 electric train sets were ordered, formed of a high-powered electric loco, classified as 91, coupled to one end of a rake of Mk4 passenger vehicles. Driving facilities at the non-powered end were provided by a fleet of Driving Van Trailers (DVTs).

The Government's orders for this new stock became very staggered for various reasons, with the locomotives being ordered prior to the passenger stock and the DVTs, mainly due to major modifications required in passenger vehicle bogie design.

To enable the Class 91s to be introduced prior to the delivery of either the Mk4 passenger rakes or the DVTs, a decision was made to adapt a small number of IC125 power cars to act as temporary DVTs. The project was masterminded by the Engineering Development Unit at the Railway Technical Centre, Derby, and coincided with major research and development into Time Division Multiplex (TDM) control systems using 'coded' messages, transmitted in time slots over the train lighting cables and decoded in remote vehicles, with up to 64 channels of data able to be passed over a single pair of cables. The TDM system was supplied by Brush.

To enable the power cars to be operated within non-IC125 consists, some major modification work was required. First, the streamlined front end had to be modified to house conventional buffing equipment. The emergency 'eye' coupling was removed and a conventional draw-hook installed; no coupling was attached, but an emergency screw coupling was carried in the engine bay. A standard air brake pipe and two main reservoir pipes were fitted, plus a standard electric train supply jumper/socket and a UIC jumper. As the work was very much experimental, the EDU oversaw the project of rebuilding two trial vehicles, Nos 43014 and 43123, in the autumn of 1987. To maintain as much as possible of the streamlined appearance of the original vehicles, only the lower section of the front skirt was removed. Conventional oval buffers were installed on extended headstocks fitted to the main dragboxes of the vehicle underframe.

To enable this equipment to operate, a TDM control cubicle was fitted in the original HST luggage compartment, and a small additional desk panel was mounted slightly above the original driving

Upper right:
The first of the EDU conversions to 'Surrogate DVT' form, No 43123, is seen well under way in this 16 September 1987 illustration. The new headstocks have been fitted, enabling buffers to be installed, while a new tri-note horn cluster has been fitted. The side and front skirts were later modified to fit. *CJM*

Right:
The inner end of prototype 'Surrogate DVT' No 43123. It can be seen that a new ETS jumper cable has been provided, and two UIC coach lighting jumpers for TDM operation. It is interesting to see that the ETS cable has been brought out of the vehicle from a new panel in the upper body section. *CJM*

desk in the cab. This equipment is detailed in the accompanying photograph caption and was operational only when the power car was coupled to a TDM-fitted electric loco. At the vehicle's inner end, two three-pin TDM jumpers were installed, with a high-level control jumper on the two Derby prototypes.

Originally it was announced that the two prototype conversions, which were to undertake testing on the WCML and a trial introduction into passenger service from December 1987, would have their power units retained as ballast weight, but with the equipment isolated and all power and auxiliary supplies fed by the powering locomotive. The DM&EE department at Derby was very unsure about allowing the power cars to be hauled around the network dead with traction equipment in situ, as research had previously shown that prolonged rotation of traction motors without power being applied could lead to glazing of the commutators, which in turn could lead to traction motor flash-overs when power was returned. However, it was the wish of the operators to retain the ability to be able to use the power car engine if needed, so the traction motors had to be left untouched.

When the project first started to convert a small fleet of 'Surrogate DVTs', a fleet size of ten vehicles was put forward, and their classification was originally to have been Driver Trailer Luggage Van (DTLV) with renumbering authorised in the 8209x series; indeed, records show that Nos 43014/123 were actually allocated the numbers 82098/99 in August 1987. After it was agreed that the power units would be retained and maintained as operational, the DTLV renumbering was cancelled and a new sub-class, 43/2, was authorised, with the modified vehicles becoming 43201 onwards; with power retained, the official type code would have been DMLV — Driving Motor Luggage Van — but as time has come to prove, this was never carried out, the original numbering being retained.

The first vehicle to be released from the EDU at Derby, No 43123, emerged in October 1987 and commenced a period of static and dynamic testing on the WCML from Willesden. For several days in November 1987 the vehicle, shut down in terms of traction, was coupled at the London end of a rake of four Mk2s with a Class 86 at

the north end. Testing was then conducted between Willesden (Stonebridge Park) and Rugby. A number of teething troubles were experienced and the remote driving vehicle returned to Derby for rectification.

The second of the Derby conversions, No 43014, emerged in November and underwent major testing at Derby before being transferred to the London area. Testing of the 'Surrogate DVTs' progressed into early 1988, and a further six conversions were authorised by the BRB. These rebuilds were carried out at Stratford Diesel Repair Shop in East London, the vehicles involved being Nos 43013/065/067/068/080/084. The first of these Stratford conversions was No 43084, which emerged in March 1988. A modification made during the rebuilding of the two Derby conversions was the removal of the standard ETS jumper and sockets, with the original three-phase power supply socket retained. The very short-lived launch into passenger service on the West Coast route took place in December 1987, with vehicle No 43014 working at the London end of a Mk2 rake powered by Class 86 No 86228.

By the time these vehicles were modified, it was agreed to keep the 'Surrogate DVT' conversions in the main HST power car fleet and renumbering was abandoned. The batch of eight buffer/TDM vehicles were based at Bounds Green, North London, where training and test running commenced in the spring of 1988 in preparation for the deployment of one or two from July 1988 on King's Cross-Peterborough commuter services, powered by the Class 89 locomotive;

Right:
The modified cab equipment on the eight 'Surrogate DVTs' consisted of an oblong box attached to the top sill of the driver's desk above the speedometer. This housed eight button indicators: from left to right these were 'sand apply', 'anti-slip brake', 'tractive effort boost', 'pantograph down', 'pantograph up/line light indicator', 'fire fight delay', 'dynamic brake not failed' and 'traction braking current indicator'. In each case these referred to the condition of equipment on the TDM-fitted electric locomotive at the remote end of the train. While the equipment was designed to operate with Class 91s, it also performed the same tasks with Classes 86, 87, 89 and 90. The only other change was a revision to the brake test switch; other cab equipment remained the same as on a conventional power car. Modified No 43014 is shown.
Brian Morrison

these were usually the 07.16 Peterborough-King's Cross and 17.36 return.

To enable the 'Surrogate DVTs' to operate at the remote ends of Mk3 HST formations powered by a Class 91, a number of modified rakes of HST stock were marshalled in the latter half of 1988, each being formed with a modified Trailer Guard's Second (TGS) at one end. These were adapted with conventional buffers at the guard's end and a standard drop-head buck-eye coupling at the passenger end, enabling easy coupling to a Class 91 slab end. The coaches rebuilt were Nos 44021/056/058/059/086/097/098/101.

The Class 91, Mk3 and 'Surrogate DVT' operation on the East Coast commenced on the King's Cross-Leeds route from March 1987.

By this time agreement had been reached between InterCity and the DM&EE that the HST power car would be used to provide three-phase train auxiliaries, such as heat and light, with the Class 91 just providing traction power. This method of operation continued for several weeks until a further change of plan was announced, whereby the HST power cars were to be authorised to provide traction power, operating under full TDM, meaning that the driver of either the Class 91 or Class 43 had *full* control over both electric and diesel traction.

The mixed train formations remained in traffic for only a relatively short period until sufficient Mk4 passenger stock and Mk4 DVTs were commissioned. Once released from the ECML, the buffer-fitted power cars had the TDM equipment removed and the vehicles became part

Right:
Test running using the TDM system with a 'Surrogate DVT', four Mk2s and a Class 86/2 commenced on the West Coast main line in early November 1987. One of the first test runs is seen on 7 November passing Kenton, powered by No 86240.
Brian Morrison

of the standard InterCity fleet. They remained allocated to the East Coast route for a short while until the batch were transferred to Edinburgh Craigentinny for deployment on the Cross Country routes.

Upon privatisation, the buffer-fitted power cars were all 'allocated' to Porterbrook Leasing and deployed on the CrossCountry operation, later taken over by Virgin Trains. The drawgear, which at one time during a quest for standardisation was considered for removal, remained in situ and has proved very useful in recent times, making it easy to attach an assisting loco in case of failure; the power cars have tended to operate on the longer-distance CrossCountry duties where

there is an increased likelihood of en route failures. In the summer of 2000, during the West Coast modernisation works at Euston, Willesden and Manchester, each of the West Coast HST formations was marshalled with one buffer-fitted power car to assist quick recovery in case of failure.

Most of the buffer-fitted TGS vehicles remain in traffic and are now allocated to GNER, Virgin and First Great Western. They have again proved very useful, especially if HST passenger rakes have been required to operate with conventional locomotives. It is not unknown for these vehicles to be used as barrier vehicles if necessary.

Left:
Most of the original WCML test runs were carried out between Willesden Yard and Stafford and were used to prove the integrity of the UIC control system and the coding/decoding equipment on the power car. With No 43014 at the helm, a test train is seen awaiting departure from Stafford on 7 December 1987. *T. R. Moors*

Left:
A very brief introduction into passenger service on the WCML was made in mid-December 1987. On 14 December No 43014 is seen leading the 11.26 Wolverhampton-Euston at Birmingham International. Class 86/2 No 86228 is providing traction at the rear. *Chris Morrison*

Above:
Doing the work for which it was intended, HST power car No 43067 leads a Mk3 formation past Helpston Junction on 30 August 1989, acting as the south end driving car, with Class 91 No 91007 providing power at the rear end. The trace of exhaust above the power car shows that the engine is running, providing additional traction power. *CJM*

Below left:
After their useful life working on the East Coast with Mk3 sets powered by Class 91s, the 'Surrogate DVTs' were used in all HST areas, with all eight eventually transferring to Cross Country use. On 4 February 1993 No 43123 leads a 2+7 formation past Duffield on the 13.28 Sheffield-St Pancras. *CJM*

Below right:
Powering south through St Denys and approaching Southampton, buffer-fitted No 43080 leads the 05.17 Manchester-Bournemouth on 20 May 1995. *CJM*

Left:
Looking rather grubby and obviously not having been through a mechanical washing plant recently, No 43068 passes North Queensferry and heads towards the Forth Bridge and Edinburgh on 6 January 1993 with the 07.55 Aberdeen-King's Cross working. *CJM*

Below:
Painted in full Virgin livery, No 43123 makes ready to depart from Glasgow Central on 12 August 1999 with the 11.20 Glasgow-Penzance service. The presence of buffers on the long-distance CrossCountry routes has paid off on numerous occasions when failures have occurred, an assisting loco being much easier to attach with conventional drawgear. *CJM*

Left:
Buffer-fitted TGS No 44056 at Doncaster, marshalled in a standard HST formation. *CJM*

9. HST Performance: On the Road with the Class 43s
by John Heaton FCIT, Railway Performance Society

It is late on a dowdy autumn afternoon in drab commuterland west of London. Slough station slumbers in that half-light that signals the departure of the day. At the west end of the station a diesel unit slinks off the Windsor branch into the bay platform. The doors thud open and a heterogeneous collection of humanity decants. Office workers, tourists, schoolchildren and shoppers spill across the width of the down main platform.

Suddenly the urgent yet familiar warning of a two-tone horn comes from the east end of the canopy. An InterCity 125 appears, sounding the horn again, the second note being held to emphasise urgency. Viewed from head-on its approach is deceptively stately, but as the angle becomes less acute the station explodes in a cacophony. The roar of the front power car kills conversation. The branch-line passengers shrink from the platform edge, cowering near the safety of the buildings.

There is just time to glimpse the driver of the High Speed Train, motionless, intense, insouciant; man and machine in common endeavour. The eight coaches flash past in a blur of green and gold allowing only a moment's relaxation before the intimidating roar of the rear power car heralds the return of routine. Half a minute later and the HST is over a mile away, its 430-tonne mass hurtling westwards at 125mph to the first stop at Reading, 36 miles from London in just 22min.

Allocation

To many, the Great Western is the natural home of the HST. Brunel's 'billiard table' profile, with its sweeping alignment, offers the perfect surface to exploit the HST's performance. It is true to say that the WR deserved to be allocated the first batch of the production sets. There is little doubt that the Eastern Region, with its longer-distance high-speed routes, could have maximised the units' potential, and the trains of the WR spent long periods languishing in Cornwall and west of Cardiff. Even the Berks & Hants route to Plymouth could not offer a single stretch of track at over 90mph west of the Reading panel box area until the major re-signalling at Westbury and Exeter in the mid-1980s.

However, it was decided that the WR offered more scope. Certainly, it offered a greater margin over existing motive power. After an unsuccessful dalliance with diesel-hydraulic power, the Western had been left with a ragbag fleet of Class 47s and 50s. The Eastern also relied on the flexible, if uncharismatic, Class 47s, but it could boast impressive headline times for key trains employing 'Deltics' on light loads. On good days these machines were capable of averaging 100mph over 100 miles. On one such day the 'Bradford Executive' recouped 18min between South Kirkby Junction and King's Cross with a 100mph run from Tuxford to Stevenage without exceeding 104mph.

Right:
Passing Alexandra Dock Junction, west of Newport, set No 253029, led by power car No 43127, forms the 11.15 Paddington-Cardiff on 14 July 1980. On the left Class 47 No 47029 is shunting to gain access to Ebbw Junction, while behind the HST a Class 31 heads west with a freight. *CJM*

Upper left:
Marshalled with a Standard Class refreshment vehicle, WR set No 253016, painted in original livery, drops down Dainton bank towards Aller Junction on 27 June 1981 forming the 09.05 Penzance-Paddington. *CJM*

Lower left:
After running for over 5 hours, set No 253021 with power car No 43043 leading (now working for Midland Mainline) forms the 12.35 Paddington-Penzance passing Scorrier on the final leg to Penzance on 21 June 1980. *CJM*

late, with its non-stop run to London hampered by temporary speed restrictions of 40, 100, 30 and 50mph. In preparation for these delays 133mph was reached between Hullavington and Little Somerford. This figure was attained for a second time at Goring. A signal stop outside Reading did not prevent the Berkshire town being passed at 71mph. A delay, probably signals, from 117mph to 112mph between Twyford and Shottesbrooke seemed to ruin the driver's calculations for a punctual arrival, but in compensation speed was whipped up to 138mph at Slough, dipping to a mere 126mph at Hayes but reviving to 133mph as late as Hanwell. The actual time from Newport to Paddington was 86min 43sec on a 93min timing, just a half minute late. The recorder calculates the net time as 78min at an average of 102.6mph.

Such exploits are now impossible. First, governors were introduced to cut off power from the rear power car at 128mph. Automatic Train Protection (ATP) superseded this installation, warning a driver if speed exceeds 128mph and intervening if the situation deteriorates. The result is that it is now commonplace for GW HSTs not to reach even 125mph. On the RPS mass timing day on 17 September 1988, 15 down HSTs were timed between Paddington and Reading. Only two failed to reach 125mph. In contrast, a recent sample of 15 down non-stop runs over the same section yielded only six 125mph maxima. The addition of an eighth coach to cater for the demand that faster schedules have created has, of course, reduced the accelerative capacity of the WR fleet.

Sharp schedules
The effect of the extra coach should not be over-estimated. On 5 February 1990 a run with the down 'Torbay Express' from Paddington to Reading was completed in 21min 27sec against a schedule of 23min, with 125mph by West Drayton in 9min 21sec. The top speed was a shade under 129mph. The train was booked a remarkable net time of 38min to Bath, plus 3min recovery time. Despite reaching 127mph at Cholsey and averaging 126mph for the 23 miles from Didcot to Shrivenham, passing Swindon at 97mph, reaching 128mph at Dauntsey and entering Box at 115mph, the run took 38min 41sec. Shall we ever see the like of this again?

It appeared that the custodians of Western punctuality in the 1980s believed that tight timings kept staff on their toes. Perhaps the spirit of Gerry Fiennes still stalked the boardroom! Examination of the computer-produced figures indicated that it was normal for fractions of a minute to be rounded down rather than up. Indeed, it was the recommended practice early in a journey. Certainly it was rare to meet an unmotivated driver during this period.

South Wales
One look at the RPS 'Fastest Times' publication is sufficient to emphasise the point about performance standards at the turn of the 21st century. Of 26 station-to-station start-to-stop times between Paddington and Swansea in the down direction, 24 were set in the 1980s. The most modern one is in the furthest west, a 1992 record

Great Western

The '140 Club'
The arrival of HSTs in fleet service on the WR was eagerly awaited by those interested in recording traction performance. Fortunately, the introduction of the trains coincided with the arrival of digital stopwatches. Even so, the greater mental dexterity required to record quarter-mile timings in 7.2 seconds at 125mph was taxing when compared to a leisurely 9.47sec of a Class 47 cruising at its top speed.

It was soon obvious that the excitement that had affected amateur ranks had also infiltrated the professional corps. It did not take long for drivers to experiment. They were quick to exploit the lack of a speed governor at the 125mph maximum. Even the disciplined, conservative, possibly staid Great Western footplatemen vied to join the unofficial '140 Club'. Now, 140mph in trials, under supervision and with special maintenance conditions, is one thing. 140mph with a normal service train is quite another. However, the efficient braking system offered to drivers who were only a few years from a railway that depended on vacuum, the splendid signal sighting of the former broad gauge main line, and good weather conditions — well, the temptation occasionally proved too much.

One Railway Performance Society (RPS) log records a run when a bid for 'membership' was made. On 23 May 1977 the 11.52 from Newport, a standard 2+7 set grossing 405 tonnes, left Newport 7min from Neath to Swansea. Of course, many of these 26 sections are no longer timetabled. The growth in importance of Reading (and Heathrow), Swindon and Bristol Parkway has resulted in additional stops, and clockface patterns mean that this arrangement often applies throughout the peak. Formerly, non-stop runs with full trains were made in the peak hours. The introduction of Class 180s with more intensive frequencies *should* lead to the restitution of a more adventurous stopping pattern for HSTs.

Many of the high water temperature problems that beset the HSTs are attributed to the vicious start/stop pattern to which these machines have been subjected. It is possible, therefore, that fewer stops could lead to a swansong of improved availability.

An examination of South Wales schedules shows a clear picture. In 1987 the 16.00 Paddington-Swansea was allowed 156min gross, 146min net, with two stops before Cardiff. By 1993 this had become 170min gross, 157min net, with three stops before Cardiff. In the summer of 1999 the figures were 175 and 159 with three stops. West of Cardiff HST performance is challenged by low maximum speeds, frequent stops and a few steep gradients. The fastest (albeit rare) HST time recorded non-stop between Cardiff and Swansea is 43min 10sec. The advantages that 'Sprinters' can offer such routes, comfort aside, are demonstrated by a fastest time 11% better at 38min 27sec.

The Berks & Hants

On the Berks and Hants route, from Reading to Taunton via Newbury, the picture mirrors that of South Wales, although it is not quite so grim. Was the 'Cornish Riviera' really booked to Exeter in 115min gross, 111min net? Yes, it was, and renowned performance specialist Peter Semmens recorded 110min 11sec in 1990. By 1993 it was timed for 122min gross, 117 net, with an extra stop at Reading, which does not explain the 7min gross time increase. By 1999 the schedule had expanded by a further minute.

The crack train on this route in diesel days was always the 'Golden Hind', now reduced by First Great Western to the status of drinks in plastic cups. At the end of the BR era the train had tablecloths, silver service, teapots and hot towels. In the late 1980s WR management decided that this train was to have absolute priority. It was not unusual for an Area Manager to be rung at home to give a personal explanation of a signal check! The theory was that opinion-formers used *only* a few trains, and that if 'their' train was on time they would act as ambassadors of the railway. Although this might sound fanciful, the following remark was recently overheard on the 'Golden Hind' as it stood outside Reading awaiting Railtrack's convenience: 'When I moved to Taunton 13 years ago this train was *always* on time.'

The Exeter drivers who worked this train during that period were far from immune to this infectious spirit. Two of the most outstanding runs were recorded by the same driver, now long retired. However, because of the speeds involved, it is probably wiser to suppress his name. Approaching the end of his career he was still at the peak of his abilities; keen, alert, calculating, aware of just where he could safely 'pinch a bit back'. He was an ex-GWR driver, which was unusual in a period where most of the top link 'fast' drivers were former Exmouth Junction (Southern) men.

The 'Golden Hind' has traditionally run non-stop from Taunton to Paddington. The typical schedule of recent years has been 100min for the 142.5 miles with an average speed of 85.5mph. A Reading stop was inserted after the Southall accident, a strange move after all these years, now that Heathrow passengers can reach the airport faster via Paddington and the Heathrow Express than by the Reading coach link. The B&H has a maximum permissible speed of 110mph, and even this is limited to three short stretches. The large number of intermediate restrictions and changes of gradient require a driver to exercise anticipation and clear judgement.

On the first of the two runs the departure from Taunton was only a few seconds late. It was a surprise to note speeds of 111mph at Athelney and 108mph at Somerton Tunnel, both on 100mph-limited track. In 1990, though, the track maintenance standards were undeniably better than now. The 90mph restriction at Cogload Junction was taken at 95mph, as was the similar restriction at Castle Cary. The minimum speed at Bruton was 97mph, with 112mph attained between Clink Road Junction and Fairwood Junction. The reason for such haste then became evident as three temporary speed restrictions (TSRs) were encountered before Newbury, compensated by only 2min of recovery before Reading. Although five further recovery minutes were available between Southall and Paddington, drivers always attempted to get 'their' path at Reading, without the assistance of the large allowance. Then there was no point trying to dissipate so much time over the last nine miles. At the time the number of TSRs was described as 'unusually high'. In Railtrack's regime, even prior to the crisis that followed the Hatfield crash in October 2000, the number seems surprisingly low. Having run hard and encompassed the delay from the TSRs, the running towards London was more restrained, although 106mph was recorded at Aldermaston. Once through Reading the 13.75 miles from Burnham to Hanwell were covered at a flying average of 128.9mph. Despite a 2min signal check at Westbourne Park, Paddington was reached in 93min 52sec, 6min early.

The second occasion was on a Monday morning in 1991 following the weekend when axle-counters had been installed on the Dawlish sea-wall. The 'Hind' arrived at Exeter 12min late and left Taunton 11min down with the seemingly impossible task of reaching Paddington in 89min at a 96mph average.

It might be expected that the driver would have adopted the same approach, but it was a measure of the man that the running was much more restrained. He was 41sec down on the first run at Bruton (94mph) with a maximum of 106mph and speeds of 91mph on the two 90mph permanent speed restrictions. The unified management structure of BR had served to ensure that there were no TSRs on the B&H, so that drivers had a fighting chance of minimising the delays that might result from the axle-counter work. The express had a clear run towards the 110mph section after Heywood Road Junction, managed 117mph before Lavington but hit the 90 restriction beyond the viaduct at 91mph. The missing second TSR put this run 65sec in front of the first at Pewsey, and the absence of the third TSR improved the margin to 3min, but still 6min down on schedule, at Reading.

There was no need of heroics from Reading to Paddington and the Burnham-Hanwell average was a mere 125.6mph. With a clear run to Paddington and 5min recovery, the driver was able to arrive a wholly satisfactory 1min early in 88min 9sec at a 97mph start-to-stop average.

West from Exeter

Between Exeter and Plymouth the interest in HST performance is often focused on the way the steep banks are tackled. Westbound the two fiercest climbs are between the former Aller Junction and Dainton, with gradients of 1 in 36, and from Totnes to Rattery, pitching at 1 in 46. However, the Tigley-Rattery section from MP2251/2 eases to 1 in 90/95, and HSTs have to be eased to comply with the 60mph limit. Eastbound, Hemerdon poses the more difficult task with 1½ miles at 1 in 42, sometimes severely blighted by autumnal leaf-fall. Dainton is just as steep on the final throw to the summit, but there is the respite of a brief level section, known colloquially as 'the shelf'. HSTs can manage minima of 55mph at Dainton, both ways, and at Tigley, but not without an illegal run at the banks. Just how impressively HSTs can perform on Hemerdon is demonstrated by the fact that they often need to be eased to comply with the 60mph restriction at the top as the gradient flattens out to a

paltry 1 in 75. A Class 47 on seven Mk2s would typically crest the summit at about 42mph.

The net schedules in each direction between Exeter and Plymouth are 52min, although the eastbound one has recently been eased from 51min. The RPS fastest times are 47min 53sec westbound and 46min 5sec eastbound. The latter was attained from the unlikely down main platform 4 at Plymouth with the 17.30 Penzance-Paddington in 1999. The set was said by the driver to be weak and managed only an 80/58mph climb of Hemerdon in 6min 48sec. Speed rose to 72mph a number of times on the 60mph limits to Totnes, being eased back to 62-64mph each time. The maximum was 73 mph down the bank at Tigley to pass Totnes in 21min 22sec. The underpowered set managed 55mph at Dainton, but only by achieving 65mph on the 55mph restriction on the bank. Newton Abbot was passed in 29min 46sec, whence speeds to Exeter were not excessive. The 90mph limit to Teignmouth was reached, but the 80mph step to the 60mph restriction at Teignmouth were taken at 79mph and 60mph respectively. The set nearly managed to reach 75mph on the two stretches authorised for this speed to Dawlish Warren. After 85mph on the 80mph restriction to Starcross, the 75mph restriction on the curve was taken at no more than 77mph. With 102mph on the final 100mph leg, Exeter was reached in 46min 5sec, despite catching sight of double yellows before Exeter City Basin. The previous record had been 47min 42sec. Undoubtedly more aggressive driving with a stronger set could have achieved a 45min timing.

The run is less of a testament to excessive speed than an indictment of the inaction by Railtrack and GW in improving the infrastructure. The present standard is way below the capabilities of the staple HST motive power on which both GW and Virgin Trains rely. This is not the end of a branch line, it is part of the main InterCity core network. The nebulous plans for improving the speed profile of this route have yet to secure funding. Only six paths per hour are available between Plymouth and Newton Abbot, yet the section has *not* been classified as a bottleneck. This situation is unacceptable.

Cornwall

One might expect that Cornwall would exhibit the same pattern of lethargy as Wales beyond Cardiff. The same combination of low maximum speeds, short distances between stops and steep gradients applies, complicated by disruptive single-line sections. It is certainly true that the majority of the RPS fastest times for the standard down

Above:
HSTs have been used on a number of charter and railtour specials, sometimes traversing tracks not usually associated with the HST fleet. On 13 December 1997 Hertfordshire Rail Tours' 'Teign Taw Turkey' visited some of the Devon branch lines, and is seen pulling away from Newton Abbot towards Heathfield on the usually freight-only branch. *Charles G. Woodland*

Right:
For many years in the 1980s an instruction was issued that if an HST set was operating on one power car, with just 2,250hp available, it had to be assisted west of Exeter over the steep Devon banks, thus numerous assisted HSTs were seen, especially in the period of power car problems. On 22 August 1980 Class 47 No 47251 pilots set No 253019 through Dawlish Warren with the 12.35 Paddington-Plymouth. *CJM*

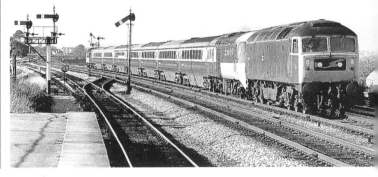

Below:
Running adjacent to the grounds of Powderham Castle and the banks of the River Exe, set No 253019, forming the 12.03 Penzance-Paddington, crosses with 'Peak' Class 46 No 46015 on a St Blazey-bound mixed freight on 21 August 1980. *CJM*

Left:
Midway between Totnes and Plymouth is the growing town of Ivybridge, which in the early 1990s was given the privilege of having its station reinstated. Rather than use the site of the original GWR station close to the town, a new park-and-ride station was built a few miles away. On 14 September 1994 the 14.35 Plymouth-Paddington passes the station led by No 43020 *John Grooms*. *CJM*

stopping pattern were achieved in 1984 with 2+7 sets. The story is different on the up line, where 18 out of 34 HST sectional fastest times have been set in the 1990s! Many of these have been achieved by Penzance-based GW drivers whose familiarity with the precise undulations of the route in conjunction with speed limits is born from the fact that they drive the road to Plymouth virtually every day of their lives.

The other striking point about the Cornish trains is that the HSTs have generally managed to maintain an advantage over the 'Sprinters'. Their fastest times beat all other forms of diesel traction on 21 out of 25 down main-line sections from Plymouth to Penzance.

Technicalities

The B&H runs serve better than most to illustrate the difficulty of differentiating between the technical characteristics of HST power cars. Take the Mirrlees power cars of the late 1980s/early 1990s, for instance. There are few logs in existence with two together, and the cars were soon separated. The same applies in many ways to the VP185-fitted cars. The performance of the other power car, which might be performing badly or very well, prevents conclusions from being drawn. A poor power car with a good driver will often give better start-to-stop times than a good power car with a poor driver. Throw into the equation differences in gross load, whether one power car has a notch strapped out to prevent high water temperature, headwinds and railhead conditions and we have half a dozen factors that appear to outweigh marginal differences in engine output.

Drivers have said that the Mirrlees power cars were more powerful, but there is little empirical evidence to support this. One wonders if this is a perception caused by the deeper, more throaty noise rather than differences in the acceleration curve. Even when the variable of driver performance is removed from the equation, conclusions are unreliable. Drivers say that they work round the whole fleet and are not aware of one power car being better than another over a long period of time. Minor adjustments to the setting of the fuel racks can make huge differences in power output. There is the belief that VP185 engines are slower to pick up revs and get away slightly slower than Paxmans. It is also said that the VP185s are deliberately downrated for fuel economy, longer life, lower maintenance costs, reduced fuel emissions and because the full power cannot be effectively transmitted to the wheel by the original traction motors.

Centre left:
Slightly off the usual HST network, power car No 43076 passes Lapford on 3 March 1990 heading a Hertfordshire Rail Tours charter that had taken an HST to Barnstaple. To provide the necessary standard of catering the set had been re-formed with two refreshment vehicles. *CJM*

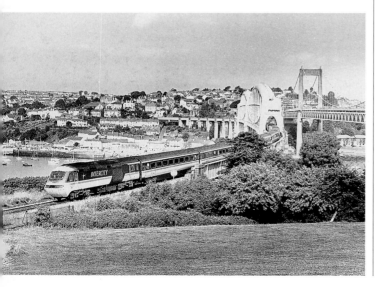

Lower left:
Passing over the superb Royal Albert Bridge, designed by Isambard Kingdom Brunel and linking Cornwall with Devon, a Cross Country formation led by power car No 43098 forms the 07.52 Penzance-Edinburgh on 12 June 1992. This was one of two Cross Country HST sets that visited Cornwall each day. *CJM*

Above:
At the east end of Newport station the four-track GWR main line crosses over the River Usk as it approaches Maindee West junction. Traversing the up main line on 1 March 1995, No 43142 leads the 09.32 Swansea-Paddington. *CJM*

Driver's-eye Wiew

There is also a degree of scepticism that the so-called 'supernotcher' power cars that are supposed to deliver full power immediately make much difference to running times. If traction power is applied too quickly wheelslip will occur, and wheelslip protection will operate, often resulting in slower times. One driver has said, 'They all give power very quickly. I tell trainees to apply notch 1 and release the brake, then get through the notches as quickly as possible. If it's a good car, the ammeter and speedometer needles will both be vertical, at about 70mph. If one power car suffers from high water temperature, it is sometimes advisable to drive in notch 4 all the way as you might reach your destination on eight notches out of ten instead of five with one power car shut down. One of the biggest factors that affects performance is not the power from the engine, but the speed the brakes release. If it is quick, the driver can rely on it responding quickly to sharp braking followed by fast acceleration. This is very important running into stations with short platforms such as many in Cornwall, where it is important to stop the train precisely. With a brake that is slow to come off, drivers will run in a lot slower to be sure of getting it released before stopping short.'

Perhaps these are areas for a deeper study by the RPS, but one that would take higher levels of organisation, coverage and co-operation with both train operating companies and rolling stock companies than it is probably realistic to expect.

Above:
Carrying Trainload Construction livery, Class 47 No 47079 was called upon to assist the 07.18 Newcastle-Paignton on 4 June 1988 following a serious failure of the rear power car, which was removed en route. The unusual formation of No 47079, hauling power car No 43150 and just seven Mk3 trailers, is seen at Dawlish running 70min late. *CJM*

Above:
The 09.18 Edinburgh-Penzance caused problems for the operators on 17 September 1982 when both power cars were declared failures at Bristol. The local Bristol Bath Road depot provided Class 47 No 47254 to pilot the train throughout to Penzance, seen here passing Powderham, west of Exeter. *CJM*

Below:
Following a power car failure at Bristol Temple Meads, the 06.42 Dundee-Penzance, led by power car No 43092, is seen piloted by EWS Class 47 No 47634 through Cowley Bridge Junction on 15 October 1997. The train later terminated at Plymouth to allow repairs to be undertaken at Laira depot. *CJM*

Lower left:
Sporting the short-lived privatised livery of Great Western with the 'Merlin' logo on the bodyside, power car No 43169 *The National Trust*, fitted with a Paxman VP185 engine, leads the 10.30 Paddington-Penzance summer Saturday service towards Teignmouth on 5 September 1998. *CJM*

Above:
With a rake of InterCity 'Swallow'-liveried stock behind, Great Western 'Merlin'-liveried power car No 43190 leads the 10.05 Penzance-Paddington towards Whiteball Tunnel and the crossing of the county line between Devon and Somerset on 27 March 1997. *CJM*

Above:
The first ever HST to visit Exmouth did so on 20 September 1996, when a special was run from Birmingham to Exmouth to mark the naming of power car No 43071 *Forward Birmingham* after the Exmouth-based RNLI lifeboat of the same name. Buffer-fitted No 43080 passes Lympstone Village station with the return train to Birmingham. *CJM*

Left:
In good lighting there can be few better locations to photograph an HST set than on the sea-wall section near Dawlish. On 29 August 1999, in almost perfect light, power car No 43131 *Sir Felix Pole* leads the 09.40 (summer Saturday) Paignton-Paddington holiday express towards Dawlish Warren. *CJM*

Above:
Two generations of East Coast 'racehorse' stand side by side at King's Cross on 30 March 1980. On the left HST No 254031, with power car No 43116 nearest the camera, is under shore supply and awaiting departure with the 17.00 to Edinburgh. On the right 'Deltic' No 55013 dozes on the buffer line after bringing in empty stock from Ferme Park. *CJM*

Below:
An East Coast 2+8 formation, led by No 43050, painted in InterCity 'Swallow' livery, approaches Alexandra Palace station on 17 February 1989, in the immediate pre-electrification period, with the 14.30 King's Cross-Edinburgh. *CJM*

East Coast Main Line

Of HSTs and 'Deltics'

While HSTs are probably associated with the East Coast main line second only to the WR, it is sobering to reflect that they enjoyed only a decade of dominance on the racing grounds of the King's Cross-Edinburgh route. In retrospect it is also fair to say that the initial impact of HSTs was not so monumental as on the WR. The 1978 schedules on the Eastern were already sharp, with 'Deltics' on eight or nine coaches working to high-speed timings. The HSTs undeniably made an improvement even on the 'top flight' trains, but their main effect was to improve the second and third tier of services, some of which were timed for Class 47s on 11-coach trains that rarely averaged 90mph for long distances. The net King's Cross-York via Selby schedule in 1982/3 was 110min. 'Deltics' on nine needed 129min. In contrast a Class 47 on 11 would have required around 146min.

In the latter years of the 'Deltics' they worked all-stations King's Cross-York trains. When these were withdrawn, the off-peak stops were absorbed by Leeds HSTs, pulling down averages of these trains with fewer stops. In 1976/77 it was possible to leave London behind a 'Deltic' at 11.25 and reach Leeds at 13.57. In 1982 the 11.50 down HST, with only two extra stops, was booked into Leeds at 14.09. In the up direction the 1976/77 12.30 'Deltic' from Leeds was scheduled to arrive in King's Cross at 15.13. Six years later the 12.45 HST, again with only two extra stops, was due in the capital at 15.07. Neither example represents revolutionary exploitation of the new motive power.

Of HSTs and Class 91s

By 1988 the Class 91s were rolling off the production line at Crewe. With trains that eventually amounted to nine coaches and a DVT,

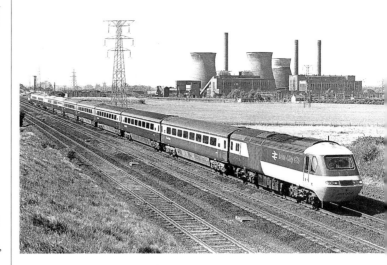

they began to assume responsibility for the bulk of main-line trains, including the crack expresses such as the 15.00 from King's Cross, which eventually became the 'Scottish Pullman' to Glasgow Central with a London-Edinburgh schedule that was honed down to 3hr 59min. Spare HSTs were reallocated to other routes with a small allocation retained to serve Scottish cities north of Edinburgh, and English destinations off the electrified network such as Harrogate, Hull and, prior to Aire Valley electrification, Bradford.

An examination of the net point-to-point timings for the King's Cross-Edinburgh route provides an interesting comparison. The 15.00 to Glasgow Class 91 is allowed 100min net, 102min gross, to reach York. The 16.00 King's Cross-Aberdeen HST is allowed 103½ min net, 108½ gross, or a net average of 109mph compared to the electric's phenomenal 113mph. The RPS fastest HST time is 103min 14sec, compared to only 97min 10sec for a Class 91. HSTs are scheduled to make the faster start to Alexandra Palace, half a minute quicker than the electrics, in 6min, but are half a minute behind by Woolmer Green in 16½ min. Observation suggests that HSTs normally reach Alexandra Palace in 5½ min, Class 91s a few seconds longer. The HSTs often make Woolmer Green in 16min with the Class 91 formations a few seconds in front. The improvement on the computer predictions is possibly due to minor liberties in early acceleration from the King's Cross throat restriction.

Between York and Newcastle the net timing for Class 91s is 47min compared to 48½ min for the 12.00 King's Cross-Inverness 'Highland Chieftain', net averages of 102mph and 99mph respectively. It is interesting to note that the RPS fastest time from York to Newcastle is 47min 5sec. There are very few RPS fastest times where the HST beats a Class 91. The HST schedules are based on those issued for the 2+9 formations that GNER once had aspirations to provide. The difference between Cross Country 2+7 timings and GNER 2+9 timings between Doncaster and Newcastle is a single minute. The difference between a weak set and an average one is greater than this.

For the record, the comparable fastest 'Deltic' times are 138min 41sec from King's Cross to York (average 81.5mph) and 63min 13sec on to Newcastle (average 76mph), but it should be remembered that 'Deltics' ran via Selby with its swing bridge, not via the new Hambleton line.

Newcastle to Edinburgh

It is between Newcastle and Edinburgh that the HSTs have made the biggest inroads on the former 'Deltic' timings, with the help of

infrastructure improvements implemented well before privatisation to exploit the capabilities of HSTs. The RPS fastest 'Deltic' time from Newcastle to Edinburgh is 99min 40sec recorded on 30 June 1978 with No 55007 *Pinza* on the 08.00 King's Cross-Edinburgh and ten bogies.

The train had been booked for an HST but reverted to 'Deltic' haulage on extended timings allowing a memorable requiem. No 55007 had already taken the Stevenage-Peterborough record in 32min 39sec (89.6mph average) with 108mph at Arlesey and 109mph down the bank from Abbots Ripton. North of Newcastle 102mph was achieved at Alnmouth. A 20mph restriction at Chathill inhibited progress, but the driver had his eye on an early arrival in Edinburgh. Grantshouse was taken at a full 75mph, but it is notable that such a fast run was inhibited from reaching more than 91mph by line speeds north of the border. A 3min-late departure from Newcastle was transformed into an early arrival of no less than 14min.

Yet such events were eclipsed by the HSTs. The RPS HST fastest time was set on 25 April 1992 with 79min 36sec, a full 20min faster than *Pinza*. Against *Pinza's* 91mph maximum, the combination of an HST on modern infrastructure was able to average no less than 94mph from Berwick to Waverley.

The West Riding

Performance on the West Riding main line from Doncaster to Leeds gives Class 91s fewer chances to display their prowess, and HSTs with a good start can easily match their electric rivals. The Wakefield-Leeds

Above:
Carrying *The Great Racer* stick-on name, power car No 43096 leads a full GNER-liveried HST set out of Edinburgh Waverley with the 10.00 Aberdeen-King's Cross service on 13 February 1999. *Chris Dixon*

Above:
With slightly more modern station facilities on the northbound platform than the southbound, the 09.12 Aberdeen-Plymouth slows for the station stop at Inverkeithing on 6 January 1993 with power car No 43127 on the front. *CJM*

Above:
Under clear signals, the northbound 'Northern Lights', 10.30 King's Cross-Aberdeen, pulls over the single-line viaduct on the approach to Montrose on 16 May 1996. *CJM*

Right:
With a mass of exhaust indicating that the driver has the power controller wide open, the 09.55 Aberdeen-King's Cross is seen south of Nigg Bay on 29 March 1996 with power car No 43108 at the front and 43038 on the rear. *CJM*

electric and HST RPS fastest times stand at 11.04 and 11.02 respectively. In the other direction they are 10.43 and 10.29. Between Doncaster and Wakefield Westgate the HST time is nearly half a minute slower than the Class 91s' 14min 10sec record, but the latter included a burst to 123mph at South Kirkby, compared to the mere 108mph by the HST, both over 100mph track.

West Coast Main Line

Deployment

'The West Coast main line' and 'HSTs' are phrases that are not readily associated in the enthusiast's mind. South of Stafford the penetration of HSTs is limited to the Euston-Holyhead services and the odd fill-in turn to and from Manchester. Even these depend largely on the availability of HSTs, which appear to have an inadequate maintenance allocation. From Stafford northwards the WCML sees CrossCountry 2+7 sets on Anglo-Scottish workings, padding out the service north of Preston, which is by far the most sparse of the radial routes from London.

Until the Railtrack/Virgin alliance provides 125/140mph upgrades of infrastructure and stock, the maximum speed for the route will remain at only 110mph. It is rare for electric traction, even the capable Class 90s, to exceed this limit by more than a handful of miles per hour. The interface of the pantograph with the overhead wire is a fragile one, the consequences of a dewirement seeming to successfully inhibit wild excesses. The same cannot always be said for HSTs. One summer morning in 1992 the down Holyhead express reached 127mph on the former LMS racing ground between Madeley and Betley Road. Presumably the driver wanted to tell his grandchildren he had driven trains at 125mph and this looked like his best opportunity. Freed from the problems of electrical contact, speeds of between 110mph and 120mph are routinely encountered.

North Wales Trains

South of Stafford most of the RPS HST fastest times slightly exceed their electric counterparts. This is partly because there are fewer chances to time them over most of the sections. Some are very close, such as Euston-Nuneaton, which is 62min 28sec for HSTs with a Class 87 having been recorded just 1sec faster.

On the North Wales coast, the 75mph maximum speed inhibits HSTs from delivering faster journey times. A 90mph limit has long been promised, but the relatively simple signalling alterations that are required seem mired in Railtrack's investment authorisation procedures. First North Western's new 100mph 'Coradia' units have had their introduction delayed by teething troubles, but they have still beaten the half-hearted attempts to deliver the infrastructure improvements they, and HSTs, need.

In practice 80mph Class 37 loco-hauled trains can outrun HSTs on this route. For instance, RPS fastest loco-hauled times for Chester-Prestatyn and Chester-Rhyl beat the best HST efforts with 20min 58sec and 21min 31sec for the former and 24min 11sec and 25min 41sec for the latter.

It is normal practice for both types of train to cruise the coastline at speeds in the 75-80mph range, but occasionally there is a rush of blood. The maxima for Class 37s in these circumstances tend to peak in the low 90s, whereas at least one 'ton' has been credited to HSTs eastbound after Abergele.

The Northern Fells

Over the Northern Fells it is fair to say that the HSTs give a more reliable performance than the electrics. This is due to the prevalence of damp rails and the fact that power is deployed in two portions, one at each end of the train. The rear HST power car usually has a drier and cleaner rail on which to lay down its tractive effort. Nevertheless, in dry weather the electrics can show HSTs a clean pair of heels. The RPS fastest times from Carlisle to Penrith for HSTs and electrics are 13min 46sec and 13min 4sec respectively. The Penrith-Oxenholme figures are 23min 11sec and 22min 23sec. The pattern is reversed between Oxenholme and Lancaster with figures of 12min 36sec for the HST and 12min 57sec for electric. However, all three of these HST records were attained on the same journey in March 1999 with three separate 120mph maxima south of Oxenholme. All three electric records are held by Class 90s, despite the frequency of Class 87s on Glasgow services during the 1990s. The timetablers expect the HSTs to be quicker. The net combined running time for Carlisle-Penrith-Oxenholme-Lancaster-Preston stopping trains is 68min compared to an equivalent 69min for E385 electric timings.

Compared to Class 50s

The most interesting performance interface probably lies between HSTs and the two Class 50 locomotives working in multiple that electrification displaced. Fast runs with Class 50s over the Preston-Carlisle section were rare. Loads were heavy, 12 Mk2s being typical. Sometimes only one Class 50 was used. Worse, two might be provided but only one would be working. Engineering work was frequent, often involving single-line working. On the other hand, non-stop HST and electric workings for the 90-mile section are also rare. The authorities appear to have given up the battle for London-Glasgow business traffic and filled the void with extra stops at intermediate stations for leisure traffic.

Above:
Formed of a full Western Region 2+8 formation with power cars Nos 43164/165, the 14.26 Holyhead-Euston traverses the North Wales Coast route at Mostyn on 13 August 1996. HST sets on this route are soon to be replaced by Class 220 and 221 Virgin 'Voyager' stock. *Charles G. Woodland*

A rare example of a non-stop HST run over the northern sections of the WCML was on the 'Water of Luce' 06.10 Leicester-Stranraer charter train in March 1993 with Nos 43043/43076 on a 2+9 set (strengthened by an extra kitchen). Delayed by a points failure at Slade Lane Junction, then by following a Buxton-Blackpool service, the special was 30min late from Preston. This put it 2min ahead of the 06.15 Euston-Glasgow Central, but with a clear road.

Right:
Led by InterCity-liveried power car No 43197 *Railway Magazine Centenary 1897-1997*, with a rake of VT-liveried stock and IC power car No 43006 on the rear, the 06.50 Edinburgh-Bournemouth, which is routed by way of Carstairs and the WCML, is seen passing Lowgill on 27 June 1999. *Chris Dixon*

The crew made a superb effort to reach 118mph at Oubeck and pass Lancaster in 14min 12sec. With a 116mph run at the climb from Carnforth it was possible to take the MP9½ summit at no less than 109mph. The maximum into the dip was 119mph, compared to a pair of Class 50s at around 102mph at this point, and the HST passed Oxenholme at 90mph in 25min 1sec. Unfortunately a track circuit failure at Grayrigg caused a double stop to telephone the signaller. This also meant that the climb of Shap had to be started at 97mph instead of the 105mph maximum, but there was still no difficulty in taking the summit at the authorised 80mph limit. There was another burst of speed, this time to 115mph at Calthwaite, to reach Carlisle in 64min 05sec, or 59½ min net, a gross average of 90.9mph.

Beattock Bank

North of Carlisle, whether the train is bound for Glasgow or Edinburgh, the principal interest lies in the climb of Beattock bank, 10 miles at 1 in 69 to 1 in 88. The HST charter detailed above passed Beattock station at 104mph and appeared to balance at 76mph before easing for a temporary speed restriction at the summit. The estimated rail horsepower was 3,390. This was the same as had been attained on Grayrigg and slightly higher than on Shap. A 2+7 formation would

probably have sustained about 79mph on Beattock, although it is open to question whether these figures represent a true balancing speed. Another RPS recorder has clocked 85mph at Beattock summit, from 108mph at the foot.

North from Edinburgh

North of the Forth/Clyde valleys the influence of HSTs seems to be that of half a dozen exotic interlopers in a world of 'Sprinter' derivatives. This impression can be misleading since the HSTs have seen off all the traction that was on the Aberdeen and Inverness lines when they first arrived. The original service pattern and timetables have evolved little over the years, constrained by a lack of infrastructure improvements and the development of ScotRail's clockface interval services.

Both routes feature high line speeds, much at 90mph, and some at 100mph. But there are many lower limits that prevent lengthy HSTs from accelerating away as quickly as the shorter 'Sprinters'. One of the fastest stretches is between Dundee and Arbroath where a 100mph average can be recorded between Balmossie and Elliot Junction, 10 dead level miles of a 17-mile run.

Speed limits between Dundee and Aberdeen have recently been given a 'tweak' to allow a slight improvement in speed over a number of key restrictions, a process that seems to have stalled south of the border. Differential speed limits, now often shared by 'Sprinters', have also been fully exploited in Scotland.

The power-to-weight ratio of the HSTs outguns most other traffic in the region, but they are hampered by gradients and curvature. On the 1 in 70 to Druimuachdar an Inverness-bound HST on full power will easily exceed 70mph, faster than the uphill limit allows. On the Aberdeen line the frequent changes in gradient and speed limits test a driver's sense of anticipation and the traction's response to an urgent request for full power.

Some remarkable runs

There is a tendency for these conditions to produce overspeeding. If the speed limits are properly treated as absolute maxima a driver hitting the foot of the climb to Druimuachdar with power off would suffer a guaranteed loss of 5mph to the top of the bank and a consequential loss of time. Similarly the driver who approaches Inverkeilor at 90mph, braking into the dip to the north, will fall below 80mph on the climb beyond. The Aberdeen line is especially prone to such traps. There is no suggestion that running in Scotland is reckless, and it is rare for any liberties to be taken with the most severe curves.

Some remarkable times can be achieved. A run with the 19.55 Aberdeen-Edinburgh in July 2000 is of note, running to Stonehaven in 14min 40sec for 16.11 miles, 19min 12sec to Montrose (24.44 miles) and 12min 46sec to Arbroath (13.61 miles). Excellent braking was the key to such outstanding runs. Easing for the 75mph restriction above Dunnottur and right on the limit from Carmont to Drumlithie, the train accelerated quickly to leave the 95mph limit at precisely that speed before reaching 100mph at Fordoun.

The RPS fastest times on this line show 13min 9sec on the extremely curved section from Kirkcaldy to Inverkeithing, with speeds of 80mph on the 65mph limits before Kinghorn (45mph limit observed) and after Dalgetty Bay. Speeds of 53mph at Aberdour and 38mph at Burntisland were only marginally over the 50mph and 30mph limits that apply at these locations. The impetus for this initiative came from a delay at Leuchars caused by the senior conductor locking himself out of the train. He eventually gained access by squeezing through an open drop-light!

On the Highland line the Inverness crews used to exploit every inch of 'their' railway. Travelling on the 'Highland Chieftain' with

Top:
Unusually carrying its running number on the nose end while painted in InterCity 'Swallow' livery, No 43099 approaches Glasgow Central on 21 August 1992 with the 07.52 service from Penzance, a journey that will have taken almost 11 hours to complete. *CJM*

Above:
In the summer of 1997 one of the Regional Eurostar sets, No 373307/08, spent several weeks working tests in the Glasgow area while outbased at Polmadie, in preparation for the introduction of through Glasgow-Paris workings, which in the event were never launched. Posed next to VT-liveried No 43155 *The Red Arrows*, Eurostar set No 373308 is seen at Polmadie on 5 June 1997. *CJM*

Nos 43039/43111 on an 85min-late run in August 1993, Pitlochry-Perth was covered in an unchecked 24min 57sec, with 90mph at Murthly, 104mph before Dalguise, 100mph after Guay and 99mph at Moulinearn — the driver was clearly in a hurry! Only 3 miles 50yd of the Highland line is authorised for 100mph through Balavil, where 108mph is not unknown. The highest authenticated speed achieved on the Highland line is no less than 115mph.

Left:
With Chesterfield in the background, identified by the twisted spire of the church, a full MML-liveried set, with power cars Nos 43076/059, passes Hasland on 30 May 1997 with the 17.27 Sheffield-St Pancras. *Charles G. Woodland*

Midland Main Line

Replacing the 'Peaks'

Since its introduction in October 1982, the HST has proved to be the catalyst that has allowed a dramatic relaunch of the Midland main line, taking it from as it was in the 1970s into what we see in the Third Millennium.

Contemplating the route in the year 2001, it is easy to forget exactly how antiquated and investment-starved the Midland main line was until 1982. The 'Bed-Pan' electrification had been completed earlier that year, but as a suburban electrification scheme it could never promise long-distance travellers anything more than improved infrastructure. Even the MML's first 100mph track provided by the scheme was of no immediate benefit because of the 90mph maximum of the Class 45s. More importantly, the scheme had left what was known as the 'Leicester Gap', a 40-mile wilderness of semaphore signalling between the northern limit of the new West Hampstead panel box at Sharnbrook and the southern extremity of the 1960s Trent installation at Hathern.

The HST introduction not only allowed the exploitation of the 100mph track south of Bedford but provoked introduction of 100mph track in the multiple-aspect-signalled area north of Leicester. Even more importantly, it stimulated major passenger growth, forcing other improvement schemes on to the agenda. As a direct result of the 'HST Effect', journey times improved, and with the 'Leicester Gap' resignalling scheme further line speed improvements were authorised in 1984, and a 110mph maximum speed was introduced in 1991/2.

Topography

The topography of the MML has always made the line a difficult one to work, requiring both locomotives of the finest pedigree and a limit in the trailing loads in order to remain competitive with the almost parallel M1 motorway. South of Leicester there is virtually no level track, the line consisting of a series of switchbacks that have always provided a stern test of locomotive capabilities. The route sees a succession of summits heading down from London at Elstree, Sandridge, Sharnbrook, Desborough and Kibworth, all with gradients of steeper than 1 in 200, Sharnbrook and Desborough being as steep as 1 in 120. In the opposite direction it is necessary to add the summit at Milepost 34 (north of Leagrave) to the above, and remove Sandridge. Class 45s with their normal load of eight or nine coaches usually breasted these summits at around 75mph, assuming that the ascent was unchecked and began at or around 90mph. However,

72mph was closer to normal for the steeper climbs of Sharnbrook and Desborough.

These factors ensured that the best net schedule of the day was 80min for the prestigious 17.20 'Master Cutler' St Pancras-Sheffield for the 99.1 miles to Leicester, representing a start-to-stop average of 74mph. Most of the other services had an 83min net schedule. Stopping services were given around 120min with six intermediate stops. North of Leicester, the best schedule was 65min for the 59.43 miles direct to Sheffield, with two stops making the complete journey from London in 150min. However, most services took closer to 180min taking the route via Derby, 6.35 miles longer. The dramatic effect of the HST was plain to see when the full service came into being in May 1983. The London-Leicester time was immediately reduced to a net 68min for fast services (a 22% improvement and a start-to-stop average of 87mph) and 91min for stopping services (a 25% improvement and a start-to-stop average of 65mph), the type of improvement hitherto associated with main-line electrification. By 1989 the net schedule had been further reduced to an incredibly tight 64min (a 92mph average), despite the increase in the trailing load from seven to eight coaches in readiness for the line speed upgrade to 110mph. The advent of the Passenger's Charter in the mid-1990s saw schedules eased to a more reasonable net 67min. North of Leicester improvements were more modest, but the best schedule came down to as low as 133min for the 158.44 miles to Sheffield, usual times being around 145min.

So how were these dramatic improvements possible? The HST was able to flatten the route to a degree that made cruising at line speed possible for long distances as never before. Leaving London heading north, Elstree summit will be passed at 100mph, slightly limited by a speed restriction through the adjacent tunnel (a flat-out speed would be around 105mph), and Sandridge at slightly under the 100mph, but also impeded, this time by a 95mph restriction round the St Albans curves. Most impressive, though, will be the drop of only 10mph from the foot of Sharnbrook Bank to breasting the summit at more or less dead on 100mph. A strong set should be able to hold as high as 104mph over the top. Desborough and Kibworth Summits will normally be passed in the mid-90s due to restricted approaches and the inherent curvature. A good set and a determined driver will be able to hold 98mph over Desborough and 100mph over Kibworth. North of Leicester, the only serious gradient challenge is the 1 in 100 ascent to Bradway Tunnel. A Class 45 formation would have done well to accelerate beyond 60mph from a Chesterfield stop, whereas an HST will achieve the 80mph line speed at the bottom of the bank and comfortably retain it all the way up.

Going south it is a similar story. A good set will reach 75mph climbing the 1 in 100 out of Sheffield — 72-73mph would be more normal before the 50mph restriction at Dore — but a Class 45 formation would have struggled to reach anything above 50mph all the way up. It is then a case of reaching and holding line speed until the gradients set in south of Leicester. Leaving Leicester, it is unusual for an HST not to reach 100mph on the ascent to Kibworth, although speed often falls back at the actual summit to about 98mph compared to around 75mph with a Class 45. The climb to Desborough is severely inhibited by a 60mph restriction at Market Harborough, and while a Class 45 would accelerate up the 1 in 120 to around 66mph at the top, an HST will reach 84mph. A strong set will

Right:
Pulling away from its
Loughborough station stop and
passing the Brush Traction factory
in the background, MML's 10.25
St Pancras-Sheffield is seen
powered by No 43059 at the front
and 43066 on the rear on
7 September 1999. *CJM*

manage around 87mph, but anything above that is very unusual. It is the same story for the ascent to Sharnbrook Summit, the restriction of 65mph through Wellingborough forcing a flat-out acceleration. A Class 45 would maintain 65mph, while the HST will achieve 87mph over the top, a good set as high as 92mph. The final ascent from Bedford all the way to Milepost 34 at a ruling grade of 1 in 200 with a slight dip at Flitwick is arguably the most interesting. An average HST can pass Bedford at 110mph and, after easing to 100mph for a restriction at Ampthill Tunnel, pass Flitwick at 106mph, holding that speed flat out for the 6 miles to the summit. Very occasionally a strong HST set can accelerate to as high as 109mph after Flitwick and maintain that speed up the grade.

Impressive Results

This evidence refutes any suggestion that the lack of 125mph track on the MML means that the HST is given an easy ride. Nothing can be further from the truth. The route with its gradients, speed restrictions and awkwardly positioned station stops presents serious challenges and the sets are worked flat out for considerable periods. The results are impressive and well worth recording. Overspeeding is rare, but when it does occur, coupled with a strong HST set, the results can be spectacular. A recent down run on the 14.55 St Pancras-Nottingham saw 121mph reached twice, the second time at the foot of Sharnbrook Bank. This impetus, combined with a storming ascent, saw the top breasted at an amazing 108mph. It must be stressed, however, that this is exceptional.

The advent of the HST on the Midland main line has awakened this sleeping giant. The 1980s saw many improvements that could be credited to the 'HST Effect', the upgrade of schedules being dramatic and rarely witnessed on a non-electrified route. The impetus has continued to the present day when the route now sees its most intensive ever timetable of four trains per hour south of Leicester. The people of the East Midlands and South Yorkshire do indeed have a great deal for which to thank the HST. Schedules are 25% better because performance is equally better — it is as simple as that.

Southern

Background

The introduction of HSTs on the former Southern Region came with the summer timetable of 1991, trials having initially taken place the previous year, and they have normally been formed of the standard Cross Country 2+7 formation. Over the subsequent years the

number of services operated by HSTs has varied, with the majority running during the middle part of the day, with the early morning and late evening services worked by the venerable Class 47s and rakes of Mk2s. These 47s are now in their fifth decade of operation on the SR. One of the problems has always been overnight stabling and fuelling, since the space in Bournemouth depot is somewhat limited. In spite of this, there has been some overnight berthing from the early days.

While offering a substantial increase in power to weight compared to the Class 47s, and indeed the Class 442 'Wessex Electric' units, there has generally been little chance for HSTs to show their capabilities to full effect on the SR. This is in part due to pathing constraints, increasingly a problem, and the stop-go nature of operations. The longest non-stop section is that between Basingstoke and Winchester, all of 18.75 miles. At the time of the Worting Junction-Eastleigh resignalling in the mid-1990s the opportunity to increase the line speed was not taken, although the potential time-saving for an HST would have been only minimal, and it thus remains at 100mph.

Roundwood

In spite of the limitations, the Blue Riband for an HST on the SR lies with a run recorded by RPS member David Sage in July 1993, with the Basingstoke-Winchester section covered in an excellent 13min 1sec, an average of 86.7mph. The southbound start from Basingstoke admirably illustrates the difference in power. On this occasion the 7.99 miles from Basingstoke to the north portal of Litchfield Tunnel were covered in just over 6min 22sec at an average of 75.2 mph, with 100mph being attained before Steventon and a speed of 108mph through the tunnel. A time of 6min 55sec to Litchfield is good for a Class 442, while the best other diesel traction, in this case a Class 159, can roughly equal a Class 442. The HST ran up to 112 mph on this occasion and, while higher speeds have been recorded, it is not the custom. As a point of reference, the best RPS Class 442 time for this section is 13min 48sec, while for the Class 159 it is 14min 40sec.

Likewise, the starts north out of Winchester show the HST in a good light. The 6.36 miles to Weston relay room normally take an HST 5min 30sec, just reaching 100mph. A Class 47 is nearly a minute slower and manages only 82mph on the ruling 1 in 252 gradient. There have been rumours of drivers 'forgetting' and achieving the full operational 125mph up to Roundwood, although no such instances have been recorded by members of the RPS and it is considered that it

Left:
Perhaps one of the more unusual HST assistance pictures is this of Freightliner Class 57 No 57003 arriving at Reading on 27 March 2000, piloting VT power car No 43013 (a buffer-fitted example) forming the 12.20 Bournemouth-Edinburgh following an AWS failure in the South West. As the train reversed at Reading with No 43195 leading, the assisting Freightliner loco was detached there. *Darren Ford*

would be almost impossible, certainly without a full south-westerly gale! Again for reference, the best RPS time for an HST in this direction is 13min 55sec, which compares to 14min 37sec for a Class 442 and 14min 45sec for a Class 159, the best 'other diesel'.

The New Forest

Although the better times, in terms of speed, are between Basingstoke and Winchester, there can be other good spots. A determined start south from Winchester can see even time attained in the 3.12 miles to Shawford, and indeed times below 3min have been achieved, at a passing speed of 100mph. The New Forest, although not generally regarded as a speedway, can witness some admirable runs and it is interesting to note that the best HST and Class 442 times between Southampton and Brockenhurst are identical, at 11min 26sec, which represents an average of 71.1mph. From being all but 5sec behind at Lyndhurst Road, passed in 6min 14sec, the HST was 7sec ahead by Woodfidley, thanks to its power and the 104mph top speed. The difference to the Brockenhurst stop lies with the braking. The Class 442s have excellent brakes, certainly in dry conditions, and can easily stop from 90mph in half a mile. While the comparative up runs are slower, the Class 442 has the edge with 11min 47sec, compared to 11min 57sec with the HST.

Brockenhurst and Bournemouth

West of Brockenhurst a down HST has been recorded to Bournemouth in 12min 29sec during April 1993. The start against the grade to Sway was excellent, passed in 3min 8sec at 85mph; speed then rose easily into the mid-90s, seeing the 8.5 miles to Hinton Admiral covered in 6min 35sec. Two typical bursts of HST power brought 108mph before Christchurch, then an acceleration from 66mph to 82mph up the 1 in 99 grade to Pokesdown. This was a fine performance for an average speed of 73.1 mph. A corresponding Class 442 time of 12min 44sec was also noteworthy, although, like the HST run, very much reliant on exceeding the line speed. In the up direction pathing has always bedevilled HST performance, and an HST time of 13min 26sec compares less than favourably with another timing of 11min 57sec for a Class 442 — although obviously it could be bettered.

Expansion on the SR came later on in the 1990s with a round trip to Portsmouth, and this is illustrated in the section covering the exploits of power car No 43008.

It remains a frustration to those interested in traction performance that the HSTs have never been given the opportunity to shine on the SR. However, these achievements illustrate the potential that, due to operational constraints, has never been reflected in the schedules.

Left:
Standing at Bournemouth station prior to its major refurbishment, with damage incurred during the 1987 hurricane still visible, Virgin XC-liveried power car No 43063 *Maiden Voyager* makes ready to depart on 3 February 1997 with the 14.21 to Manchester Piccadilly. *CJM*

Right:
Led by power car No 43197 *Railway Magazine Centenary 1897-1997*, the 05.30 Manchester Piccadilly-Bournemouth passes through Eastleigh on 16 February 1999. After being repainted in VT livery at the end of 2000, this power car was renamed *The Railway Magazine* in February 2001. *CJM*

Right:
The recent almost hourly services from Poole, Bournemouth and the South Coast to Birmingham and the North have provided a superb nationwide link without the need for passengers to travel through London, and this has been especially welcomed by the leisure travel market. On 3 March 1995 the 12.19 Bournemouth-Newcastle approaches Southampton powered by No 43069. *CJM*

CrossCountry from Bristol to York

Slow Speeds

The failure of BR sector management, Organisation for Quality and privatisation to raise speeds and lower journey times on the CrossCountry route has been a source of concern for over 15 years. The advent of HSTs has at least added some zest to acceleration from the proliferation of intermediate restrictions and station stops.

It is sobering to reflect that the net non-stop HST schedule for Birmingham New Street-Bristol Temple Meads is 72min, but 20 years ago a Class 45 on the 12-coach 'Cornishman' could run the section in a net 80min.

The maximum speed for the whole route from Bristol to York via Leeds is *never* more than 100mph, discounting the main line between Colton Junction and Chaloner's Whin outside York at 125mph. Indeed, between Stoke Works Junction and Rotherham there are only two 100mph sections totalling no more than 10 miles, between Derby and Clay Cross. Small wonder then that HSTs have not been able to transform the fortunes of what, at least until the Virgin 'Voyagers' arrive, will continue to be a Cinderella route.

Lickey

The chief aspect of interest south of Birmingham is the climb of the Lickey Hills, which requires two working power cars, unless a clear run can be guaranteed from Oddingley to the Blackwell summit. On two such occasions when this situation was personally experienced, the HST had to stop for assistance, the first because a temporary speed restriction was in force on the bank, the second because the signaller chose to give priority to a 'Sprinter' with a Bromsgrove stop.

A typically healthy HST set will pass the foot of the 2-mile 1 in 38 climb at Bromsgrove at the maximum speed of 80mph and have a shade in hand over 60mph at the summit. In a paradox with Shap, 75mph is allowed at Blackwell, which even HSTs cannot achieve, whereas the 80mph at Shap causes modern express passenger traction to be eased.

The fastest climb that has come to notice is one of only 98sec from Bromsgrove to Blackwell. Admittedly the bank was charged at 94mph, and the minimum speed was 69mph, recovering to 70mph at the summit. It is often the case that there is a slight rise in speed with modern traction just before the summit, especially if recording in the rear of the train, as the front traction unit hits the easier grade!

Into Yorkshire

One of the stretches that has been accelerated in recent years is the Swinton and Knottingley line to Moorthorpe. This compensates for the loss of the Midland route via Cudworth and enables the important traffic node of Wakefield to be served without major time penalties. Cured of colliery subsidence, speeds of 100mph can now be regularly recorded near Hickleton.

The RPS fastest time for Sheffield-Wakefield Westgate now stands at only 23min 10sec (net schedule 24½ min). After the Cudworth route had been modernised in the early 1970s and adopted as the standard route, Wakefield Westgate was reached somewhat sinuously via Oakenshaw and Wakefield Kirkgate, the journey taking typically 37min (net schedule 35min). The fastest loco-hauled time via Moorthorpe is 26min 54sec (net schedule 26min).

In both directions between Leeds and York the net schedules are often the least cause for consideration. They look sharp on paper at 22min eastbound and westbound, but extra allowances often have to be added. The problem of finding a path between Arriva/Northern Spirit expresses and stopping trains, avoiding conflicting movements at the throat of York station and finding an unoccupied platform at Leeds all add their own contribution to the congestion. The crack 06.40 Dundee-Penzance 'Cornishman' has a York-Leeds schedule of 27½ min, which requires an average speed of only 55.8mph. Virgin 'Voyagers' will need to command better paths than this to realise their potential.

HSTs leaving Leeds for York are at a considerable disadvantage compared to 'Sprinters', as their ten vehicles wend their way over a crippling 10mph speed restriction. This has improved under the Leeds remodelling, but still does not allow free acceleration. At present the RPS fastest times for HSTs are 20.48 eastbound and 21.35 westbound. The equivalent Class 158 records are 20.16 and 21.38 respectively.

The Future

Will we still be measuring HST performance as they complete their Golden Jubilee in 25 years time? The answer is almost certainly not. Different formations, new safety features and more modern engines are all possibilities to achieve life extension, but it is difficult to envisage any new franchise being awarded to a company committed to no more than refurbishing 25-year-old trains. Regardless of the politics of franchising, the investment case is likely to favour new builds.

In the short term it is likely that safety features such as Automatic Train Protection will successfully harness excess speeds. The current system does not even allow a skilled driver to legally regain the maximum amount of time, as its on-board equipment requires drivers to brake earlier than necessary. It does, however, protect passengers from the rare over-adventurous or negligent act. The Train Protection and Warning System will be less effective unless extended to monitor maximum speed from the original concept of regulating the approach to stop signals.

Data recording equipment will dampen performance even further. At present it is intended to evaluate three systems on ten Great Western power cars. Experiments in the 1980s proved unsuccessful. Drivers understand that the records will be routinely downloaded as a part of the assessment process and as recommended by the Health & Safety Executive. Where this is done at present, such as on the Class 159s on South West Trains, overspeeding is rare, even when running downhill and late. In the future HSTs and their replacements are likely to run SNCF-style, where an excess of 1km/h over the maximum speed gives cause for comment.

Odds and Ends

On One Power Car — Literally

It is a relatively regular occurrence for HSTs to run with only one operative power car. It is far more rare for one to run with the rear power car missing altogether. One such incident happened on 9 February 1994 when the 07.20 Penzance-Edinburgh 'Cornish Scot' was brought to a stand at Totnes with suspected wheelflats on rear power car No 43013. A spare driver rode in the power car to Exeter, where a broken spring was diagnosed and No 43013 was detached. After allowing the 09.35 Plymouth-Paddington to overtake, No 43092 was sent forward *alone* with its seven Mk3 coaches.

The train was limited to 100mph because brake application is slower without air being supplied from an E70 valve in the rear power car. Leaving Exeter on a yellow, the start was subdued. It was surprising to see adverse signals from the preceding Paddington train at Tiverton Parkway, after a maximum speed of 91mph at Cullompton. Starting from Tiverton Parkway and attacking the 1 in 115 gradient to Whiteball, the HST made good progress, passing the site of the former Whiteball box in 4min 41sec, only 1min longer than a healthy 2+7 set. The power-to-weight ratio of 6.9hp per tonne was very similar to a standard Class 47/4 on seven Mk2s.

It was beyond Taunton that the true capability of this strange train was shown, with 105mph, under clear signals and in good visibility, before Highbridge. Bristol Panel chose to play safe by giving precedence to the 09.40 Paignton-Cardiff out of Weston-super-Mare, checking the HST to 49mph. Speed seemed to balance at 93mph on the 1 in 146 gradient from Nailsea to Flax Bourton. There was a slight check approaching Bristol, which offset the fact that the 90mph area had been entered at 94mph.

The net scheduled running time from Exeter to Bristol amounted to 53min. Having left Exeter 31min late, the train was only 35min late at Bristol. The actual gross running time was 62min 28sec, but the net time after checks was no more than 58min.

Working on One Power Car

You are stood waiting for a southbound HST at York. It is announced to be 20min late. Ten minutes later it is announced as 25min late. Your heart sinks. It must be on one power car — an all too familiar event. Steps are necessary to reschedule connections and rearrange your diary.

It is one of the HST's strengths that it is flexible enough to operate on half power, and sometimes even keep in touch with its schedule, although the authorities must be careful to monitor the fuel situation because the one working engine consumes a disproportionately high amount of diesel.

Above:
Only on a very few occasions have HST sets operated with one power car completely missing, and this has usually been due to en route failure or a dire shortage of power cars. On 11 November 1988 Laira had such a shortage, and the 10.35 Paignton-Paddington was only able to have one power car, No 43036. With the train unable to work its booked empty stock service from Laira to Paignton via a change-of-direction move at Newton Abbot, it started from Newton Abbot and is seen traversing the Dawlish sea-wall section. The Mk2 coach on the rear was attached to enable a conventional coupling to be available on the rear of the train for the empty stock movement from Paddington to Old Oak Common. *CJM*

In the late 1980s a performance logger had two runs with up Leeds expresses that allowed comparisons to be made of HSTs on one power car against a loco-hauled alternative. On 12 October 1979 the 14.45 Leeds-King's Cross was 20min late from Doncaster, having made extra stops to cover a failed train. It was announced that the anticipated London arrival would be 33min late, a feat of prediction that sounded like folly. A similar run on 15 September 1978 with No 47527 on 306 tonnes net (320 gross) had taken 119min without exceeding its 95mph maximum. There had been temporary speed restrictions to 40mph at Highdyke, 53mph on Stoke bank and 20mph at Knebworth, costing perhaps 7min. The Class 47's speed at Askham and Abbots Ripton was 78mph and 80mph respectively.

With a notably clear run except for a minor check to 82mph at Welwyn Garden City, the single-power-car HST covered the 156 miles in exactly 105min at an average of 89mph. Very low maxima were attained on uphill sections, with 85mph at Askham and 87mph at Abbots Ripton. However, power-to-weight ratios counted for nothing on the downhill stretches, and the HST was able to reach 113mph at Essendine. The RPS fastest HST time for Doncaster-King's Cross is 87min 55sec.

On 6 March 1993 the 09.55 Aberdeen-King's Cross was on one power car from York and managed only 101mph to Doncaster. There the senior conductor announced that the fault had been rectified, but this was clearly optimistic. After a 50mph check at Black Carr Junction, speed did not exceed 94mph before the climb to Askham, taken at a miserable 74mph. A brighter 108mph at Bathley Lane preceded a more respectable 81mph at Highdyke. The train then proceeded to run freely down Stoke bank, averaging 117mph from Essendine to Tallington. Peterborough was reached in 54min 12sec, 75sec faster than the RPS fastest 'Deltic' time, representing a net loss of only 5min on the net 47min HST schedule. A speed of 84mph at Abbots Ripton proved that the ailing power car had not received a miracle cure. There followed a lengthy delay for engineering work at Offord, and 82mph on the 1 in 200 from Hitchin seemed disappointing, but it probably represented the theoretical balancing speed, while 107mph at Oakleigh Park made some compensation. On an extended Saturday afternoon schedule, with 25½min allowed in excess of the net schedule from Peterborough, arrival in King's Cross was only 21½min late.

Occasionally, however, a train with only one power car can surprise the observer. One late summer evening, the down 'Golden Hind' suffered a rear engine shut-down at Reading. The driver came back to inspect and shrugged his shoulders as he returned to the front. Hopes of a tight connection home from Exeter evaporated, but this particular driver was one who would 'have a go' and we only had seven trailers. Only 5min late from Reading, speed rose slowly to 80mph by Theale, 87mph at Thatcham and 90mph at Newbury, another minute lost. A speed of 92mph on the Kintbury 90 speed restriction and a last-minute brake application took speed to precisely the booked 75mph through Hungerford and 86mph, compared to the 100mph maximum, was possible before 71mph on the Grafton curve 70mph restriction. This was almost maintained to Savernake, then 104mph was reached downhill through Patney, followed by severe braking into successive 60mph and 40mph temporary restrictions taken at 65mph and 40mph with notch 5 between the two. At Brewham 87mph was reached, with 97mph at Somerton and a racing 106mph down through Langport East. Taking Cogload at the regulation 90mph, the driver managed to record my sixth fastest time from Cogload Junction into Taunton station — sixth out of many hundreds.

This remarkable performance resulted in the loss of only half a minute against the gross schedule, and an actual gain of 43sec from Lavington. The climb to Whiteball lay ahead. Speed faltered at just below 70mph through Bradford to Wellington. Then there was a sudden burst to 83mph, held at 82mph into the tunnel. I rummaged through my bag for the RPS Power Output Guide. Reaching 107mph through Tiverton Parkway and running from there to Exeter only 2sec slower than the run that took the RPS Taunton-Exeter record, the 'Hind' landed in Exeter St David's only 4min late. And on one power car from Reading! Well, not quite. The driver explained that the travelling fitter had joined at Taunton and they had hatched a plan for the driver to shut off power at MP170, for the fitter to start the rear power car. What teamwork!

On One Power Car . . . Plus a Class 91
During 1989/90 there was a brief interlude when the talents of HSTs and Class 91s were combined to create some running times that remain unbeaten to this day. With Class 91s and Mk4 coaches ready for service and the wires ready and waiting, East Coast operators were inhibited from exploiting the new resources by the lack of Driving Van Trailers (DVTs). An imaginative stopgap solution (detailed in Chapter 8) was devised. Some HST power cars were fitted with buffers and attached to rakes of Mk4s as 'Surrogate DVTs'. Initially it was intended that they should provide 'train supply' power only, but electrical complications resulted in a decision to allow the HST power cars to be used for extra traction. They weighed 70 tonnes compared to the 45 tonnes of the DVTs. The combination of 6,760hp Class 91s coupled to 2,250hp HST power cars was dramatic. Add the fact that most of the formations had only eight coaches, and some seven, and the result was a power-to-weight ratio approaching 20hp per tonne — by far the highest ever seen in Britain.

Of the 34 station-to-station sections recorded with these combinations by RPS members, 13 still stand, despite the fact that there had been only a year to catch up with them and there has been a full decade to search out conventional formation performances. Taking the King's Cross-Stevenage-Peterborough-Grantham-Newark-Retford-Doncaster stopping pattern, 'Surrogate DVT' formations beat Class 91s on four out of the six sections with a net advantage of 100sec. Over short sprints they were hard to beat. On 11 March 1989 a Class 91/SDVT formation was recorded at 9min 3sec from Grantham to Newark, a 97.5mph average over only 14.71 miles. The fastest Class 91 chips in at 9min 38sec, and the fastest HST at 9min 53sec. On 1 July 1989 the pairing of Nos 91004/43068 clocked 132mph before Claypole to cover the section in 9min 28sec.

Other stunning examples of acceleration include Stevenage-Hitchin start-to-pass in 3min 22sec at 129mph involving a calculated rail horsepower of 8,000, giving 0-120mph in 170sec. Leaving Doncaster on 3 October 1989, Nos 43081/91004 reached 120mph at MP151 near Rossington, half a minute quicker than might be expected from

an HST, and 5mph faster than a Class 91 alone would manage.

Of course, for much of the journey the power of the HST car was redundant as the Class 91s were designed to cruise at 125mph without any assistance, but for that one, brief period we were able to sample acceleration standards not previously seen.

No 43197 *The Railway Magazine Centenary 1897-1997*
The author of this book has a special interest in power car No 43197. Having covered hundreds of naming ceremonies with his pen and camera, he was invited to perform the naming ceremony on No 43197. The power car, as one might expect, is a regular performer on the CrossCountry route, and its exploits have been frequently recorded, at least 35 times by the writer of this chapter alone. Most of its work is quiet, efficient, competent, even mundane, but one dark night in the winter of 1997 it grabbed the limelight.

A succession of frustrating, if not untypical, delays had pushed out the 'Devon Scot' from 7min late at New Street to 25min late at Bristol Temple Meads. The Plymouth driver knew that a series of connections was in jeopardy and that if he followed the 21.31 stopper from Exeter he would be very late home. Coupled with No 43121, *The Railway Magazine* shot out of Bristol to pass Nailsea in an astonishing 6min 4sec. It was pitch black, there were no audible rail joints and global positioning systems were at the time not readily available. From the averages, though, it was clear that high speeds were being attained. Nailsea to Yatton was accomplished at 115.5mph as speed was eased until the tricky signal at Worle Junction was seen to be off. High speed was quickly resumed with a 115mph average from Puxton to Worle Junction, 114.9mph to Uphill Junction, 114.3mph to Highbridge and 115.8mph to Bridgwater. With 6min of allowances, 25 late at Bristol had turned into just 14min late at Taunton after a staggering 26min 59sec at an average 99.4mph for the 44.71 miles from Bristol.

Gaining half a minute at Taunton, the driver ran at Whiteball on full power from the moment he received the right away. The flying average from Bradford to Wellington was no less than 105.2mph. The 101.8mph to Whiteball Tunnel suggests 100mph might just have been held on entry. An amazing 'white knuckle' brake application resulted in an inch-perfect stop at Tiverton Parkway in only 10min 6sec, what would have been an excellent passing time, and 27sec inside the previous record. Running to Exeter was more restrained as a path in front of the stopper was now guaranteed. The observer left the train at Newton Abbot after another record run, 16min 56 sec, the only known example of a sub-17min run between Exeter St David's and Newton Abbot, where it arrived just 8min late. With an advertised arrival at Plymouth of 22.26, there was every chance it would be early!

No 43008: Britain's most travelled power car
Records reveal that HST power car No 43008 holds the record for the highest mileage of any British traction unit, currently in excess of 8,000,000. Obviously this vehicle must be fitted with a reliable electrical system as well as power unit. It has worked on a number of different routes, all of which have allowed it to tot up significant mileage when in use.

At present No 43008 is operated by Virgin CrossCountry. It holds the RPS Haslemere-Havant record, in partnership with No 43152 on the somewhat obscure 07.36 Blackpool North-Portsmouth Harbour. This train has enjoyed a wide variety of traction that has also included Class 158s and top-and-tail Class 47s. No 43008 had put in a standard performance to Guildford before recording 12min 25sec to Haslemere, itself no better than a Class 158 is able to achieve.

With 9min 13sec to passing Petersfield at 93mph one might have expected the HST to have had a substantial advantage on the 'Sprinter', but RPS recorders have beaten this passing time by 12sec with No 158851. The HST was then subjected to a 40mph gauging restriction through Buriton Tunnel that does not affect the Class 158;

Right:
Well, this must be the ultimate HST-formed train — a single power car, offering only the driving cab's two seats but with 26 waiting passengers! But it is not quite what it seems. On 25 May 1991 the leading power car of the 11.30 Newquay-Paddington (No 43035) derailed between Luxulyan and St Blazey, and as the train could travel no further, enterprising on-train staff uncoupled the rear power car and used it to shuttle the 30 or so passengers back to Luxulyan station for onward transport by road to Par. This was the amazing sight at Luxulyan after no fewer than 20 passengers had made the first 'shuttle' journey. The power car is No 43029. *Malcolm Surl*

the time cost was 1min. The Class 158 was running late and managed to avoid the timetabled conflict approaching Havant, where the HST was forced to cool its heels awaiting a path. So 22min 46sec became the fastest HST time for this section, whereas the equivalent Class 442 and Class 158 times are 19min 18sec and 19min 16sec respectively.

Specially Staged Runs

From time to time specially staged runs have been made with HSTs to grab publicity for rail. The old BR public relations machine was peculiarly adept at this. On one occasion a whole episode of the TV music show *Top of the Pops* was used to feature a Paddington-Bristol Temple Meads record attempt prior to the eponymous naming of No 43002 *Top of the Pops*. Of course it was far easier for the command structure of the old railway to organise such events, which needed special paths, clever regulation, the one-off easing of some speed limits, and usually the shortening of formations. This latter measure improved power-to-weight ratios and effectively shortened the length of intermediate speed restrictions.

The *Top of the Pops* run was detailed by Peter Semmens in *The Railway Magazine* (December 1984, p480). The 2+5 formation from Paddington to Bristol Temple Meads via Badminton was scheduled for 66min 18sec (using timings to a tenth of a minute), but the run was completed in 62min 33sec without exceeding 129mph and at an average speed of 112.7mph.

The ER/WR rivalry came to a head on 27 September 1985 when the East Coast management made an attempt to wrest back from their colleagues the record for the highest average speed. Another 2+5 formation was arranged, this time to run from Newcastle to King's Cross at speeds of up to 140mph. One suspects, however, that there was an eye on the 15-year-old 143.2mph maximum record speed of the prototype HST. Everyone involved responded magnificently. Peter Semmens recorded 144mph at Essendine (corroborated by Noel Proudlock and David Huntley) and the 168.6 miles from Newcastle to King's Cross were completed in a mere 139min 37sec at a new record average of 115.4mph — two records in one day. Peter Semmens gave full details of the run in *The Railway Magazine* (December 1985, p563). His vivid description caught the spirit of the event: 'The esprit

de corps being shown by railway staff along the line was tremendous, with many people in high visibility vests standing well back and waving us on.'

Acknowledgements

I would like to thank the following for their help with this chapter: Nigel Smedley, Alan Varley, David Sage, Tim Calow, Frank Collins, Bruce Nathan, John Morton, Lee Allsopp, David Ashley, Bill Hemstock, Bevan Price, Paul Walker and Alastair Wood.

The Railway Performance Society

The Railway Performance Society (RPS) was formed in 1979 by a group of enthusiasts interested in timing trains. Concerned at the reduction in the number of performance items appearing in the press, they were keen to ensure that there was a forum for their specialisation.

The aim of the RPS is to promote the science and art of train timing. Its activities include:

• A quarterly magazine packed with performance articles
• Publication of 'Fastest Times' supplements for members to compare their results
• Publication of line charts for British and French lines showing distances and speed limits
• Meetings in Bristol, Crewe, London and York
• Promotion of best practice and new technology
• Mass Timing Days covering as many trains as possible in one day on selected routes
• The occasional opportunity to take part in consultancy work
• Guidance on calculating power outputs
• Its own website

The Society caters for all levels of ability, from the novice to the expert. A brief Beginner's Guide is available.

Anyone interested should contact RPS Publicity Officer Rob Score, 5 Stratfield Road, Basingstoke, Hampshire, RG21 5RS, or visit the RPS website at www.railperf.org.uk.

Above:
An original David Newton-style HST plate with logo, No 43078 *Shildon County Durham*. *CJM*

Below:
A standard HST cast plate with stand-alone logo, also cast by David Newton, for No 43053 *Leeds United*. *CJM*

Above:
The bilingual plate *City of Swansea/Dinas Abertawe*, produced by David Newton for No 43019. *CJM*

Below:
Painted in traditional Great Western green and gold, the plate *Great Western* and coat of arms was a David Newton masterpiece for No 43185. *CJM*

Left:
Produced by Doric Productions as the 'new generation' of reflective plates with a silver ground, this is the replacement *Great Western* for No 43185. *CJM*

Below left & below right:
The two versions of the Doric Productions reflective plate for No 43103 *Charles Wesley*. Originally the silver-grounded plate was used, but this was later changed to the black-grounded version. *Both CJM*

10. HST Naming

Above:
A standard single-line Doric Productions silver-grounded plate, for No 43096 *The Queen's Own Hussars*. CJM

Above:
A number of non-standard special-order plates have been fitted over the years to accommodate company house styles. One was the David Newton-produced *The Black Horse*, complete with logo above and painted in house colours, fitted to No 43034. CJM

Above:
Another specially designed plate was *Dartmoor The Pony Express* for No 43158, finished in CrossCountry Trains' italic font, complete with a stand-alone logo above and a separate CrossCountry Trains plate below. CJM

In common with most other main-line traction, names were applied to HST power cars following various public requests from the late 1970s after the relaxation in the naming of BR locomotives and trains from May 1977. In terms of HSTs, these requests were at first declined, but eventually the BRB gave authorisation for the fitting of a limited number of 'suitable' names in late 1982. Considerable research was then carried out into the most suitable and effective style of nameplate for what was the flagship BR traction fleet, with various transfer and traditional cast plate styles reviewed. Nameplate expert David Newton produced a sample plate, using slightly smaller than 'standard'-size letters fitted to a plate that could also incorporate a logo or coat of arms if needed.

By early 1983 this style was accepted and the first pair of HST power car nameplates were cast by David Newton. These were *City of Newcastle* — for No 43113 — unveiled on 26 April 1983 at Newcastle Central station. The plates incorporated the city's coat of arms on the left side. To suit the style of the livery at that time, the plates were applied midway along the bodyside below the 'InterCity 125' legend and were produced in cast aluminium with shone letters and a red background.

Over the following months and years a large number of HST power cars were given names, mainly to the same design. On the original yellow/blue livery, these were always applied in the mid-vehicle position. Some names had stand-alone or secondary coats of arms or logos, and no strict rules existed for their application position, the most usual being above the nameplate.

A total change of nameplate policy and design came in December 1989 with the InterCity business sector led by Dr John Prideaux, who favoured a more stylish design of plate finished in stainless steel; these were very expensive to produce and were supplied by a London-based company, Doric Productions. At first these had a silver background with black or graphite letters and edge, but following concern over their appearance this was changed to a black background with silver letters and edge. However, this weathered very badly and a return to the original silver background style was made. Doric Productions also produced the InterCity silver/black 'Swallow' logos.

With the revision of livery and nameplate style, a change of fitting position was made, with the standard application point changed from mid-vehicle to the area between the luggage van door and radiator grille, close to the non-driving end; this was actually by far the most suitable place for fitting, being more visible and better balanced on the bodyside.

Thankfully, the application of reflective or 'tin-plate' names, as they became known, was relatively short-lived, as from October 1992, when Chris Green took over as Managing Director of the InterCity business, cast nameplates were again stipulated. In a number of cases power cars that were named in the original cast style prior to 1989 had reflective names produced in the 1989-92 period; some were fitted while others were stored. In more recent years some new cast plates have replaced reflective names.

In the immediate pre-privatisation period some non-standard cast names were applied, mainly to the Cross Country fleet where italic letters became the house style; on some vehicles a secondary Cross Country Trains plate was added.

Under the full privatised banner, the application of names has continued. However, on GNER the cast and reflective plates were all removed on repainting into corporate colours and subsequent namings have seen the use of transfer or sticky-backed letters applied direct to the bodyside. On Virgin Trains, cast nameplates of various designs have been applied. A worrying change of policy was introduced by the first Virgin Trains Chief Executive, Brian Barrett, in mid-1998 when he stipulated a 'new' design of grotesque transfer name incorporating a drawing or picture, in place of proper metal nameplates. Thankfully, upon the appointment of Chris Green as Chief Executive of Virgin Trains, he agreed that naming should continue and authorised a return to cast plates. On (First) Great

Western and Midland Mainline, cast names are still applied in varying designs.

Many of the cast and reflective names also have secondary plates, usually above the main name, either showing a coat of arms or secondary wording; in the main these are in the same style as the main plate.

Today the policy of applying names to selected power cars continues, and with Virgin soon to be introducing new multiple-unit trains to replace the HSTs, some of the present names might be transferred in a new style to the modern stock. First Great Western, Midland Mainline and GNER have all confirmed their intention to retain names at the present time.

Above:
In Virgin Trains style with thicker letters and edge is David Newton's *The Red Arrows* for No 43155 (43068), complete with stand-alone highly detailed RAF shield above. *CJM*

Above:
The *railway children* charity name applied to No 43098, cast by Newton Replica's new owner John Garton, is one of very few with such a large secondary plate carrying no fewer than 42 words. *CJM*

Above:
The new order of stick-on Virgin Trains names was thankfully short-lived. No 43157's *HMS Penzance* is illustrated, which also incorporated a drawing of the Royal Navy minesweeper of the same name. *CJM*

Above:
To mark the 150th anniversary of *The Irish Mail*, this name in sticker form was applied to No 43101. *CJM*

Above:
Midland Mainline continued the practice of cast plates under privatisation, but used a new style, produced by John Garton. This is *Midland Pride*, No 43058. *CJM*

Above:
GNER's answer to loco naming is little more than sticky-back letters fitted to the bodyside, as seen here with *The Great Racer*, No 43096. *CJM*

Right:
Not a protection against possible nameplate thieves, but Penglaz, a hobby horse from the Golowan Festival in Penzance, who attended the naming of *CrossCountry Voyager*. This was a special plate with logo above to launch a new marketing drive of long-distance cross-country travel. *CJM*

Below:
The Captain and Ship's Company from the Royal Navy minesweeper of the same name stand by the cast nameplate *HMS Penzance*, applied to No 43198 after the transfer name on No 43157 fell out of favour. *CJM*

Above:
Perhaps one of the all-time classic line-ups of modern traction, the pre-production gas-turbine-powered APT-E and the prototype HSDT sit side by side at Swindon in July 1975, when the Class 252 was operating on the Paddington-Bristol route and the APT-E was performing high-speed tests over the Didcot-Swindon route. *CJM*

Left:
The two prototype HSDT power cars were used for testing on the WR main line in June 1976 coupled to a rake of production HST passenger cars. This most unusual formation is seen near Swindon on 24 June 1976, working a special from Old Oak Common to Swindon and return. *Brian Morrison*

11. HST Liveries

During the advanced stages of construction of the prototype HSDT, it was decided to outshop the train in pearl grey and blue livery, but applied in reverse style to the standard application to passenger stock of the period, reflecting that of the Pullman colours worn by the Metro-Cammell sets on the Western Region and loco-hauled stock of the ER/LMR. This saw a predominately grey body, offset by a BR blue band extending the full vehicle length at slightly deeper than window height. Branding and numbering was applied in white on the lower grey panels, while the BR double arrow logo was applied the full height of the dark blue band on power cars towards the cab end.

While the Pullman or APT livery was very pleasing to the eye, the BRB decided that the production sets would revert to a more traditional livery style, at least in terms of the passenger vehicles. These were all finished in standard BR blue and grey, offset by white running numbers applied to the lower blue panel and a white 'Inter-City 125' legend at the left-hand end of the body, again on the blue panel. The HST power cars, with their impressive body lines, received a special livery styling, with a number of designs evaluated. Eventually the first finished production power car, No 43002, was painted in a two-tone yellow and black scheme towards the driving end, yellow being applied as the lower body colour and black at window height. The black band carefully continued the profile of the upper grey band on the coaching stock.

Having the predominant yellow colour on the driving end both below the cab window and on the cab roof, the application of a high-visibility yellow warning end was not necessary. The black upper band on the side carried the 'Inter-City125' legend in grey outline 'skeleton' letters. Towards the inner end of the power car, bisecting the radiator panel, a subtle change of livery on a diagonal was made, changing to the conventional blue/grey colours.

For some weeks after application, the then BR design panel reviewed the appearance of No 43002; the black upper panel did not meet all aspirations and was not totally acceptable, with several members suggesting that BR blue would look more pleasing. Eventually, before the power car took to the road, it was returned to the Crewe paint shop where BR blue replaced the black. The outline 'Inter-City125' legend remained, but surprisingly with black infill. Subsequent sets emerged in this revised livery style, but from No 43004 the letter infill became the body colour.

Originally, as the sets were to be maintained as multiple-unit formations, set numbers were applied using black numbers on the hinged front coupling cover. As time progressed and the set identities ceased to exist, the 253xxx numbers for Western Region and 254xxx numbers for Eastern/Scottish sets disappeared. A handful of power cars did receive five-digit TOPS numbers applied to their ends below the cab window.

The first change to the IC125 livery story came in autumn 1983 when, following the business sectorisation of the railway and the formation of the InterCity operation, a new identity was desired. The new IC function carried out a major market research campaign, which

Right:
The first time the public saw the production HST was at BREL Crewe Works Open Day on 20 September 1975, when power car No 43002 of set 253001 was parked inside the main erecting shop. It carried the very short-lived yellow and black livery, with a black cab roof, which looked very smart. *CJM*

Left:
Prototype set No 252001 departs
from Bristol Temple Meads on
6 May 1975, the second day of
full public service, with the 10.15
Paddington to Weston-super-
Mare. *Terry Nicholls*

resulted in the new livery being devised. This was first applied by the RTC Derby to BR Research Division-operated car No RDB977089, the original prototype TRUK No 10100. It was painted in the new exterior colours, closely following the then APT-E scheme. The IC senior directorate visited Derby a number of times in early 1983, with the trial vehicle operating on the main line to Marylebone for the first time on 13 April where the BRB Chairman inspected the new corporate scheme.

Closely following the trial-repainted coach, full authorisation for the new identity was granted with surprisingly few significant changes. Externally the colours were two-tone grey, offset by a red and white mid-height body band; 1st Class vehicles were given a deep yellow stripe at cant-rail height, while refreshment vehicles had a red band. On the bodyside the 'InterCity 125' legend was carried in black on the lower body panel at one end.

For the power cars, the same style as originally applied was followed in terms of the yellow, but the upper blue band at the leading end was replaced by InterCity executive grey, on to which the InterCity 125 legend was applied in stencil white lettering together with the BR double-arrow logo. In the main, set numbers were applied in white on the grey panel below the front window. At the inner end of the first five vehicles to be repainted, Nos 43125/126/129/130/151, the change to passenger colours was at the inner end of the cooler group side grilles, which were painted in yellow/grey. On subsequent repaints the same angle split in the cooler group area as originally used was followed, with the coaching stock colour scheme taking over. This livery became known as the 'Executive' colour scheme, as it was mainly applied to trains such as the APT and now the HST, which were deemed as the VIP element of the UK rolling stock fleet. The 'Executive name' was used at this time, rather than the InterCity title, as the InterCity brand was still largely associated with the blue and grey colour scheme.

The first squadron application was made in August/September 1983, with the above-mentioned five power cars and two passenger rakes from the Western Region allocation repainted as part of a refurbishment by BREL Derby. The livery was officially 'launched' on 24/25 September with the running of a VIP filming train to relaunch the InterCity operation, using the scenic but non-InterCity Copy Pit line.

Some minor variations to the Executive livery appeared, with a handful of power cars having a hyphen between the 'InterCity' and '125' legends on the power car sides, but generally all subsequent repaints followed the new style.

After a couple of years of application, a further revised paint style for power cars was authorised, with the lower bodyside yellow being replaced by the light InterCity grey and the continuance of the red/white bands along both sides and around the leading end.

The next and probably the most significant livery change came in 1987 when the then IC Business Director, Dr John Prideaux, and Marketing Director Rob Mason oversaw a re-launch of the UK main-line passenger operation. The basic livery style was refined, with the power cars adorned with just the word '*INTERCITY*' in italic capitals on the upper section on both sides, together with a 'Swallow' logo devised by design consultancy Newell & Sorrell; these were applied in stainless steel, facing the driving end just behind the cab section. In the InterCity 'Swallow' style, the coaching stock livery of light and Executive grey continued to the radiator-side grilles, which were finished in the dark Executive grey at an angle; forward from this, the lower body panel was finished in off-white, the red and white mid-height body bands continuing all around the power car, with a novel application of black to the front of the angled cab-side window to improve aesthetic appearance. The new 'Swallow' livery was released in mid-1987 in time for the 21st anniversary of InterCity.

In the main, neither power car numbers nor set numbers were carried on the front in this livery style, but some odd exceptions were recorded.

During the development of what became the standard InterCity livery, some Western Region power cars emerged from overhaul at Landore, Swansea, with the bright red bodyside band replaced with a maroon or 'Executive red' stripe, but after a very short time these were replaced with the conventional colour.

With a fleet of almost 200 Class 43s, some small variations to the applied livery style were inevitable, and some of the more significant deserve mention. On a few vehicles the front horn grille was painted yellow in place of black. No 43029 operated for several years in the 1990s without the '*INTERCITY*' legend on the bodyside, while No 43038 received a white cab roof in 1990, reportedly to test the durability of white roofs in everyday service; this vehicle also received a

Right:
With the massive yards at Old Oak Common in the background, Old Oak Common signalbox on the left and the line from North Pole Junction in the left foreground, yellow-and-blue-liveried HST set No 253014, led by power car No 43029, passes what is now North Pole Eurostar depot on its way into Paddington on 31 October 1978 with the 09.10 service from Bristol Temple Meads. *CJM*

full yellow warning end. Various revisions were recorded to the style and position of running numbers: originally the 43xxx number was applied on the light grey band at the inner vehicle end, but from September 1989 running numbers were applied at the nose end, just below the red band, centrally beneath the cab side window. Some variations have even been seen to this style, with for example No 43013 having its number to the rear of the cab side doors after a repaint in 1990.

A slight variation to the standard InterCity livery came in 1988 when the TDM-modified power cars or 'Surrogate DVTs' were introduced, for these were given full yellow warning ends.

In terms of coaching stock, the InterCity livery scheme as originally implemented saw the InterCity 125 legend applied to the left-hand end of the trailer vehicles on the light grey panel below the first passenger window. Following the adoption of the InterCity 'Swallow' colours, the word '*INTERCITY*' was applied in the same position using the standard IC italic font. A number of variations on this vehicle-side theme have been recorded in terms of the position and style of items such as coach letters, the class of travel and window decals showing No Smoking or 1st Class. A livery chart showing the 'correct' locations for the IC 'Swallow' livery is shown on page 134, and details of other brandings and positions can be referenced from the illustrations.

Centre right:
In the days before TGS vehicles were added to formations, West of England set No 253032 storms away from Whiteball Tunnel towards Tiverton Junction on 5 April 1980 with the 07.40 Paddington-Plymouth service. When this picture was taken the now closed down Whiteball freight loop was still in use. *CJM*

Right:
With power car No 43081 at the head, painted in the original yellow and blue livery, the 08.40 Newcastle-King's Cross is seen departing from Doncaster on 20 November 1984. Soon after their introduction on the ER, most HST sets lost their nose-end 254xxx numbers, with power cars and coaches being identified as individual assets. *CJM*

The privatised railways have given rise to the most significant change in terms of livery, with all 25 of the passenger train operators adopting their own identities and colour schemes. In terms of HSTs, a wide and diverse variation in colour schemes has abounded with the sets allocated to Great North Eastern Railway, Virgin Trains, (First) Great Western and Midland Mainline.

The Great North Eastern Railway (GNER), with only a small HST fleet, was the first to repaint all its charges, using the house colours of dark blue offset by a broad waist-height band of red/orange. The company coat of arms in either cast or transfer form is applied centrally on the lower body panel. Power cars are painted in a like scheme, with yellow warning ends to conform with Railtrack Group Standards. Running numbers on GNER vehicles are often hard to see, being applied in spindly numbers in dark blue on the bright body band. To show ownership, a large 'GNER' is applied to the power car sides at the driving end; originally these were in silver/grey, but later they were standardised to gold.

Arguably the most distinctive privatisation livery is that of Virgin, which adopted the company red as its prime colour. Power cars were painted all-over red towards the driving end, with an angled change to graphite grey close to the radiator side grilles, with three white bodyside horizontal stripes breaking up the grey in the former brake-van area. Yellow warning ends have been retained, some extending over the cab roof and others applied only to the cab end section. The trailer vehicles are finished in red for the main body section, offset by three longitudinal white bands running the vehicle length on the lower body panel; all coaches have graphite grey applied towards the ends, with an angled divide from above the bogie angling backwards towards the coach end.

All decals on VT stock are applied in white, with the large Virgin 'signature' adorning power car sides and a smaller impression on passenger vehicles. On the first few repaints into VT colours the 'XC' CrossCountry branding was also applied to the bodysides, but this was quickly dropped after the Virgin Group was awarded the West Coast franchise, and a form of common user allocation was launched.

Great Western decided to use a traditional green as its base colour, offset by an ivory, almost white, lower body band, on to which a 'Merlin' logo was applied on trailer cars. On power cars the 'Merlin' was applied on the upper dark green body panel. The Great Western livery was very smart, but following the sale of the entire business to First Group, a revised livery scheme was introduced. To avoid full repainting, the same basic colour scheme was followed, but a series of dark green horizontal stripes were applied in transfer form on the lower body ivory panel, with a wide gold stripe applied just below window height on which the First Group logo and Great Western names were applied. On power cars, the thin green stripes were also applied and a revision made to the front skirt colour, the original Great Western name and 'Merlin' logo being removed in preference of a First Group 'First' and letter 'F' in gold.

The launch of the revised First Group livery took place on 9 June 1999, when power cars Nos 43147/172 were returned to traffic from Bristol St Philips Marsh, and within just six months the entire fleet was in the new standard identity.

In July 2001 First Group unveiled the now standard house colours of dark blue offset by a pink and white swirl at the cab end on vehicle 43029, the very last power car to carry InterCity colours. For a special roll-out on Bristol on 25 July 2001, the car was renumbered 43001. One passenger coach was also re-liveried at the same time.

Perhaps one of the most controversial new liveries for the IC125

Above:
With Teignmouth's picturesque St Michael's Church in the background, a 2+7 WR HST set passes along the sea-wall heading towards Dawlish on 5 July 1984 with the 07.25 Plymouth-Paddington. *CJM*

Right:
The undulating and curvaceous route between Exeter and Penzance is not ideal for any form of high-speed running, the major benefit of using HSTs being their supreme acceleration. On 2 July 1984, the 13.46 Penzance-Paddington is seen near Ivybridge led by No 43030. *CJM*

fleet was developed by Midland Mainline, part of the National Express Group. MML adopted a tri-colour scheme, with a light grey base and teal green upper colour, offset by three deep orange longitudinal stripes, with a small 'Midland Mainline' name applied at cant-rail height on passenger stock. The power cars followed the same basic colours, with the teal green angling down to below the front light cluster unit at the nose end and the orange bands merging into a whisker. Yellow ends were retained and a large 'MIDLAND MAINLINE' name applied in block capitals on the engine room bodyside. Rather than try and camouflage the side radiator grilles, the MML scheme highlighted these in black. Just to the rear of the cab doors is the Midland Mainline logo of a jumping deer.

In all cases, underframes of the vehicles, either in BR ownership or the private sector, have used black as the colour, with electrical conduits picked out in orange. FO and TSO bogie springs are usually highlighted in yellow, while refreshment vehicles have green springs.

Above:
One of the most photogenic locations in the West, especially with semaphore signals, was Dainton Tunnel between Newton Abbot and Totnes. On 1 July 1984 the 13.45 Paddington-Penzance breasts the summit and starts the descent to Totnes led by power car No 43011, the vehicle written off in the 1999 Ladbroke Grove accident. *CJM*

Left:
Painted in the interim 'Executive' or InterCity livery, adopted to coincide with the first refurbishment of the fleet, set No 253028 with power car No 43125 leading passes along the banks of the River Teign near Bishopsteignton on 7 July 1984 with the 08.35 Penzance-Paddington. This vehicle sports the continuance of the yellow through the radiator grille, whereas on squadron repaints the radiator grille was finished in grey. *CJM*

Right:
Photographed during the transition between blue and grey and early InterCity colours, power car No 43028 leads a mixed-livery formation past Aller Divergence near Newton Abbot on 24 May 1989 with the 14.22 Paignton-Newcastle. *CJM*

Right:
Another of the mixed-livery formations, led by power car No 43040, is seen passing Clay Cross Junction, south of Chesterfield, on 18 September 1987, forming the 12.10 Newcastle-Plymouth Cross Country service. *CJM*

Right:
In full InterCity 'Swallow' livery, and looking extremely smart, the 16.21 Sheffield-St Pancras Midland main line service passes Clay Cross Junction on 6 July 1993, led by power car No 43045. *CJM*

Left:
Power car No 43064, a vehicle originally built for the Eastern Region and thus a Class 254, is seen passing Sharnbrook on 14 March 1994 with the 08.34 Leeds-St Pancras. *CJM*

Upper right:
Pulling out of Westbury station and rejoining the westbound main line at Fairwood Junction, No 43030 leads the 11.35 Paddington-Plymouth on 22 September 1994. *CJM*

Below right:
Showing the full IC 'Swallow' livery, with a similar rake of stock, the 15.35 Plymouth-Paddington is seen near Exminster on 30 June 1994 led by No 43163. *CJM*

Not to Scale

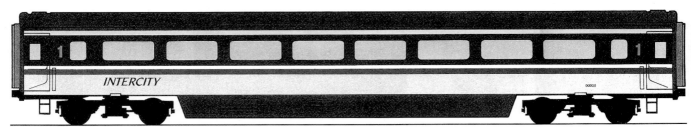

Not to Scale

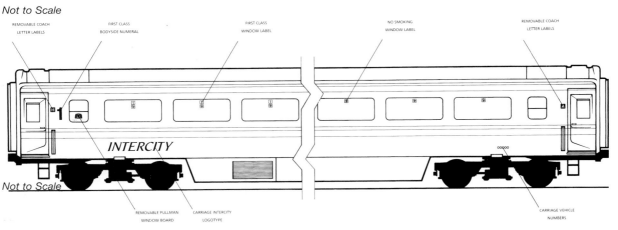

Not to Scale

REMOVABLE COACH LETTER LABELS	FIRST CLASS BODYSIDE NUMERAL	FIRST CLASS WINDOW LABEL	NO SMOKING WINDOW LABEL	REMOVABLE COACH LETTER LABELS

REMOVABLE PULLMAN WINDOW BOARD

CARRIAGE INTERCITY LOGOTYPE

CARRIAGE VEHICLE NUMBERS

InterCity livery and detail fitting chart as produced by the Director of Design.

Above:
Of the privatised liveries, Virgin, with its red, grey and black colours, arguably shows up the body lines of the HST at their best. Power car No 43097 stands at Carlisle on 4 October 2000 with the 09.15 Aberdeen-Plymouth service. *CJM*

Below & Right:
The very first power car painted in Virgin livery for the launch of the privatised company, No 43063, is seen at Ribblehead on its journey from Leeds Neville Hill to Edinburgh Craigentinny. This power car had the cab roof finished in yellow and the 'XC' branding on the side, seen in greater detail on the right. *CJM*

Above:
The external livery of the GNER's fleet of HSTs, Class 91s and Mk4s never seems to do justice to the high quality of the trains' interiors and service provision. Looking rather drab, No 43111 leads the 07.00 Edinburgh-King's Cross past Shipton-by-Beningbrough north of York on 20 January 2000. *CJM*

Right:
On its way to Edinburgh, the southbound 09.50 Aberdeen-King's Cross, formed of a full GNER-liveried set with power car No 43167 at the front, slows for the tight curves at Burntisland. *CJM*

Above:
The Midland Mainline turquoise, orange and grey colours look very striking, especially when seen far from home as here on 8 August 1998, when a set led by power car No 43064 was photographed crossing the harbour at Cockwood in South Devon, hired-in by Virgin Trains on a summer Saturday when the company had insufficient assets to operate a full service. *CJM*

Right:
Midland Mainline branding on an HST power car bodyside. *CJM*

Below:
Operating the wrong way round with the 1st Class carriages at the north end, an MML-liveried set with power car No 43043 is seen arriving at Derby on 17 April 1999 with the 09.25 Sheffield-St Pancras. *CJM*

Above:
The original Great Western livery of green and ivory looked very handsome as long as it was kept clean, which was rather difficult as the light colour was at the base of the body. A full GW-liveried set, led by power car No 43135 with No 43019 at the rear, climbs towards Whiteball Tunnel on 9 April 1997 with the 13.04 Exeter-Paddington. *CJM*

Right:
In full First Great Western colours, which perhaps look a little less stark than the original livery, the 09.35 Paddington-Plymouth approaches Aller Divergence on 4 March 2000 with power car No 43004 *Borough of Swindon* leading. *CJM*

Above left:
One of the most unusual liveries ever applied to an HST power car was this, on No 43028, which resembles Indian warpaint more than a livery. The front-end treatment was done by Manchester Longsight when a separate livery was being considered for the West Coast dedicated power cars used on Holyhead and Blackpool services. No 43028 is seen at Crewe on 5 October 1997 powering the 13.35 Holyhead-Euston. *Chris Dixon*

Above right:
In 1993 some trials were undertaken on the Western Region to replace the red body band on HST power cars with InterCity maroon. The colour change was applied only to a handful of cars and unless inspected carefully it was difficult to detect. After a short while the instruction was issued from the IC Board to retain the red band. No 43010 shows the maroon band alongside coach 41127 with a red band at Swansea. *CJM*

Below:
In July 2001, First Group applied their blue, white and pink swirl livery to an HST power car and one trailer vehicle for a press preview of the projected modernised fleet. The power car chosen for repaint was No 43029, which had recently been transferred from Virgin Trains to FGW use and was the last power car to carry full InterCity colours. the repainting was carried out at Bristol St Philips Marsh depot. For the official roll out the vehicle was renumbered 43001, a number which was actually allocated to a prototype train set power car and not a production vehicle. The identity of No 43029 was returned before entry into traffic. The TS repainted was No 42361, which for the launch was renumbered 42000. The power car and a new FGW Class 180 No 180103 is seen outside St Philips Marsh on 25 July 2001. *CJM*

A most welcome feature of the HST was the inclusion of new-generation catering cars. Apart from eight kitchen vehicles built to run with the Mk2 Pullman sets for the 1966 West Coast electrification, used on premier business services between Euston, Manchester and Liverpool, no other Mk2 catering cars were built. Much later, some spare Mk2 FOs were converted into lounge or bar cars for overnight sleeper and Cross Country services. Thus there was a 14-year gap in catering car builds from 1962, when the last of the Mk1 cars (which used gas for cooking) was completed, to the appearance of the new Mk3 HST vehicles in 1976.

Reluctance to build Mk2 catering cars was probably caused by the old BR regarding train catering as a loss-making activity. The food and beverage service was provided by a railway-owned subsidiary — British Transport Hotels — and train catering deficits were clearly shown as a loss in the annual report and accounts. It was only later that what we now call 'on-board service' was regarded as an essential 'added value' element to protect and promote ticket sales. To be fair, one should note that the logistics are such that very few railways worldwide cover the direct costs of a full on-board dining service, although take-away bar and trolley sales usually cover their costs.

The decision to build new Mk3 HST catering cars showed that a more enlightened view was gaining ground. In BR days the Treasury, which scrutinised all rail investment projects, was always poised to strike out any items that it considered to be unnecessary or frivolous expenditure. Fortunately, catering cars survived this scrutiny.

Journey time is the key factor that determines on-board service, and food and beverage needs. Thus, given the significant travel time reductions that HSTs would offer, on many routes only one meal sitting would be possible. Partly to make best use of on-train space, but also to provide enhanced levels of customer care, it was initially decided to provide meal service for 1st Class passengers at their seats; a separate facility was provided for bar and take-away service. Meal service for Second/Standard Class passengers would be provided in 'unclassified' seating next to the kitchen.

Three HST catering car types were built:

TRUK (Trailer Restaurant Unclassified Kitchen): Based on a classic restaurant car configuration, the TRUK comprised a high-capacity kitchen at one end and a 24-seat dining saloon at the other. Although Standard Class customers would be served in this car, 1st Class seats were installed. The working area consisted of a 12ft 1in pantry with a sink next to a 15ft 2in kitchen area, providing space for two cooks to work should this be necessary on peak trains. The equipment in the all-electric kitchen included Microaire ovens for faster cooking — an important consideration with reduced journey times and quick turnrounds at terminal stations. Service was through a side hatch from the kitchen into the 24-seat saloon and through to the two adjoining

Right:
The interior of an original HST TRSB, showing the serving counter. Note the glass racks above head height, a feature long since gone. *CJM*

48-seat 1st Class cars. A TRUK could produce 120 meals at one sitting, which was often necessary on busy trains such as the morning 'Yorkshire Pullman' from Leeds and the 'Tees Tyne Pullman' from Newcastle to King's Cross.

TRSB (Trailer Restaurant Standard Buffet): The forerunner of today's multi-purpose catering service car, the TRSB was conceived as a means of providing an on-board environment suitable for business travellers, social drinkers and leisure passengers with families. Initially the cars made a strong visual impact, but it is now over 25 years since they entered service and during that time many changes to the decor have been made, and more are in prospect. There is a 13ft 7in bar area and counter at one end, a 11ft 1in kitchen area in the centre, and an 28ft 5in seating area at the opposite end. As originally designed this space was used to locate 35 Second Class seats in a 2+2 configuration; for a few months some WR cars were fitted with 1st Class seats. Although smaller than the TRUK kitchen, the TRSB car — which was similarly equipped with items such as Microaire ovens — was able to produce a range of hot snacks including toasted items, pizzas, burgers and light meals. Bar service included draught beer, but this was later removed for both technical reasons and a problem with staff honesty. At one stage the former GW InterCity business unit used the cars to provide a simpler version of the Great British Breakfast. All sandwiches for sale on the train were prepared on-board.

Not long after the Great Western HST service was launched, it became apparent that the two-car catering concept exceeded the needs of the majority of its journeys. Breakfast sales were fine, but given journey times of between 1hr 30min and 2 hours on evening HSTs out of Paddington to Bristol and South Wales, dinner sales were small; the TRUK was only fully used on morning services. Accordingly, BR decided to restrict the construction of TRUK cars to just 20 vehicles, which would be transferred to the East Coast route where longer journeys generated a stronger demand for evening dinner service.

TRUB (Trailer Restaurant Unclassified Buffet): As the TRSB kitchen was not large enough to cover breakfast service on most GW routes, BR designers produced a third HST catering car version — the TRUB. While the 13ft 7in bar area was the same as the TRSB, the kitchen was extended from 11ft 1in to 16ft 4in, the seating area at the opposite end being reduced to 21ft 3in. On-board equipment was the same as other HST catering cars. Essentially the TRUB was an updated version of the classic bar-plus-kitchen configuration used for the large number of Mk1 locomotive-hauled vehicles dating from the 1950s.

One of the most difficult aspects of the publicly owned BR era was the impact of short-term economic downturns on public sector expenditure levels. During these economic troughs, the state-owned industries would have to cut back both on long-term investment and subsidies necessary to sustain unremunerative services retained for social reasons. BR was obliged to make across-the-board cuts usually without regard to the longer-term consequences on its passenger business. Because it was still seen as a loss-leader, catering was a prime case in point; prices were increased and service levels cut back. This was the situation in the early 1980s. Although Great Western and East Coast HST services had generated considerable levels of new business, there was now an economic downturn, and BR had to cut costs. It was against this background that BR made a number of changes to HST catering.

As related earlier, BR had already decided to dispense with the TRUK/TRSB on GW routes, and had agreed to adapt the TRUB as the standard HST catering car; 58 of these were built and some were designated TRFB. As new cars came off the production line the fleet was reorganised. Great Western received the new TRUBs in exchange for its TRUKs, which went to the East Coast, and TRSBs, which were placed in the new sets for Cross Country. For some months the East Coast retained 20 TRUK/TRSB sets for its busier trains supported by 12 sets, including one of the new TRUB cars. Regrettably, the East Coast two-car catering set-up survived for only a few months, and all but three TRUKs were taken out of HST work; two were retained to cover the 'Tees Tyne' and 'Yorkshire' Pullmans and the third was converted into an Executive saloon that could be hired and attached to HST sets for group travel. As the saloon had to be marshalled into a standard HST set during its overnight visit to a depot, its use was very restricted. Some of the remaining cars were converted for use in the Royal Train, but most were converted into locomotive-hauled modular catering cars for the West Coast electrified network.

Modular Catering: 'Cuisine 2000'

As new-generation high-speed trains began to replace classic 100mph services, some European railways decided to replace traditional restaurant cars serving food cooked on-board in a train kitchen with airline-style tray meals. In many respects, high-speed trains are like aircraft. Space is limited, vehicle weight must be minimised, and turnround times are short so that in-service revenue earning is maximised. With reduced journey times, there is little time to prepare and cook a meal on board.

Following studies undertaken for InterCity, which suggested that costs could be reduced and food quality improved, BR launched a new project, 'Cuisine 2000', incorporating some features of airline catering. Most hot food courses were prepared on shore where they were chilled, taken to the train, and regenerated in the train kitchen. Because the end product would be unsatisfactory, steaks, eggs and toast were excluded from the 'cook-chill' process. Whereas aircraft meals are served on trays, Cuisine 2000 retained china plates and traditional silver service. Advocates of the system claimed that food wastage would be reduced, a higher standard and variety of dishes would be offered, and staff could concentrate on serving the passenger rather than on food preparation. Traditional tasks — such as washing up — were transferred to the train catering depot, and sandwich production would be contracted out to private suppliers.

Cuisine 2000 was adopted for general use on the West Coast main line and a number of vehicles — surplus HST trailers — were converted for the new system. Cuisine 2000 did produce a number of useful benefits, but there was a serious disadvantage — product wastage. The use-by time of a 'cook-chill' dish is quite short, to the extent that items not used by the end of a journey had to be disposed of.

At one stage, InterCity planned to convert all of its HST catering cars to 'Cuisine 2000'; a prototype conversion was completed and tested for some time on the 'Master Cutler' between Sheffield and St Pancras. However, given the cost of conversion and the ambiguity surrounding the possible benefits, InterCity did not proceed with this full-scale conversion.

Towards Privatisation

It is now 25 years since the first HSTs entered service on the old Western Region, and it is easy to overlook the impact these trains made on the long-distance domestic travel market. It is no exaggeration to say that without them, long-distance rail would have lost its market share to the domestic airline, private car and long-distance coach. Initially, journey time reduction was the main thrust of BR's HST marketing, but this was just one aspect of the total travel experience. Others — such as catering and on-board service — were equally important. First Class customers were now judging InterCity by the standards of airline 'Club Class'; those buying budget price tickets were also looking for better service. As the new InterCity business sector, set up in 1982, found its stride, a number of innovations were introduced. The key to this was a strengthened in-house catering department — Inter City On Board Service (ICOBS). Despite jokes about railway food service standards on HSTs and the other classic routes, InterCity service standards were greatly improved, providing an excellent starting point for the new privatised companies.

Many thought that the enduring InterCity branding for quality 100mph-plus trains would be retained by the new operators. This did not happen; each of the new HST operators — First Great Western, Midland Mainline, Virgin and GNER — set out to establish its own branding and identity. Changes to external liveries and internal refurbishment have been described earlier, but customer service styles were also changed. In the main each of the private operators upgraded internal fittings to the customer service side of refreshment vehicles during refurbishments.

Midland Mainline and Virgin West Coast have moved towards airline-style pricing. On these routes full restaurant service is now restricted to 1st Class customers, the price of which is included in the ticket. This entitles passengers to a full 'Great British Breakfast' on morning services and a snack service including alcoholic and other drinks at other times. Midland Mainline offers complimentary tea and coffee to Standard Class passengers. Virgin CrossCountry offers complimentary food items and refreshments to 1st (Club) Class customers, but these have to be collected from the bar.

Right:
The TRBF kitchen layout, showing the almost sole use of stainless steel. This view is from the counter end. *CJM*

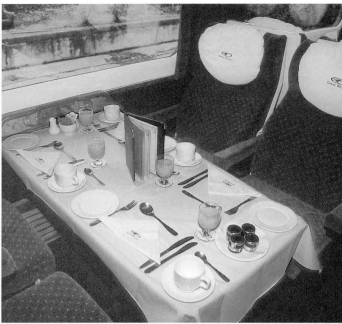

First Great Western continues to offer a full restaurant service on many trains — with meals charged separately — and open to both 1st and Standard Class. There are two styles of service: Pullman Restaurant, serving full meals in classic style, and Pullman Bistro, providing an informal budget price service. Non-alcoholic drinks and biscuits and light snacks are complimentary in 1st Class.

Of all the new HST operators, GNER has achieved the highest standards of on-board service. To enhance its restaurant cars, the company engaged the services of the McCoys, owners of a famed restaurant in North Yorkshire. Except on some peak Pullman services,

access to restaurant cars is open to all customers, and meals are charged separately. In addition, the quality and content of the buffet range has been upgraded with successful results.

A final point: after 25 years the two-car catering set-up first envisaged by BR for the HST has found new favour. The new Virgin West Coast 'Pendolino' will have a similar arrangement with a 1st Class kitchen at one end of the train and a shop for Standard Class passengers at the opposite end. Others are likely to adopt this configuration for new trains. The two-car catering concept was clearly ahead of its time.

13. Technical Details

Prototype Power Cars

Number range	43000-43001
	(originally 41001 and 41002)
Built by	BREL Crewe
Introduced	1972
Design codes	430AA Paxman 'Valenta' engine,
	Brush traction motors. Guard's/rear
	driver's accommodation fitted
Wheel arrangement	Bo-Bo
Weight	68.5 tonnes
Height	12ft 10in (3.90m)
Length	56ft 4in (17.16m)
Width	8ft 11in (2.73m)
Wheelbase	42ft 4in (12.90m)
Bogie wheelbase	8ft 7in (2.60m)
Bogie pivot centres	33ft 9in (10.28m)
Wheel diameter	3ft 4in (1.02m)
Minimum curve negotiable	4 chains (80.46m)
Engine type	Paxman 'Valenta' 12RP200
Engine output	2,250hp (1,680kW) at 1,500rpm
Power at rail	1,770hp (1,320kW)
Maximum tractive effort	17,980lb (80kN)
Continuous tractive effort	10,340lb (46kN)
Cylinder bore	7¾in (197mm)
Cylinder stroke	7½in (190mm)
Maximum speed	125mph (201km/h)
Brake type	Air
Brake force	49 tonnes
Route availability	6
Bogie type	BP9a
Heating type	As built: Electric train supply
	Modified: 415V three-phase
	(IC125 stock only)
Multiple working	Within class (one either end of train)
Main alternator type	Brush BA1001B
Auxiliary ETS alternator	Brush BAH601B
Traction motor type	Brush TMH68-46, frame-mounted
No of traction motors	4
Gear ratio	59:23
Fuel tank capacity	1,210 gallons (5,500 litres)
Cooling water capacity	163 gallons (741 litres)
Lubricating oil capacity	75 gallons (341 litres)
Sanding equipment	Not fitted
Luggage capacity	2.5 tonnes evenly distributed

Production Power Cars

Number range	43002-43198
Built by	BREL Crewe
Introduced	1976-82
Design codes*	430AA: Paxman 'Valenta' engine,
	Brush traction motors, Guard's
	accommodation
	430CA: Paxman 'Valenta' engine,
	Brush traction motors, Guard's
	accommodation removed
	430DA: Paxman 'Valenta' engine,
	GEC traction motors
	430FA: Paxman 'Valenta' engine,
	Brush traction motors, modified with
	nose-end drawgear
	430GA: Paxman 'Valenta' engine,
	GEC traction motors, Guard's
	accommodation, ATP fitted
	430HA: Paxman 'Valenta' engine,
	Brush traction motors, ATP fitted
	430JA: Paxman 'Valenta' engine,
	GEC traction motors, ATP fitted
	430LA: Paxman VP185 engine,
	Brush traction motors
	430MA: Paxman VP185 engine,
	Brush traction motors, ATP fitted
Wheel arrangement	Bo-Bo
Weight	70 tonnes
Height	12ft 10in (3.90m)
Length	58ft 5in (17.80m)
Width	8ft 11in (2.73m)
Wheelbase	42ft 4in (12.90m)
Bogie wheelbase	8ft 7in (2.60m)
Bogie pivot centres	33ft 9in (10.28m)
Wheel diameter	3ft 4in (1.02m)

Right:
In their early years working on the Western Region, Old Oak Common depot in West London played a major role in HST fleet maintenance, with an extension of the depot specially constructed to deal with the fleet. Power cars from sets 253007 and 253011 share depot space in this September 1979 illustration. *Darren Ford collection*

Above:
TRBS No 40427, operated by Virgin Trains on its CrossCountry operation, is seen from the buffet end. Recently the small windows in the top of the serving counter area have been painted in body colours, as the area inside is now modified and the windows can no longer be seen. *Darren Ford*

Centre:
GNER meets Virgin: GNER No 43113 storms through the middle road at Doncaster on 16 June 2000 with the 08.00 Aberdeen-King's Cross, while Virgin No 43155 *City of Aberdeen* awaits departure southbound with the 12.08 Newcastle-Plymouth. *Darren Ford*

Lower:
It is very rare to see an HST power car operating under its own power on its own, mainly due to the fact that if a failure occurred nothing could assist the vehicle without an adapter coupling. However, on 31 March 1986 power car No 43188 was recorded passing Clay Mills near Burton upon Trent returning light to BREL Derby Locomotive Works during a test run following classified overhaul and prior to painting. *John Tuffs*

Minimum curve negotiable	4 chains (80.46m)
Engine type	As built: All fitted with Paxman 'Valenta' 12RP200L
	Nos 43167-170 experimentally re-engined with Mirrlees Blackstone MB190 (1987-96)
	Present day: All Paxman 'Valenta' 12RP200L *except* 43047/059/074/075/168-170/177, fitted with Paxman VP185
Engine output	Paxman 'Valenta' 12RP200L: 2,250hp (1,680kW) at 1,500rpm
	Mirrlees Blackstone MB190: 2,400hp (1,788kW) at 1,500rpm
	Paxman VP185: 2,500hp (1,680kW) at 1,500rpm
Power at rail	1,770hp (1,320kW)
Maximum tractive effort	17,980lb (80kN)
Continuous tractive effort	10,340lb (46kN)
Cylinder bore	'Valenta': 7¾in (196mm)
	MB190: 7½in (190mm)
	VP185: 7¼in (185mm)
Cylinder stroke	'Valenta': 7½in (190mm)
	MB190: 8¼in (210mm)
	VP185: 7¾in (196mm)
Maximum speed	125mph (201km/h)
Brake type	Air
Brake force	50 tonnes
Route availability	6
Bogie type	BP16
Heating type	Electric train supply: 415V three-phase (IC125 stock only)
Multiple working	Within class (one either end of train)
Main alternator type	Brush BA1001B
Auxiliary ETS alternator	Brush BAH601B
Traction motor type	43002-123/153-198: Brush TMH 68-46, frame-mounted
	43124-152: GEC G417AZ, frame-mounted
No of traction motors	4
Gear ratio	59:23
Fuel tank capacity	1,030 gallons (4,680 litres)
Cooling water capacity	163 gallons (741 litres)
Lubricating oil capacity	75 gallons (341 litres)
Sanding equipment	Not fitted
Luggage capacity	2.5 tonnes (when built 1.5 tonnes) evenly distributed
Owners	Angel Train Contracts: hired to First Great Western, Great North Eastern Railway, and a handful to Virgin Trains for WC operation.
	Porterbrook Leasing: hired to Virgin Trains, Midland Mainline
Special fittings	National Radio Network telephone, Driver-Guard radio, Automatic Train Protection (FGW sets only)

Notes Power cars Nos 43013/014/065/067/068/080/084/123 fitted with nose-end drawgear.
Originally fitted with Guard's office/luggage van — now out of use

*Design codes show position at May 2001

Prototype Trailer Vehicles — Class 252

Type	FO	TSO	TRSB	TRUK
Number range	11000-11003	12000-12003	10000	10100
Revised number range	41000-41002	42000-42002	40000	40500
Built by	BREL Derby	BREL Derby	BREL Derby	BREL Derby
Length	75ft 4in (23.00m)	75ft 4in (23.00m)	75ft 4in (23.00m)	75ft 4in (23.00m)
Height	12ft 4in (3.81m)	12ft 4in (3.81m)	12ft 4in (3.81m)	12ft 4in (3.81m)
Width	8ft 11in (2.74m)	8ft 11in (2.74m)	8ft 11in (2.74m)	8ft 11in (2.74m)
Wheelbase	52ft 5in (16.00m)	52ft 5in (16.00m)	52ft 5in (16.00m)	52ft 5in (16.00m)
Bogie wheelbase	8ft 7in (2.60m)	8ft 7in (2.60m)	8ft 7in (2.60m)	8ft 7in (2.60m)
Weight	33.5 tonnes	33.5 tonnes	35 tonnes	37 tonnes
Bogie design	BT10	BT10	BT10	BT10
Seating	48F	72S	35S	24U
Layout	2+1	2+2	2+2	2+1
Notes	11001 rebuilt as Royal stock	12001 rebuilt as Royal stock		

Production Trailer Vehicles — Classes 253 and 254

Type	FO	TSO	TGS	TRSB	TRBS
Number range	41003-41180	42003-42363	44000-44101	40001-40037	40401-40437
Design code	GH1G	GH2G	GJ2G	GK2G	GK2G
Built by	BREL Derby	BREL Derby	BREL Derby	BREL Derby	BREL Derby
Length	75ft 4in (23.00m)	75ft 4in (23.00m)	75ft 4in (23.00m)	75ft 4in (23.00m)	75ft 4in (23.00m)
Height	12ft 4in (3.81m)	12ft 4in (3.81m)	12ft 4in (3.81m)	12ft 4in (3.81m)	12ft 4in (3.81m)
Width	8ft 11in (2.74m)	8ft 11in (2.74m)	8ft 11in (2.74m)	8ft 11in (2.74m)	8ft 11in (2.74m)
Wheelbase	52ft 5in (16.00m)	52ft 5in (16.00m)	52ft 5in (16.00m)	52ft 5in (16.00m)	52ft 5in (16.00m)
Bogie wheelbase	8ft 7in (2.60m)	8ft 7in (2.60m)	8ft 7in (2.60m)	8ft 7in (2.60m)	8ft 7in (2.60m)
Weight	33.6 tonnes	36.6 tonnes	33.5 tonnes	36 tonnes	36.1 tonnes
Bogie design	BT10	BT10	BT10	BT10	BT10
Seating	(48F) 46-48F*	(76S) 65-76S	(65S) 61-65S	35S	33S
Layout	2+1	2+2	2+2	2+2	2+2
Notes					

Type	TRB	TRUB	TRBF	TRFM	TRUK
Number range	40204-40233**	40300-40357	40700-40757	40619	40501-40520
Design code	GN4G	GL1G	GK1G	GK1G	GL1G
Built by	BREL Derby	BREL Derby	BREL Derby	BREL Derby	BREL Derby
Length	75ft 4in (23.00m)	75ft 4in (23.00m)	75ft 4in (23.00m)	75ft 4in (23.00m)	75ft 4in (23.00m)
Height	12ft 4in (3.81m)	12ft 4in (3.81m)	12ft 4in (3.81m)	12ft 4in (3.81m)	12ft 4in (3.81m)
Width	8ft 11in (2.74m)	8ft 11in (2.74m)	8ft 11in (2.74m)	8ft 11in (2.74m)	8ft 11in (2.74m)
Wheelbase	52ft 5in (16.00m)	52ft 5in (16.00m)	52ft 5in (16.00m)	52ft 5in (16.00m)	52ft 5in (16.00m)
Bogie wheelbase	8ft 7in (2.60m)	8ft 7in (2.60m)	8ft 7in (2.60m)	8ft 7in (2.60m)	8ft 7in (2.60m)
Weight	36.1 tonnes	38 tonnes	38.1 tonnes	38.1 tonnes	37 tonnes
Bogie design	BT10	BT10	BT10	BT10	BT10
Seating	(22U) 21-22U	17U	17F	17F	24F
Layout	2+1	2+1	2+1	2+1	2+1
Notes					Further 7 ordered, not built

Type	TLUK
Number range	40513
Design code	GL1G
Built by	BREL Derby
Length	75ft 4in (23.00m)
Height	12ft 4in (3.81m)
Width	8ft 11in (2.74m)
Wheelbase	52ft 5in (16.00m)
Bogie wheelbase	8ft 7in (2.60m)
Weight	33.6 tonnes
Bogie design	BT10
Seating	24 Lounge
Layout	Lounge
Notes	

* Actual seating dependent on present operator. As-built figure in brackets.

** Actual vehicle numbers 40204-13/21/28/31-33

Above:
At first glance this looks as if Great Western might have been short of trains and was using this to form a passenger service! In fact it is a stock transfer move from Laira to St Philips Marsh, formed of Class 47 No 47832, power car No 43167, a barrier car and power car No 43190 on the rear. The train is seen passing Cockwood on 5 February 1995. *CJM*

Above left:
The first XPT to take to the main line, with vehicles XP2000, XF2200 and XF2201, is seen at Wollongong, Australia, on 5 September 1981. The UK HST design ancestry of these trains is immediately recognisable in terms of the power cars, although the passenger saloons are of a totally different design. *J. Costigan*

Above right:
A full Australian XPT 2+5 formation is seen on an early complete train formation test run. It is interesting to see that the cab side windows are much larger than on the UK train and are curved towards the front. The headlight/tail/fog light cluster is of course slightly different, being a little below the point of the nose end rather than above it. *L. Carver*

Above:
The 'Riverina XPT' service was introduced on 23 August 1982 between Sydney and Albury. It covered the journey in 7hr 20min with nine intermediate stops, slashing 80min off the previous timing. Due to speed restrictions the only section of the route where the full 160km/h could be achieved was on the approaches to Albury on the New South Wales-Victoria border. This view shows a train near Goulburn. *Graham Turner*

Left:
With power car No XP2008 *City of Goulburn* leading, an XPT formation in original livery is seen at Sydney in the summer of 1991. Unlike the UK train, three high-intensity headlights are mounted on the roof line in addition to the nose-end running lights, fog lights and tail lights. The inner end of the XPT power car is largely different from that of a UK HST in having no guard's and luggage compartment. *Martyn Porter*

14. The Australian Xpress Passenger Train 'XPT'

British Rail and its engineering partners could see huge export potential for the HST concept, and BR's Transmark arm was entrusted with selling the product overseas. In the event, only one customer was actually found, the New South Wales Railway in Australia, which introduced UK HST-look-alike trains in 1982.

Public transport was a major issue in the New South Wales state elections of 1976, and this gave rise between September 1977 and January 1978 to a call for tenders for the construction of 40 loco-hauled cars for country use, 16 two-car railcars for outer suburban and inter-urban use, and 25 high-speed railcars similar to Westrail's *Prospector*. Early in 1978 Commonwealth Engineering (Comeng) put forward a single alternative bid for a high-speed train based on the BR InterCity 125.

Comeng was a licensee of Bombardier, and a modified version of the Canadian VIA Rail LRC was also put forward. The HST option was eventually selected by the Government, and in February 1979 the Premier announced that 100 vehicles would be ordered for country and inter-urban services to Wollongong, Nowra, Kempsey, Grafton, Armidale, Orange, Wagga Wagga and Canberra. There would be 26 diesel-electric power cars, 66 stainless steel trailer cars and eight driving trailers. These would form eight inter-city train sets in 2+5 formation and six inter-urban sets in 1+4 form — power car, guard/trailer, trailer, trailer, driving trailer. The new trains were to be marketed under the 'InterCity XPT' (Xpress Passenger Train) branding. The contract, valued at A$39 million, was signed in March 1980 for just 30 vehicles to form four 2+5 sets with two spare power cars.

Closely based on the UK HST was the 'Countrylink XPT', introduced in New South Wales from 1982. The power cars, which look similar to the Class 43s, are fitted with a Paxman 'Valenta' power unit set to deliver 2,000hp, allowing a top speed of 100mph (160km/h). By the mid-1990s the original power units were starting to show signs of their age and a re-engineering programme commenced in 1999, with No XP2016 being the first to be re-engined at the A. Goninan & Co works in Newcastle using the new Paxman VP185. The power cars are 17.3m long, 4.22m high and 2.89m wide, with an all-in weight of 76 tonnes. Construction, which was undertaken in Australia under licence, uses similar methods to the UK train. Radiators are formed in aluminium and fitted with hydraulically driven fans. The cooling group is larger than in the UK counterpart in order to cope with the higher temperatures.

To combat the high dust levels encountered in Australian conditions, the engine compartment is fitted with additional secondary air filters, and to keep the compartment cool two exhaust ventilating fans are fitted. The driving cab is fully air-conditioned to cope with hot Australian conditions, with an emergency ventilation and heating system provided in case of air-conditioning failure.

At the front end, superior headlights are fitted for night running, and two amber fog lights, white marker lights and red tail lights are provided.

Compared to the UK train, gearing is slightly revised due to the terrain. The bogies are similar to the UK BP9a bogies, but the primary suspension is modified to have increased vertical movement and the secondary suspension is softer, with increased lateral movement. These modifications were necessary to cope with a variety of track conditions.

A 'Westcode' air brake system is fitted, with an eight-step brake valve incorporating an EP service brake with a back-up emergency system. Disc braking is employed throughout and all axles are fitted with wheelslip/slide detectors.

The first two vehicles, power car No XP2000 and trailer No XF2200, were finished on 23 August 1981, prior to which a tour train was arranged to show off the new train before it commenced pre-service testing. The tour train consisted of XP2000, XF2200 and XF2201, and visited many locations between 5 and 18 August 1981, and shortly afterwards a new Australian speed record of 114mph (183km/h) was set between Table Top and Gerogery on 6 September. Another test run of a full set, which included the first use of an XPT buffet car, operated from Sydney to Taree and back on 29 January 1982.

The entire first batch of vehicles was delivered by October 1982, with XPT vehicles given the prefix 'X' in their coding, 'P' indicating a power car, 'B' 1st Class, 'F' economy class, 'R' a buffet and 'H' a guard's compartment. The passenger cars were assembled from a maintenance-free and lightweight skin of stainless steel, with a length of 24.2m, width of 2.92m, and height of 4.04m. Weights were 40 tonnes for the saloon cars, 48 tonnes for sleeping cars and 44 tonnes for buffet cars. The following list shows the vehicle delivery dates and original names:

Right:
Showing the two main liveries for the XPT, No XP2012 *Tamworth* (right) and No XP2014 *Grafton* (left) are 1984-built vehicles for the XPT extension to the North Tablelands and Canberra. This view was taken at Sydney in 1991. *Martyn Porter*

Number	Delivery date	Name
XP2000	27 August 1981	*City of Maitland*
XP2001	20 October 1981	*City of Dubbo*
XP2002	22 December 1981	*City of Armidale*
XP2003	9 February 1982	*City of Taree*
XP2004	22 February 1982	*City of Kempsey*
XP2005	23 April 1982	*City of Newcastle*
XP2006	29 May 1982	*City of Wagga Wagga*
XP2007	2 July 1982	*City of Albury*
XP2008	20 August 1982	*City of Goulburn*
XP2009	3 October 1982	*City of Canberra*
XBH2100	6 November 1981	
XBH2101	23 December 1981	
XBH2102	3 April 1982	
XBH2103	20 August 1982	
XBR2150	27 November 1981	
XBR2151	21 March 1982	
XBR2152	24 May 1982	
XBR2153	13 August 1982	
XF2200	27 August 1981	
XF2201	4 September 1981	
XF2202	28 October 1981	
XF2203	15 December 1981	
XF2204	8 January 1982	
XF2205	29 January 1982	
XF2206	5 March 1982	
XF2207	16 April 1982	
XF2208	24 April 1982	
XF2209	29 May 1982	
XF2210	9 June 1982	
XF2211	11 July 1982	

Regular XPT services commenced on 4 April 1982, with one set replacing the locomotive-hauled 'Central West Express' between Sydney and Dubbo. A day return from Sydney to Dubbo ran on Monday, Wednesday and Friday, with a day return to Orange on Tuesday, Thursday and Saturday, the services now being named the 'Central West XPT'. From 23 November 1983 alterations saw the service run to Dubbo on Monday to Saturday. All trains operated as one class, passengers paying a 1st Class fare plus surcharge.

The second XPT service was the 'Mid-North Coast XPT', providing a day return from Kempsey to Sydney on Monday to Saturday from 31 May 1982. The third service to go to XPT operation was the 'Riverina XPT' to Albury, which commenced daily operation from 23 August 1982. Unlike the others, this was not a day return service and two trains were needed.

After the initial success of XPT running to Dubbo, Kempsey and Albury, it was agreed to extend services to the North Tablelands and Canberra. Twenty additional vehicles were ordered in 1983, five power cars (XP) and 15 trailers, now fitted with rotating seats. The type letter 'D' was used to indicate this modification:

Number	Delivery date	Name
XP2010	15 February 1984	*City of Orange*
XP2011	12 March 1984	*City of Sydney*
XP2012	19 May 1984	*City of Tamworth*
XP2013	31 May 1984	*Municipality of Casino*
XP2014	29 June 1984	*City of Grafton*
XDH2104	2 November 1983	
XDH2105	4 November 1983	

Number	Delivery date	Name
XDH2106	27 November 1983	
XDH2107	2 December 1983	
XDH2108	16 December 1983	
XDH2109	22 January 1984	
XDH2110	21 February 1984	
XDH2111	13 March 1984	
XDH2112	30 March 1984	
XDH2113	7 June 1984	
XDR2154	29 January 1984	
XDR2155	5 March 1984	
XDR2156	19 May 1984	
XD2212	3 July 1984	
XD2213	28 September 1984	

These additional vehicles permitted the formation of six 2+5 sets with three spare power cars and five spare trailers. Services to Canberra, the 'Canberra XPT', started on 29 August 1983 with a daily day return between Canberra and Sydney, the journey taking 4 hours. With the introduction of the extra stock many other service alterations were made to expand the network.

Pressure had been placed on the authorities to form XPTs with two classes of travel, and from 13 May 1985 this was introduced, and the surcharge for 1st Class travel was abolished. The passenger trailers had to be internally modified for 1st and Standard Class use, and the changes were:

Vehicle numbers	Designation
XBH2100-2103	1st Class
XDH2104-2110	Standard Class
XDH2111-2113	1st Class
XBR2150-2153	1st Class
XBR2154-2156	1st Class
XF2200-2205	Standard Class
XF2206-2210	1st Class
XF2211	Standard Class
XD2212-2213	1st Class

Progressively, modifications saw the Standard Class saloons given fixed (non-rotating) seats in the 2+2 layout. First Class became a mix of rotating 2+2 and fixed 2+1.

After the normalisation of the XPT and the introduction of standard fares, passenger numbers grew by around 33% by August 1985. Comeng was immediately given an order to build 12 extra trailers to allow six train sets to be formed in the 2+7 layout:

Number	Delivery date
XD2214	20 August 1986
XD2215	1 September 1986
XD2216	15 September 1986
XD2217	20 October 1986
XD2218	30 October 1986
XD2219	28 November 1986
XD2210	17 November 1986
XD2221	5 December 1986
XD2222	12 December 1986
XD2223	21 December 1986
XD2224	22 December 1986
XD2225	30 January 1987

Sadly, from 14 October 1985 the 'Mid-North Coast XPT' was withdrawn and the 'Northern Tablelands XPT' was altered to operate three days a week. These alterations allowed a new daily service to Grafton to be launched, titled the 'Holiday Coast XPT', and over the next few months growth over the route was staggering with a 300% increase in train journeys.

The re-formation of the XPTs to 2+7 was carried out by February 1987, except for the sets working the 'Central West XPT', which remained 2+5. Some further changes to interior coach layouts were made over the coming years.

After the formation of 'Countrylink' in 1989, it was agreed to alter services throughout the state. The 'Holiday Coast XPT' was extended to Murwillumbah from 17 July 1989, operating on a two-day out-and-back duty. It was further extended to Brisbane from 22 July 1989, with a major new timetable launched from 11 February 1990. This saw a new XPT service to Brisbane and Murwillumbah running daily in each direction, while the 'Northern Tablelands XPT' was cut back to Tamworth, as a 2+5 formation. The 'Riverina XPT' ran daily, but the 'Canberra XPT' was withdrawn.

A new 'Countrylink' livery of dark blue, turquoise, white and silver was applied to the set XP2000, 2100, 2223, 2155, 2106 and XP2003 when it was outshopped in January 1990, and this livery was progressively applied to all vehicles, the final one, No XP2014, emerging in July 1992.

By 1992 growth on XPT services was such that further additional rolling stock was sought and major refurbishment of existing stock required in preparation for the services to be extended to Melbourne from 1993. ABB Transportation of Dandenong, Victoria, was contracted to build four extra power cars, five de luxe trailers and eight sleeping cars. At the same time, A. Goninan & Co of Newcastle was contracted to refurbish the existing fleet of trailers. Nos 2100-2103 were rebuilt to match the new de luxe vehicles, while Nos 2150-2156 were modified with buffet compartments, and Nos 2111 and 2225 were rebuilt as buffet cars. The remaining trailers were refurbished with new carpets, curtains and seats.

The new ABB stock was:

Number	Delivery Date	Name
XP2015	31 August 1992	*City of Melbourne*, later renamed *City of Bathurst*
XP2016	19 November 1992	*City of Cootamundra*
XP2017	17 December 1992	*City of Melbourne*
XP2018	8 January 1993	Not named
XL2228	5 March 1993	
XL2229	11 March 1993	
XL2230	2 April 1993	
XL2231	2 April 1993	
XL2232	2 April 1993	
XAM2175	21 May 1993	
XAM2176	15 July 1993	
XAM2177	15 July 1993	
XAM2178	31 July 1993	
XAM2179	31 July 1993	
XAM2180	26 October 1993	
XAM2181	6 November 1993	
XAM2182	28 October 1993	

These alterations saw 2+5 formations used on Dubbo and Tamworth services and 2+7 formations on Melbourne, Brisbane and Murwillumbah trains. By this stage most XF trailers contained 1st Class seats. Conversions were still taking place, but vehicles had not yet been recoded.

A number of vehicle layout changes were made in the mid-1990s to meet customer needs, and this saw an amount of trailer vehicle renumbering.

Above:
Displaying the 1990s 'Countrylink' livery, power car XP2004 *Kempsey* is seen at Sydney Central station on 27 September 1996. *Iain Mackenzie*

Below:
Original power car No 2000 was repainted in the mid-1990s to advertise the 2000 Olympics to be held in Sydney; showing this superb colour scheme the vehicle is seen at Melbourne at 07.00 on 30 September 1996. *Iain Mackenzie*

As part of a test programme with power cars XP2003/15 and three trailers on a run to Albury, an attempt was made to reach 200km/h for the first time in Australia on 18 September 1992, but it failed with a top speed of 119mph (193km/h) between Table Top and Yerong Creek.

Sleeping cars were first used on the Brisbane and Murwillumbah trains from 30 July 1993, the nine compartments accommodating 18 passengers, or 27 1st Class passengers sitting up during daylight running.

With the delivery of all new rolling stock a number of service changes were introduced from the autumn of 1993, replacing the Tamworth service with new *Xplorer* railcars to Armidale and Moree. Daylight and overnight XPTs were introduced to Melbourne and the weekly 'Grafton Express' was replaced by a daily XPT. The new *Xplorer* railcars replaced the Tamworth XPT from October 1993.

The first regular 'Melbourne XPT' service on the Sydney-Melbourne corridor departed from Sydney on 21 November 1993, returning the following day. The new 'Grafton XPT' service commenced on 25 November 1993, and the first daylight XPT running between Sydney and Melbourne commenced on 13 December 1994.

Coaches of a Swedish tilting X2000 train were hired for trials in Australia in 1995 and these were powered by modified XPT power cars XP2000 and XP2009.

Appendix I.
The IC125 Trailer Stock Fleet in Numerical Order

10000	See 40000
10100	See 40500
11000	See 41000
11001	Built as Prototype FO, rebuilt as Royal Train stock 2903
11002	See 41001
11003	See 41002
12000	See 42000
12001	Built as Prototype TSO, rebuilt as Royal Train stock 2904
12002	See 42001
12003	See 42002
40000	Built as Prototype TRSB originally numbered 10000, rebuilt as Departmental 975984
40001	Built as TRSB, rebuilt to TRBS 40401, owned by Porterbrook, with VT CrossCountry pool
40002	Built as TRSB, rebuilt to TRBS 40402, owned by Porterbrook, with VT CrossCountry pool
40003	Built as TRSB, rebuilt to TRBS 40403, owned by Porterbrook, with VT CrossCountry pool
40004	Built as TRSB, rebuilt as TRBS 40404, rebuilt to TRB 40204, owned by Angel Trains, with FGW
40005	Built as TRSB, rebuilt as TRBS 40405, rebuilt to TRB 40205, owned by Angel Trains, with FGW
40006	Built as TRSB, rebuilt as TRBS 40406, rebuilt to TRB 40206, owned by Angel Trains, with FGW
40007	Built as TRSB, rebuilt as TRBS 40407, rebuilt to TRB 40207, owned by Angel Trains, with FGW
40008	Built as TRSB, rebuilt as TRBS 40408, rebuilt to TRB 40208, owned by Angel Trains, with FGW
40009	Built as TRSB, rebuilt as TRBS 40409, rebuilt to TRB 40209, owned by Angel Trains, with FGW
40010	Built as TRSB, rebuilt as TRBS 40410, rebuilt to TRB 40210, owned by Angel Trains, with FGW
40011	Built as TRSB, rebuilt as TRBS 40411, rebuilt to TRB 40211, rebuilt to TRBS 40411, owned by Porterbrook, with VT CrossCountry pool
40012	Built as TRSB, rebuilt as TRBS 40412, rebuilt to TRB 40212, rebuilt to TRBS 40412, owned by Porterbrook, with VT CrossCountry pool
40013	Built as TRSB, rebuilt as TRBS 40413, rebuilt to TRB 40213, owned by Angel Trains, with FGW. Wrecked in Ladbroke Grove collision 5.10.99, stored Bombardier Crewe pending disposal
40014	Built as TRSB, rebuilt as TRBS 40414, owned by Porterbrook, with VT CrossCountry pool
40015	Built as TRSB, rebuilt as TRBS 40415, owned by Porterbrook, with VT CrossCountry pool
40016	Built as TRSB, rebuilt as TRBS 40416, owned by Porterbrook, with VT CrossCountry pool
40017	Built as TRSB, rebuilt as TRBS 40417, owned by Porterbrook, with VT CrossCountry pool
40018	Built as TRSB, rebuilt as TRBS 40418, owned by Porterbrook, with VT CrossCountry pool
40019	Built as TRSB, rebuilt as TRBS 40419, owned by Porterbrook, with VT CrossCountry pool
40020	Built as TRSB, rebuilt as TRBS 40420, owned by Porterbrook, with VT CrossCountry pool
40021	Built as TRSB, rebuilt as TRBS 40421, rebuilt to TRB 40221, owned by Angel Trains, with FGW
40022	Built as TRSB, rebuilt as TRBS 40422, owned by Porterbrook, with VT CrossCountry pool
40023	Built as TRSB, rebuilt as TRBS 40423, owned by Porterbrook, with VT CrossCountry pool
40024	Built as TRSB, rebuilt as TRBS 40424, owned by Porterbrook, with VT CrossCountry pool
40025	Built as TRSB, rebuilt as TRBS 40425, owned by Porterbrook, with VT CrossCountry pool
40026	Built as TRSB, rebuilt as TRBS 40426, owned by Porterbrook, with VT CrossCountry pool
40027	Built as TRSB, rebuilt as TRBS 40427, owned by Porterbrook, with VT CrossCountry pool
40028	Built as TRSB, rebuilt as TRBS 40428, rebuilt to TRB 40228, owned by Angel Trains, with FGW
40029	Built as TRSB, rebuilt as TRBS 40429, owned by Porterbrook, with VT CrossCountry pool
40030	Built as TRSB, rebuilt as TRBS 40430, owned by Porterbrook, with VT CrossCountry pool
40031	Built as TRSB, rebuilt as TRBS 40431, rebuilt to TRB 40231, owned by Angel Trains, with FGW
40032	Built as TRSB, rebuilt as TRBS 40432, rebuilt to TRB 40232, rebuilt to TRBS 40432, owned by Porterbrook, with VT in CrossCountry pool
40033	Built as TRSB, rebuilt as TRBS 40433, rebuilt to TRB 40233, rebuilt to TRBS 40433, owned by Porterbrook, with VT in CrossCountry pool
40034	Built as TRSB, rebuilt as TRBS 40434, owned by Porterbrook, with VT CrossCountry pool
40035	Built as TRSB, rebuilt as TRBS 40435, owned by Porterbrook, with VT CrossCountry pool
40036	Built as TRSB, rebuilt as TRBS 40436, owned by Porterbrook, with VT CrossCountry pool
40037	Built as TRSB, rebuilt as TRBS 40437, owned by Porterbrook, with VT CrossCountry pool
40204	See 40004
40205	See 40005
40206	See 40006
40207	See 40007
40208	See 40008
40209	See 40009
40210	See 40010
40211	See 40011
40212	See 40012
40213	See 40013
40221	See 40021
40228	See 40028
40231	See 40031
40232	See 40032
40233	See 40033
40300	Built as TRUB, rebuilt as TRBF 40700, owned by Porterbrook, with MML
40301	Built as TRUB, rebuilt as TRBF 40701, owned by Porterbrook, with MML
40302	Built as TRUB, rebuilt as TRBF 40702, owned by Porterbrook, with MML
40303	Built as TRUB, rebuilt as TRBF 40703, owned by Angel Trains, with FGW
40304	Built as TRUB, rebuilt as TRBF 40704, owned by Angel Trains, with GNER
40305	Built as TRUB, rebuilt as TRBF 40705, owned by Angel Trains, with GNER
40306	Built as TRUB, rebuilt as TRBF 40706, owned by Angel Trains, with GNER
40307	Built as TRUB, rebuilt as TRBF 40707, owned by Angel Trains, with FGW

40308	Built as TRUB, rebuilt as TRBF 40708, owned by Porterbrook, with MML
40309	Built as TRUB, rebuilt as TRBF 40709, owned by Angel Trains, with FGW
40310	Built as TRUB, rebuilt as TRBF 40710, owned by Angel Trains, with FGW
40311	Built as TRUB, rebuilt as TRBF 40711, owned by Angel Trains, with GNER
40312	Built as TRUB, rebuilt as TRBF 40712, owned by Angel Trains, with FGW
40313	Built as TRUB, rebuilt as TRBF 40713, owned by Angel Trains, with FGW
40314	Built as TRUB, rebuilt as TRBF 40714, owned by Angel Trains, with FGW
40315	Built as TRUB, rebuilt as TRBF 40715, owned by Angel Trains, with FGW
40316	Built as TRUB, rebuilt as TRBF 40716, owned by Angel Trains, with FGW
40317	Built as TRUB, rebuilt as TRBF 40717, owned by Angel Trains, with FGW
40318	Built as TRUB, rebuilt as TRBF 40718, owned by Angel Trains, with FGW
40319	Built as TRUB, rebuilt as TRBF 40719, rebuilt to TRFM, 40619, owned by Porterbrook, with VT CrossCountry pool
40320	Built as TRUB, rebuilt as TRBF 40720, owned by Angel Trains, with GNER
40321	Built as TRUB, rebuilt as TRBF 40721, owned by Angel Trains, with FGW
40322	Built as TRUB, rebuilt as TRBF 40722, owned by Angel Trains, with FGW
40323	Built as TRUB, rebuilt as TRBF 40723, owned by Angel Trains, with VT West Coast pool
40324	Built as TRUB, rebuilt as TRBF 40724, owned by Angel Trains, with FGW
40325	Built as TRUB, rebuilt as TRBF 40725, owned by Angel Trains, with FGW
40326	Built as TRUB, rebuilt as TRBF 40726, owned by Angel Trains, with FGW
40327	Built as TRUB, rebuilt as TRBF 40727, owned by Angel Trains, with FGW
40328	Built as TRUB, rebuilt as TRBF 40728, owned by Porterbrook, with MML
40329	Built as TRUB, rebuilt as TRBF 40729, owned by Porterbrook, with MML
40330	Built as TRUB, rebuilt as TRBF 40730, owned by Porterbrook, with MML
40331	Built as TRUB, rebuilt as TRBF 40731, owned by Angel Trains, with FGW
40332	Built as TRUB, rebuilt as TRBF 40732, owned by Angel Trains, with VT West Coast pool
40333	Built as TRUB, rebuilt as TRBF 40733, owned by Angel Trains, with FGW
40334	Built as TRUB, rebuilt as TRBF 40734, owned by Angel Trains, with FGW
40335	Built as TRUB, rebuilt as TRBF 40735, owned by Angel Trains, with GNER
40336	Built as TRUB, rebuilt as TRBF 40736, owned by Angel Trains, with FGW
40337	Built as TRUB, rebuilt as TRBF 40737, owned by Angel Trains, with GNER
40338	Built as TRUB, rebuilt as TRBF 40738, owned by Angel Trains, with FGW
40339	Built as TRUB, rebuilt as TRBF 40739, owned by Angel Trains, with FGW
40340	Built as TRUB, rebuilt as TRBF 40740, owned by Angel Trains, with GNER
40341	Built as TRUB, rebuilt as TRBF 40741, owned by Porterbrook, with MML
40342	Built as TRUB, rebuilt as TRBF 40742, owned by Angel Trains, with VT West Coast pool
40343	Built as TRUB, rebuilt as TRBF 40743, owned by Angel Trains, with FGW
40344	Built as TRUB, rebuilt as TRBF 40744, owned by Angel Trains, with FGW
40345	Built as TRUB, rebuilt as TRBF 40745, owned by Angel Trains, with FGW
40346	Built as TRUB, rebuilt as TRBF 40746, owned by Porterbrook, with MML
40347	Built as TRUB, rebuilt as TRBF 40747, owned by Angel Trains, with FGW
40348	Built as TRUB, rebuilt as TRBF 40748, owned by Angel Trains, with GNER
40349	Built as TRUB, rebuilt as TRBF 40749, owned by Porterbrook, with MML
40350	Built as TRUB, rebuilt as TRBF 40750, owned by Angel Trains, with GNER
40351	Built as TRUB, rebuilt as TRBF 40751, owned by Porterbrook, with MML
40352	Built as TRUB, rebuilt as TRBF 40752, owned by Angel Trains, with FGW
40353	Built as TRUB, rebuilt as TRBF 40753, owned by Porterbrook, with MML
40354	Built as TRUB, rebuilt as TRBF 40754, owned by Porterbrook, with MML
40355	Built as TRUB, rebuilt as TRBF 40755, owned by Angel Trains, with FGW
40356	Built as TRUB, rebuilt as TRBF 40756, owned by Porterbrook, with MML
40357	Built as TRUB, rebuilt as TRBF 40757, owned by Angel Trains, with FGW
40401	See 40001
40402	See 40002
40403	See 40003
40404	See 40004
40405	See 40005
40406	See 40006
40407	See 40007
40408	See 40008
40409	See 40009
40410	See 40010
40411	See 40011
40412	See 40012
40413	See 40013
40414	See 40014
40415	See 40015
40416	See 40016
40417	See 40017
40418	See 40018
40419	See 40019
40420	See 40020
40421	See 40021
40422	See 40022
40423	See 40023
40424	See 40024
40425	See 40025
40426	See 40026
40427	See 40027
40428	See 40028
40429	See 40029
40430	See 40030
40431	See 40031
40432	See 40032
40433	See 40033
40434	See 40034
40435	See 40035
40436	See 40036
40437	See 40037
40500	Built as Prototype TRUK, originally numbered 10100, rebuilt as Departmental 977089. Now scrapped — cut up by Booth-Roe, Rotherham, 2.93
40501	TRFK, owned by Porterbrook, stored at Bombardier Derby
40502	TRFK, rebuilt as Mk3 hauled stock, 10204
40503	Built as TRFK, rebuilt as Mk3 hauled stock, 10205
40504	Built as TRFK, rebuilt as Mk3 hauled stock, 10202
40505	Built as TRFK, rebuilt as TSO 41179, owned by Angel Trains, with FGW
40506	Built as TRFK, rebuilt as Mk3 hauled stock, 10203
40507	Built as TRFK, rebuilt as Mk3 hauled stock, 10206
40508	Built as TRFK, rebuilt as Mk3 hauled stock, 10209
40509	Built as TRFK, rebuilt as Mk3 hauled stock, 10210
40510	Built as TRFK, rebuilt as Mk3 hauled stock, 10211
40511	Built as TRFK, rebuilt as TSO 41180, owned by Angel Trains, with FGW
40512	Built as TRFK, rebuilt as Mk3 Royal Train vehicle 2916
40513	Built as TRFK, modified to TLUK 'Executive saloon'. Now owned by Porterbrook, stored at Bombardier Derby (reportedly sold to Irish Rail)
40514	Built as TRFK, rebuilt as Mk3 Royal Train vehicle 2917
40515	Built as TRFK, rebuilt as Mk3 Royal Train vehicle 2918
40516	Built as TRFK, rebuilt as Mk3 hauled stock, 10207
40517	Built as TRFK, rebuilt as Mk3 hauled stock, 10208
40518	Built as TRFK, rebuilt as Mk3 Royal Train vehicle 2919
40519	Built as TRFK, rebuilt as Mk3 hauled stock, 10200
40520	Built as TRFK, rebuilt as Mk3 hauled stock, 10201
40521-40527	Ordered as TRUKs, cancelled just before construction due to changed catering needs
40619	See 40319
40700	See 40300
40701	See 40301
40702	See 40302
40703	See 40303
40704	See 40304
40705	See 40305
40706	See 40306
40707	See 40307
40708	See 40308
40709	See 40309
40710	See 40310

40711	See 40311
40712	See 40312
40713	See 40313
40714	See 40314
40715	See 40315
40716	See 40316
40717	See 40317
40718	See 40318
40719	See 40319
40720	See 40320
40721	See 40321
40722	See 40322
40723	See 40323
40724	See 40324
40725	See 40325
40726	See 40326
40727	See 40327
40728	See 40328
40729	See 40329
40730	See 40330
40731	See 40331
40732	See 40332
40733	See 40333
40734	See 40334
40735	See 40335
40736	See 40336
40737	See 40337
40738	See 40338
40739	See 40339
40740	See 40340
40741	See 40341
40742	See 40342
40743	See 40343
40744	See 40344
40745	See 40345
40746	See 40346
40747	See 40347
40748	See 40348
40749	See 40349
40750	See 40350
40751	See 40351
40752	See 40352
40753	See 40353
40754	See 40354
40755	See 40355
40756	See 40356
40757	See 40357

41000	Built as Prototype FO, originally numbered 11000, rebuilt as Departmental 975814, now preserved at Peak Rail, Matlock
41001	Built as Prototype FO, originally numbered 11002, rebuilt as production FO 41170, owned by Angel Trains, with GNER
41002	Built as Prototype FO, originally numbered 11003, rebuilt as production FO 41174, rebuilt to TSO 42357, owned by Angel Trains, with VT West Coast pool
41003	FO, owned by Angel Trains, with FGW
41004	FO, owned by Angel Trains, with FGW
41005	FO, owned by Angel Trains, with FGW
41006	FO, owned by Angel Trains, with FGW
41007	FO, owned by Angel Trains, with FGW
41008	FO, owned by Angel Trains, with FGW
41009	FO, owned by Angel Trains, with FGW
41010	FO, owned by Angel Trains, with FGW
41011	FO, owned by Angel Trains, with FGW
41012	FO, owned by Angel Trains, with FGW
41013	FO, owned by Angel Trains, with FGW

41014	FO, owned by Angel Trains, with FGW
41015	FO, owned by Angel Trains, with FGW
41016	FO, owned by Angel Trains, with FGW
41017	FO, owned by Angel Trains, with FGW
41018	FO, owned by Angel Trains, with FGW
41019	FO, owned by Angel Trains, with FGW
41020	FO, owned by Angel Trains, with FGW
41021	FO, owned by Angel Trains, with FGW
41022	FO, owned by Angel Trains, with FGW
41023	FO, owned by Angel Trains, with FGW
41024	FO, owned by Angel Trains, with FGW
41025	FO, owned by Angel Trains, with VT West Coast pool
41026	FO, owned by Angel Trains, with VT West Coast pool
41027	FO, owned by Angel Trains, with FGW
41028	FO, owned by Angel Trains, with FGW
41029	FO, owned by Angel Trains, with FGW
41030	FO, owned by Angel Trains, with FGW
41031	FO, owned by Angel Trains, with FGW
41032	FO, owned by Angel Trains, with FGW
41033	FO, owned by Angel Trains, with FGW
41034	FO, owned by Angel Trains, with FGW
41035	FO, owned by Angel Trains, with VT West Coast pool
41036	FO, owned by Angel Trains, with VT West Coast pool
41037	FO, owned by Angel Trains, with FGW
41038	FO, owned by Angel Trains, with FGW
41039	FO, owned by Angel Trains, with GNER
41040	FO, owned by Angel Trains, with GNER
41041	FO, owned by Porterbrook, with MML
41042	FO, owned by Angel Trains, with FGW. Destroyed in Ladbroke Grove crash 5.10.99
41043	FO, owned by Angel Trains, with GNER
41044	FO, owned by Angel Trains, with GNER
41045	FO, owned by Porterbrook, with VT CrossCountry pool
41046	FO, owned by Porterbrook, with MML
41047	Built as FO, rebuilt to TSO 42350, owned by Angel Trains, with FGW
41048	Built as FO, rebuilt to TSO 42351, owned by Angel Trains, with FGW
41049	FO, Angel Trains. Stored following serious collision damage at Southall 9.97
41050	FO, broken up by M. R. J. Philips at Southall following collision, 9.97, previously operated by Angel Trains, with FGW
41051	FO, owned by Angel Trains, with FGW
41052	FO, owned by Angel Trains, with FGW
41053	Built as FO, rebuilt to TSO 42346, owned by Angel Trains, with FGW
41054	Built as FO, rebuilt to TSO 42347, owned by Angel Trains, with FGW
41055	FO, owned by Angel Trains, with FGW
41056	FO, owned by Angel Trains, with FGW
41057	FO, owned by Porterbrook, with MML
41058	FO, owned by Porterbrook, with MML
41059	FO, owned by Porterbrook, with VT CrossCountry pool
41060	FO, owned by Angel Trains. Seriously damaged in Ladbroke Grove collision 5.10.99, stored at Bombardier Crewe pending disposal
41061	FO, owned by Porterbrook, with MML
41062	FO, owned by Porterbrook, with MML
41063	FO, owned by Porterbrook, with MML
41064	FO, owned by Porterbrook, with MML
41065	FO, owned by Angel Trains, with FGW
41066	FO, owned by Angel Trains, with VT West Coast pool
41067	FO, owned by Porterbrook, with MML
41068	FO, owned by Porterbrook, with MML
41069	FO, owned by Porterbrook, with MML
41070	FO, owned by Porterbrook, with MML
41071	FO, owned by Porterbrook, with MML
41072	FO, owned by Porterbrook, with MML
41073	Built as FO, rebuilt to TSO 42348, owned by Angel Trains, with FGW
41074	Built as FO, rebuilt to TSO 42349, owned by Angel Trains, with FGW
41075	FO, owned by Porterbrook, with MML
41076	FO, owned by Porterbrook, with MML

41077	FO, owned by Porterbrook, with MML
41078	FO, owned by Porterbrook, with MML
41079	FO, owned by Porterbrook, with MML
41080	FO, owned by Porterbrook, with MML
41081	FO, owned by Porterbrook, with VT CrossCountry pool
41082	FO, rebuilt to TSO and renumbered 42363, owned by Porterbrook, with VT CrossCountry pool
41083	FO, owned by Porterbrook, with MML
41084	FO, owned by Porterbrook, with MML
41085	FO, owned by Porterbrook, with VT CrossCountry pool
41086	FO, owned by Porterbrook, with VT CrossCountry pool
41087	FO, owned by Angel Trains, with GNER
41088	FO, owned by Angel Trains, with GNER
41089	FO, owned by Angel Trains, with FGW
41090	FO, owned by Angel Trains, with GNER
41091	FO, owned by Angel Trains, with GNER
41092	FO, owned by Angel Trains, with GNER
41093	FO, owned by Angel Trains, with FGW
41094	FO, owned by Angel Trains, with FGW
41095	FO, owned by Porterbrook, with VT CrossCountry pool
41096	FO, owned by Porterbrook, with VT CrossCountry pool
41097	FO, owned by Angel Trains, with GNER
41098	FO, owned by Angel Trains, with GNER
41099	FO, owned by Angel Trains, with GNER
41100	FO, owned by Angel Trains, with GNER
41101	FO, owned by Angel Trains, with FGW
41102	FO, owned by Angel Trains, with FGW
41103	FO, owned by Angel Trains, with FGW
41104	FO, owned by Angel Trains, with FGW
41105	FO, owned by Angel Trains, with FGW
41106	FO, owned by Angel Trains, with FGW
41107	FO, owned by Porterbrook, with VT CrossCountry pool
41108	FO, owned by Porterbrook, with VT CrossCountry pool
41109	FO, owned by Porterbrook, with VT CrossCountry pool
41110	FO, owned by Angel Trains, with FGW
41111	FO, owned by Porterbrook, with MML
41112	FO, owned by Porterbrook, with MML
41113	FO, owned by Porterbrook, with MML
41114	FO, owned by Porterbrook, with VT CrossCountry pool
41115	FO, owned by Porterbrook, with VT CrossCountry pool
41116	FO, owned by Angel Trains, with FGW
41117	FO, owned by Porterbrook, with MML
41118	FO, owned by Angel Trains, with GNER
41119	FO, owned by Porterbrook, with VT CrossCountry pool
41120	FO, owned by Angel Trains, with GNER
41121	FO, owned by Angel Trains, with FGW
41122	FO, owned by Angel Trains, with FGW
41123	FO, owned by Angel Trains, with FGW
41124	FO, owned by Angel Trains, with FGW
41125	FO, owned by Angel Trains, with FGW
41126	FO, owned by Angel Trains, with FGW
41127	FO, owned by Angel Trains, with FGW
41128	FO, owned by Angel Trains, with FGW
41129	FO, owned by Angel Trains, with FGW
41130	FO, owned by Angel Trains, with FGW
41131	FO, owned by Angel Trains, with FGW
41132	FO, owned by Angel Trains, with FGW
41133	FO, owned by Angel Trains, with FGW
41134	FO, owned by Angel Trains, with FGW
41135	FO, owned by Angel Trains, with FGW
41136	FO, owned by Angel Trains, with FGW
41137	FO, owned by Angel Trains, with FGW
41138	FO, owned by Angel Trains, with FGW
41139	FO, owned by Angel Trains, with FGW
41140	FO, owned by Angel Trains, with FGW
41141	FO, owned by Angel Trains, with FGW
41142	FO, owned by Angel Trains, with FGW

41143	FO, owned by Angel Trains, with FGW
41144	FO, owned by Angel Trains, with FGW
41145	FO, owned by Angel Trains, with FGW
41146	FO, owned by Angel Trains, with FGW
41147	FO, owned by Porterbrook, with VT CrossCountry pool
41148	FO, owned by Porterbrook, with VT CrossCountry pool
41149	FO, owned by Porterbrook, with VT CrossCountry pool
41150	FO, owned by Angel Trains, with GNER
41151	FO, owned by Angel Trains, with GNER
41152	FO, owned by Angel Trains, with GNER
41153	FO, owned by Porterbrook, with MML
41154	FO, owned by Porterbrook, with MML
41155	FO, owned by Porterbrook, with MML
41156	FO, owned by Porterbrook, with MML
41157	FO, owned by Angel Trains, with FGW
41158	FO, owned by Angel Trains, with FGW
41159	FO, owned by Porterbrook, with VT CrossCountry pool
41160	FO, owned by Porterbrook, with VT CrossCountry pool
41161	FO, owned by Porterbrook, with VT CrossCountry pool
41162	FO, owned by Porterbrook, with VT CrossCountry pool
41163	FO, owned by Porterbrook, with VT CrossCountry pool
41164	FO, owned by Angel Trains, with VT West Coast pool
41165	FO, owned by Porterbrook, with VT CrossCountry pool
41166	FO, owned by Porterbrook, with VT CrossCountry pool
41167	FO, owned by Porterbrook, with VT CrossCountry pool
41168	FO, owned by Porterbrook, with VT CrossCountry pool
41169	FO, owned by Porterbrook, with VT CrossCountry pool
41170	See 41001
41171	See 42001
41172	See 42000
41173	See 42002
41174	See 41002
41175	See 42114
41176	See 42142
41177	See 42158
41178	See 42011
41179	See 40505
41180	See 40511
42000	Built as Prototype TSO, originally numbered 12000, rebuilt as production FO 41172, rebuilt to TSO 42355, owned by Angel Trains, with VT West Coast pool
42001	Built as Prototype TSO, originally numbered 12002, rebuilt as production FO 41171, rebuilt to TSO 42353, owned by Angel Trains, with VT CrossCountry pool
42002	Built as Prototype TSO, originally numbered 12002, rebuilt as production FO 41173, rebuilt to TSO 42356, owned by Angel Trains, with FGW
42003	TSO, owned by Angel Trains, with FGW
42004	TSO, owned by Angel Trains, with FGW
42005	TSO, owned by Angel Trains, with FGW
42006	TSO, owned by Angel Trains, with FGW
42007	TSO, owned by Angel Trains, with FGW
42008	TSO, owned by Angel Trains, with FGW
42009	TSO, owned by Angel Trains, with FGW
42010	TSO, owned by Angel Trains, with FGW
42011	Built as TSO, rebuilt to FO 41178, rebuilt to TSO 42362, owned by Angel Trains, with FGW
42012	TSO, owned by Angel Trains, with FGW
42013	TSO, owned by Angel Trains, with FGW
42014	TSO, owned by Porterbrook, with VT CrossCountry pool
42015	TSO, owned by Angel Trains, with FGW
42016	TSO, owned by Angel Trains, with FGW
42017	TSO, owned by Angel Trains, with FGW
42018	TSO, owned by Angel Trains, with FGW
42019	TSO, owned by Angel Trains, with FGW
42020	TSO, owned by Angel Trains, with FGW

42021	TSO, owned by Angel Trains, with FGW
42022	TSO, owned by Angel Trains, with FGW
42023	TSO, owned by Angel Trains, with FGW
42024	TSO, owned by Angel Trains, with FGW
42025	TSO, owned by Angel Trains, with FGW
42026	TSO, owned by Angel Trains, with FGW
42027	TSO, owned by Angel Trains, with FGW
42028	TSO, owned by Angel Trains, with FGW
42029	TSO, owned by Angel Trains, with FGW
42030	TSO, owned by Angel Trains, with FGW
42031	TSO, owned by Angel Trains, with FGW
42032	TSO, owned by Angel Trains, with FGW
42033	TSO, owned by Angel Trains, with FGW
42034	TSO, owned by Angel Trains, with FGW
42035	TSO, owned by Angel Trains, with FGW
42036	TSO, owned by Angel Trains, with VT West Coast pool
42037	TSO, owned by Angel Trains, with VT West Coast pool
42038	TSO, owned by Angel Trains, with VT West Coast pool
42039	TSO, owned by Angel Trains, with FGW
42040	TSO, owned by Angel Trains, with FGW
42041	TSO, owned by Angel Trains, with FGW
42042	TSO, owned by Angel Trains, with FGW
42043	TSO, owned by Angel Trains, with FGW
42044	TSO, owned by Angel Trains, with FGW
42045	TSO, owned by Angel Trains, with FGW
42046	TSO, owned by Angel Trains, with FGW
42047	TSO, owned by Angel Trains, with FGW
42048	TSO, owned by Angel Trains, with FGW
42049	TSO, owned by Angel Trains, with FGW
42050	TSO, owned by Angel Trains, with FGW
42051	TSO, owned by Angel Trains, with VT West Coast pool
42052	TSO, owned by Angel Trains, with VT West Coast pool
42053	TSO, owned by Angel Trains, with VT West Coast pool
42054	TSO, owned by Angel Trains, with FGW
42055	TSO, owned by Angel Trains, with FGW
42056	TSO, owned by Angel Trains, with FGW
42057	TSO, owned by Angel Trains, with GNER
42058	TSO, owned by Angel Trains, with GNER
42059	TSO, owned by Angel Trains, with GNER
42060	TSO, owned by Angel Trains, with FGW
42061	TSO, owned by Angel Trains, with FGW
42062	TSO, owned by Angel Trains, with FGW
42063	TSO, owned by Angel Trains, with GNER
42064	TSO, owned by Angel Trains, with GNER
42065	TSO, owned by Angel Trains, with GNER
42066	TSO, owned by Angel Trains, with FGW
42067	TSO, owned by Angel Trains, with FGW
42068	TSO, owned by Angel Trains, with FGW
42069	TSO, owned by Angel Trains, with FGW
42070	TSO, owned by Angel Trains, with FGW
42071	TSO, owned by Angel Trains, with FGW
42072	TSO, owned by Angel Trains, with FGW
42073	TSO, owned by Angel Trains, with FGW
42074	TSO, owned by Angel Trains, with FGW
42075	TSO, owned by Angel Trains, with FGW
42076	TSO, owned by Angel Trains, with FGW
42077	TSO, owned by Angel Trains, with FGW
42078	TSO, owned by Angel Trains, with FGW
42079	TSO, owned by Angel Trains, with FGW
42080	TSO, owned by Angel Trains, with FGW
42081	TSO, owned by Angel Trains, with FGW
42082	TSO, owned by Angel Trains, with FGW
42083	TSO, owned by Angel Trains, with FGW
42084	TSO, owned by Porterbrook, with VT CrossCountry pool
42085	TSO, owned by Porterbrook, with VT CrossCountry pool
42086	TSO, owned by Porterbrook, with VT CrossCountry pool
42087	TSO, owned by Porterbrook, with VT CrossCountry pool
42088	TSO, owned by Porterbrook, with VT CrossCountry pool
42089	TSO, owned by Angel Trains, with FGW
42090	TSO, owned by Porterbrook, with VT CrossCountry pool
42091	TSO, owned by Porterbrook, with VT CrossCountry pool
42092	TSO, owned by Porterbrook, with VT CrossCountry pool
42093	TSO, owned by Porterbrook, with VT CrossCountry pool
42094	TSO, owned by Porterbrook, with VT CrossCountry pool
42095	TSO, owned by Porterbrook, with VT CrossCountry pool
42096	TSO, owned by Angel Trains, with FGW
42097	TS0, owned by Angel Trains, with VT West Coast pool
42098	TSO, owned by Angel Trains, with FGW
42099	TSO, owned by Angel Trains, with FGW
42100	TSO, owned by Porterbrook, with MML
42101	TSO, owned by Porterbrook, with MML
42102	TSO, owned by Porterbrook, with MML
42103	TSO, owned by Porterbrook, with VT CrossCountry pool
42104	TSO, owned by Angel Trains, with GNER
42105	TSO, owned by Porterbrook, with VT CrossCountry pool
42106	TSO, owned by Angel Trains, with GNER
42107	TSO, owned by Angel Trains, with FGW
42108	TSO, owned by Porterbrook, with VT CrossCountry pool
42109	TSO, owned by Porterbrook, with VT CrossCountry pool
42110	TSO, owned by Porterbrook, with VT CrossCountry pool
42111	TSO, owned by Porterbrook, with MML
42112	TSO, owned by Porterbrook, with MML
42113	TSO, owned by Porterbrook, with MML
42114	Built as TSO, rebuilt to FO 41175, rebuilt to TSO 42354, owned by Angel Trains, with GNER
42115	TSO, owned by Porterbrook, with VT in CrossCountry pool
42116	TSO, owned by Porterbrook, with VT in CrossCountry pool
42117	TSO, owned by Porterbrook, with VT in CrossCountry pool
42118	TSO, owned by Angel Trains, with FGW
42119	TSO, owned by Porterbrook, with MML
42120	TSO, owned by Porterbrook, with MML
42121	TSO, owned by Porterbrook, with MML
42122	TSO, owned by Angel Trains, with VT West Coast pool
42123	TSO, owned by Porterbrook, with MML
42124	TSO, owned by Porterbrook, with MML
42125	TSO, owned by Porterbrook, with MML
42126	TSO, owned by Angel Trains, with FGW
42127	TSO, owned by Porterbrook, with VT CrossCountry pool
42128	TSO, owned by Porterbrook, with VT CrossCountry pool
42129	TSO, owned by Angel Trains, with FGW
42130	TSO, owned by Porterbrook, with VT CrossCountry pool
42131	TSO, owned by Porterbrook, with MML
42132	TSO, owned by Porterbrook, with MML
42133	TSO, owned by Porterbrook, with MML
42134	TS0, owned by Angel Trains, with VT West Coast pool
42135	TSO, owned by Porterbrook, with MML
42136	TSO, owned by Porterbrook, with MML
42137	TSO, owned by Porterbrook, with MML
42138	TSO, owned by Angel Trains, with FGW
42139	TSO, owned by Porterbrook, with MML
42140	TSO, owned by Porterbrook, with MML
42141	TSO, owned by Porterbrook, with MML
42142	Built as TSO, rebuilt to FO 41176, rebuilt to TSO 42352, owned by Porterbrook, with MML
42143	TSO, owned by Angel Trains, with FGW
42144	TSO, owned by Angel Trains, with FGW
42145	TSO, owned by Angel Trains, with FGW
42146	TSO, owned by Angel Trains, with GNER
42147	TSO, owned by Porterbrook, with MML
42148	TSO, owned by Porterbrook, with MML
42149	TSO, owned by Porterbrook, with MML
42150	TSO, owned by Angel Trains, with GNER
42151	TSO, owned by Porterbrook, with MML
42152	TSO, owned by Porterbrook, with MML

42153	TSO, owned by Porterbrook, with MML
42154	TSO, owned by Angel Trains, with GNER
42155	TSO, owned by Porterbrook, with MML
42156	TSO, owned by Porterbrook, with MML
42157	TSO, owned by Porterbrook, with MML
42158	Built as TSO, rebuilt to FO 41177, rebuilt to TSO 42158, owned by Angel Trains, with GNER
42159	TSO, owned by Porterbrook, with VT CrossCountry pool
42160	TSO, owned by Porterbrook, with VT CrossCountry pool
42161	TSO, owned by Porterbrook, with VT CrossCountry pool
42162	TSO, owned by Porterbrook, with VT CrossCountry pool
42163	TSO, owned by Porterbrook, with MML
42164	TSO, owned by Porterbrook, with MML
42165	TSO, owned by Porterbrook, with MML
42166	TSO, owned by Porterbrook, with VT CrossCountry pool
42167	TSO, owned by Porterbrook, with VT CrossCountry pool
42168	TSO, owned by Porterbrook, with VT CrossCountry pool
42169	TSO, owned by Porterbrook, with VT CrossCountry pool
42170	TSO, owned by Porterbrook, with VT CrossCountry pool
42171	TSO, owned by Angel Trains, with GNER
42172	TSO, owned by Angel Trains, with GNER
42173	TSO, owned by Porterbrook, with VT CrossCountry pool
42174	TSO, owned by Porterbrook, with VT CrossCountry pool
42175	TSO, owned by Porterbrook, with VT CrossCountry pool
42176	TSO, owned by Porterbrook, with VT CrossCountry pool
42177	TSO, owned by Porterbrook, with VT CrossCountry pool
42178	TSO, owned by Porterbrook, with VT CrossCountry pool
42179	TSO, owned by Angel Trains, with GNER
42180	TSO, owned by Angel Trains, with GNER
42181	TSO, owned by Angel Trains, with GNER
42182	TSO, owned by Angel Trains, with GNER
42183	TSO, owned by Angel Trains, with FGW
42184	TSO, owned by Angel Trains, with FGW
42185	TSO, owned by Angel Trains, with FGW
42186	TSO, owned by Angel Trains, with GNER
42187	TSO, owned by Porterbrook, with VT CrossCountry pool
42188	TSO, owned by Porterbrook, with VT CrossCountry pool
42189	TSO, owned by Porterbrook, with VT CrossCountry pool
42190	TSO, owned by Angel Trains, with GNER
42191	TSO, owned by Angel Trains, with GNER
42192	TSO, owned by Angel Trains, with GNER
42193	TSO, owned by Angel Trains, with GNER
42194	TSO, owned by Porterbrook, with MML
42195	TSO, owned by Porterbrook, with VT CrossCountry pool
42196	TSO, owned by Angel Trains, with FGW
42197	TSO, owned by Angel Trains, with FGW
42198	TSO, owned by Angel Trains, with GNER
42199	TSO, owned by Angel Trains, with GNER
42200	TSO, owned by Angel Trains, with FGW
42201	TSO, owned by Angel Trains, with FGW
42202	TSO, owned by Angel Trains, with FGW
42203	TSO, owned by Angel Trains, with FGW
42204	TSO, owned by Angel Trains, with FGW
42205	TSO, owned by Porterbrook, with MML
42206	TSO, owned by Angel Trains, with FGW
42207	TSO, owned by Angel Trains, with FGW
42208	TSO, owned by Angel Trains, with FGW
42209	TSO, owned by Angel Trains, with FGW
42210	TSO, owned by Porterbrook, with MML
42211	TSO, owned by Angel Trains, with FGW
42212	TSO, owned by Angel Trains, with FGW
42213	TSO, owned by Angel Trains, with FGW
42214	TSO, owned by Angel Trains, with FGW
42215	TSO, owned by Angel Trains, with GNER
42216	TSO, owned by Angel Trains, with FGW
42217	TSO, owned by Porterbrook, with VT CrossCountry pool
42218	TSO, owned by Porterbrook, with VT CrossCountry pool
42219	TSO, owned by Angel Trains, with GNER
42220	TSO, owned by Porterbrook, with MML
42221	TSO, owned by Angel Trains, with FGW
42222	TSO, owned by Porterbrook, with VT CrossCountry pool
42223	TSO, owned by Porterbrook, with VT CrossCountry pool
42224	TSO, owned by Porterbrook, with VT CrossCountry pool
42225	TSO, owned by Porterbrook, with MML
42226	TSO, owned by Angel Trains, with GNER
42227	TSO, owned by Porterbrook, with MML
42228	TSO, owned by Porterbrook, with MML
42229	TSO, owned by Porterbrook, with MML
42230	TSO, owned by Porterbrook, with MML
42231	TSO, owned by Porterbrook, with VT CrossCountry pool
42232	TSO, owned by Porterbrook, with VT CrossCountry pool
42233	TSO, owned by Porterbrook, with VT CrossCountry pool
42234	TSO, owned by Porterbrook, with VT CrossCountry pool
42235	TSO, owned by Angel Trains, with GNER
42236	TSO, owned by Angel Trains, with FGW
42237	TSO, owned by Porterbrook, with VT CrossCountry pool
42238	TSO, owned by Porterbrook, with VT CrossCountry pool
42239	TSO, owned by Porterbrook, with VT CrossCountry pool
42240	TSO, owned by Angel Trains, with GNER
42241	TSO, owned by Angel Trains, with GNER
42242	TSO, owned by Angel Trains, with GNER
42243	TSO, owned by Angel Trains, with GNER
42244	TSO, owned by Angel Trains, with GNER
42245	TSO, owned by Angel Trains, with FGW
42246	TSO, owned by Porterbrook, with VT CrossCountry pool
42247	TSO, owned by Porterbrook, with VT CrossCountry pool
42248	TSO, owned by Porterbrook, with VT CrossCountry pool
42249	TSO, owned by Porterbrook, with VT CrossCountry pool
42250	TSO, owned by Angel Trains, with FGW
42251	TSO, owned by Angel Trains, with FGW
42252	TSO, owned by Angel Trains, with FGW
42253	TSO, owned by Angel Trains, with FGW
42254	TSO, owned by Porterbrook, with VT CrossCountry pool
42255	TSO, owned by Angel Trains, with FGW
42256	TSO, owned by Angel Trains, with FGW
42257	TSO, owned by Angel Trains, with FGW
42258	TSO, owned by Porterbrook, with VT CrossCountry pool
42259	TSO, owned by Angel Trains, with FGW
42260	TSO, owned by Angel Trains, with FGW
42261	TSO, owned by Angel Trains, with FGW
42262	TSO, owned by Porterbrook, with VT CrossCountry pool
42263	TSO, owned by Angel Trains, with FGW
42264	TSO, owned by Angel Trains, with FGW
42265	TSO, owned by Angel Trains, with FGW
42266	TSO, owned by Porterbrook, with VT CrossCountry pool
42267	TSO, owned by Angel Trains, with FGW
42268	TSO, owned by Angel Trains, with FGW
42269	TSO, owned by Angel Trains, with FGW
42270	TSO, owned by Porterbrook, with VT CrossCountry pool
42271	TSO, owned by Angel Trains, with FGW
42272	TSO, owned by Angel Trains, with FGW
42273	TSO, owned by Angel Trains, with FGW
42274	TSO, owned by Porterbrook, with VT CrossCountry pool
42275	TSO, owned by Angel Trains, with FGW
42276	TSO, owned by Angel Trains, with FGW
42277	TSO, owned by Angel Trains, with FGW
42278	TSO, owned by Porterbrook, with VT CrossCountry pool
42279	TSO, owned by Angel Trains, with FGW
42280	TSO, owned by Angel Trains, with FGW
42281	TSO, owned by Angel Trains, with FGW
42282	TSO, owned by Porterbrook, with VT CrossCountry pool
42283	TSO, owned by Angel Trains, with FGW
42284	TSO, owned by Angel Trains, with FGW
42285	TSO, owned by Angel Trains, with FGW

42286	TSO, owned by Porterbrook, with VT CrossCountry pool
42287	TSO, owned by Angel Trains, with FGW
42288	TSO, owned by Angel Trains, with FGW
42289	TSO, owned by Angel Trains, with FGW
42290	TSO, owned by Porterbrook, with VT CrossCountry pool
42291	TSO, owned by Angel Trains, with FGW
42292	TSO, owned by Angel Trains, with FGW
42293	TSO, owned by Angel Trains, with FGW
42294	TSO, owned by Porterbrook, with VT CrossCountry pool
42295	TSO, owned by Angel Trains, with FGW
42296	TSO, owned by Angel Trains, with FGW
42297	TSO, owned by Angel Trains, with FGW
42298	TSO, owned by Porterbrook, with VT CrossCountry pool
42299	TSO, owned by Angel Trains, with FGW
42300	TSO, owned by Angel Trains, with FGW
42301	TSO, owned by Angel Trains, with FGW
42302	TSO, owned by Porterbrook, with VT CrossCountry pool
42303	TSO, owned by Porterbrook, with VT CrossCountry pool
42304	TSO, owned by Porterbrook, with VT CrossCountry pool
42305	TSO, owned by Porterbrook, with VT CrossCountry pool
42306	TSO, owned by Porterbrook, with VT CrossCountry pool
42307	TSO, owned by Porterbrook, with VT CrossCountry pool
42308	TSO, owned by Porterbrook, with VT CrossCountry pool
42309	TSO, owned by Porterbrook, with VT CrossCountry pool
42310	TSO, owned by Porterbrook, with VT CrossCountry pool
42311	TSO, owned by Porterbrook, with VT CrossCountry pool
42312	TSO, owned by Porterbrook, with VT CrossCountry pool
42313	TSO, owned by Porterbrook, with VT CrossCountry pool
42314	TSO, owned by Porterbrook, with VT CrossCountry pool
42315	TSO, owned by Porterbrook, with VT CrossCountry pool
42316	TSO, owned by Porterbrook, with VT CrossCountry pool
42317	TSO, owned by Porterbrook, with VT CrossCountry pool
42318	TSO, owned by Porterbrook, with VT CrossCountry pool
42319	TSO, owned by Porterbrook, with VT CrossCountry pool
42320	TSO, owned by Porterbrook, with VT CrossCountry pool
42321	TSO, owned by Porterbrook, with VT CrossCountry pool
42322	TSO, owned by Porterbrook, with VT CrossCountry pool
42323	TSO, owned by Angel Trains, with GNER
42324	TSO, owned by Porterbrook, with MML
42325	TSO, owned by Angel Trains, with FGW
42326	TSO, owned by Porterbrook, with VT CrossCountry pool
42327	TSO, owned by Porterbrook, with MML
42328	TSO, owned by Porterbrook, with MML
42329	TSO, owned by Porterbrook, with MML
42330	TSO, owned by Porterbrook, with VT CrossCountry pool
42331	TSO, owned by Porterbrook, with MML
42332	TSO, owned by Angel Trains, with FGW
42333	TSO, owned by Angel Trains, with FGW
42334	TSO, owned by Porterbrook, with VT CrossCountry pool
42335	TSO, owned by Porterbrook, with MML
42336	TSO, owned by Porterbrook, with VT CrossCountry pool
42337	TSO, owned by Porterbrook, with MML
42338	TSO, owned by Porterbrook, with VT CrossCountry pool
42339	TSO, owned by Porterbrook, with MML
42340	TSO, owned by Angel Trains, with GNER
42341	TSO, owned by Porterbrook, with MML
42342	See 44082
42343	See 44095
42344	See 44092
42345	See 44096
42346	See 41053
42347	See 41054
42348	See 41073
42349	See 41074
42350	See 41047
42351	See 41048
42352	See 42142

42353	See 42001
42354	See 42114
42355	See 42000
42356	See 42002
42357	See 41002
42358	Number not issued
42359	Number not issued
42360	See 44084
42361	See 44099
42362	See 42011
42363	See 41082
44000	TGS, owned by Porterbrook, with VT CrossCountry pool
44001	TGS, owned by Angel Trains, with FGW
44002	TGS, owned by Angel Trains, with FGW
44003	TGS, owned by Angel Trains, with FGW
44004	TGS, owned by Angel Trains, with FGW
44005	TGS, owned by Angel Trains, with FGW
44006	TGS, owned by Angel Trains, with FGW
44007	TGS, owned by Angel Trains, with FGW
44008	TGS, owned by Angel Trains, with FGW
44009	TGS, owned by Angel Trains, with FGW
44010	TGS, owned by Angel Trains, with FGW
44011	TGS, owned by Angel Trains, with FGW
44012	TSO, owned by Angel Trains, with VT West Coast pool
44013	TGS, owned by Angel Trains, with FGW
44014	TGS, owned by Angel Trains, with FGW
44015	TGS, owned by Angel Trains, with FGW
44016	TGS, owned by Angel Trains, with FGW
44017	TSO, owned by Angel Trains, with VT West Coast pool
44018	TGS, owned by Angel Trains, with FGW
44019	TGS, owned by Angel Trains, with GNER
44020	TGS, owned by Angel Trains, with FGW
44021	TGS, owned by Porterbrook, with VT CrossCountry pool
44022	TGS, owned by Angel Trains, with FGW
44023	TGS, owned by Angel Trains, with FGW
44024	TGS, owned by Angel Trains, with FGW
44025	TGS, owned by Angel Trains, with FGW
44026	TGS, owned by Angel Trains, with FGW
44027	TGS, owned by Porterbrook, with MML
44028	TGS, owned by Angel Trains, with FGW
44029	TGS, owned by Angel Trains, with FGW
44030	TGS, owned by Angel Trains, with FGW
44031	TSO, owned by Angel Trains, with VT West Coast pool
44032	TGS, owned by Angel Trains, with FGW
44033	TGS, owned by Angel Trains, with FGW
44034	TGS, owned by Angel Trains, with FGW
44035	TGS, owned by Angel Trains, with FGW
44036	TGS, owned by Angel Trains, with FGW
44037	TGS, owned by Angel Trains, with FGW
44038	TGS, owned by Angel Trains, with FGW
44039	TGS, owned by Angel Trains, with FGW
44040	TGS, owned by Angel Trains, with FGW
44041	TGS, owned by Porterbrook, with MML
44042	TGS, owned by Porterbrook, with VT CrossCountry pool
44043	TGS, owned by Angel Trains, with FGW
44044	TGS, owned by Porterbrook, with MML
44045	TGS, owned by Angel Trains, with GNER
44046	TGS, owned by Porterbrook, with MML
44047	TGS, owned by Porterbrook, with MML
44048	TGS, owned by Porterbrook, with MML
44049	TGS, owned by Angel Trains, with FGW
44050	TGS, owned by Porterbrook, with MML
44051	TGS, owned by Porterbrook, with MML
44052	TGS, owned by Porterbrook, with MML
44053	TGS, owned by Porterbrook, with VT CrossCountry pool
44054	TGS, owned by Porterbrook, with MML

44055	TGS, owned by Porterbrook, with VT CrossCountry pool
44056	TGS, owned by Angel Trains, with GNER
44057	TGS, owned by Porterbrook, with VT CrossCountry pool
44058	TGS, owned by Angel Trains, with GNER
44059	TGS, owned by Angel Trains, with FGW
44060	TGS, owned by Porterbrook, with VT CrossCountry pool
44061	TGS, owned by Angel Trains, with GNER
44062	TGS, owned by Porterbrook, with VT CrossCountry pool
44063	TGS, owned by Angel Trains, with GNER
44064	TGS, owned by Angel Trains, with FGW
44065	TGS, owned by Porterbrook, with VT CrossCountry pool
44066	TGS, owned by Angel Trains, with FGW
44067	TGS, owned by Angel Trains, with FGW
44068	TGS, owned by Porterbrook, with VT CrossCountry pool
44069	TGS, owned by Porterbrook, with VT CrossCountry pool
44070	TGS, owned by Porterbrook, with MML
44071	TGS, owned by Porterbrook, with MML
44072	TGS, owned by Porterbrook, with VT CrossCountry pool
44073	TGS, owned by Porterbrook, with MML
44074	TGS, owned by Porterbrook, with VT CrossCountry pool
44075	TGS, owned by Porterbrook, with VT CrossCountry pool
44076	TGS, owned by Porterbrook, with VT CrossCountry pool
44077	TGS, owned by Angel Trains, with GNER
44078	TGS, owned by Porterbrook, with VT CrossCountry pool
44079	TGS, owned by Porterbrook, with VT CrossCountry pool
44080	TGS, owned by Angel Trains, with GNER
44081	TGS, owned by Porterbrook, with VT CrossCountry pool
44082	Built as TGS, rebuilt to TSO 42342, owned by Angel Trains, with VT West Coast pool

44083	TGS, owned by Porterbrook, with MML
44084	Built as TGS, rebuilt to TSCD 45084, rebuilt to TSO 42360, owned by Angel Trains, with FGW
44085	TGS, owned by Porterbrook, with MML
44086	TGS, owned by Angel Trains, with FGW
44087	TGS, owned by Porterbrook, with VT CrossCountry pool
44088	TGS, owned by Porterbrook, with VT CrossCountry pool
44089	TGS, owned by Porterbrook, with VT CrossCountry pool
44090	TGS, owned by Porterbrook, with VT CrossCountry pool
44091	TGS, owned by Porterbrook, with VT CrossCountry pool
44092	Built as TGS, rebuilt to TSO 42344, owned by Angel Trains, with FGW
44093	TGS, owned by Angel Trains, with FGW
44094	TGS, owned by Angel Trains, with GNER
44095	Built as TGS, rebuilt to TSO 42343, owned by Angel Trains, with FGW
44096	Built as TGS, rebuilt to TSO 42345, owned by Angel Trains, with FGW
44097	TGS, owned by Porterbrook, with VT CrossCountry pool
44098	TGS, owned by Angel Trains, with GNER
44099	Built as TGS, rebuilt to TSO 42361, owned by Angel Trains, with FGW
44100	TGS, owned by Porterbrook, with VT CrossCountry pool
44101	TGS, owned by Porterbrook, with VT CrossCountry pool

Below:
This unusual combination was recorded on 7 January 1991 at Cullompton and consists of Class 47 No 47812 hauling power car No 43183, barrier car No 6330, HST trailers Nos 44014, 42043 and 42042, and power car No 43026. The train was en route from St Philips Marsh, Bristol, to Laira. *CJM*

Appendix II. The Present IC125 Fleet in Numerical Order with Details of Owner, Operator, Livery, Operating Pool and Seating Details

Layout Codes

BCF	Baby-changing facility	DH/BE	Drop-head/Buck-eye	L	Lavatory	S	Standard
BRF	Bike-rack fitted	DIS	Disabled	PA	Public address system	TUS	Tip-up seat
CLS	Central luggage stack	F	First	RA	Reduced airline-style seating	WCS	Wheelchair space

Refreshment Vehicles
All non-smoking

Number	(Former Number[s])	Type	Design Code	Pool	Owner	Operator	Livery	Layout
40204	(40404,40004)	TRBF	GN1020A	IWRR	Angel Trains	FGW	FGW	23F, WCS
40205	(40405,40005)	TRBF	GN1020A	IWRR	Angel Trains	FGW	FGW	23F, WCS
40206	(40406,40006)	TRBF	GN1020A	IWRR	Angel Trains	FGW	FGW	23F, WCS
40207	(40407,40007)	TRBF	GN1020A	IWRR	Angel Trains	FGW	FGW	23F, WCS
40208	(40408,40008)	TRBF	GN1020A	IWRR	Angel Trains	FGW	FGW	23F, WCS
40209	(40409,40009)	TRBF	GN1020A	IWRR	Angel Trains	FGW	FGW	23F, WCS
40210	(40410,40010)	TRBF	GN1020A	IWRR	Angel Trains	FGW	FGW	23F, WCS
40213*	(40413,40013)	TRBF	GN1020A	SCXH	Angel Trains	Stored	FGW	23F, WCS
40221	(40421,40021)	TRBF	GN1020A	IWRR	Angel Trains	FGW	FGW	23F, WCS
40228	(40428,40028)	TRBF	GN1020A	IWRR	Angel Trains	FGW	FGW	23F, WCS
40231	(40431,40031)	TRBF	GN1020A	IWRR	Angel Trains	FGW	FGW	23F, WCS
40401	(40001)	TRBS	GK2040B	ICCT	Porterbrook	VT	VT	33S, 1TUS, WCS
40402	(40002)	TRBS	GK2040B	ICCT	Porterbrook	VT	VT	33S, 1TUS, WCS
40403	(40003)	TRBS	GK2040B	ICCT	Porterbrook	VT	VT	33S, 1TUS, WCS
40411	(40211,40011)	TRBS	GK2040B	ICCT	Porterbrook	VT	VT	33S, 1TUS, WCS
40412	(40212,40012)	TRBS	GK2040B	ICCT	Porterbrook	VT	VT	33S, 1TUS, WCS
40414	(40014)	TRBS	GK2040B	ICCT	Porterbrook	VT	VT	33S, 1TUS, WCS
40415	(40015)	TRBS	GK2040B	ICCT	Porterbrook	VT	VT	33S, 1TUS, WCS
40416	(40016)	TRBS	GK2040B	ICCT	Porterbrook	VT	VT	33S, 1TUS, WCS
40417	(40017)	TRBS	GK2040B	ICCT	Porterbrook	VT	VT	33S, 1TUS, WCS
40418	(40018)	TRBS	GK2040B	ICCT	Porterbrook	VT	VT	33S, 1TUS, WCS
40419	(40019)	TRBS	GK2040B	ICCT	Porterbrook	VT	VT	33S, 1TUS, WCS
40420	(40020)	TRBS	GK2030B	ICCT	Porterbrook	VT	VT	34S, 1TUS, WCS
40422	(40022)	TRBS	GK2040B	ICCT	Porterbrook	VT	VT	33S, 1TUS, WCS

Left:
Painted in the original yellow and blue livery, power car No 43078 approaches Doncaster on the East Coast main line on 29 October 1980 with the 07.10 King's Cross-Leeds. *CJM*

Number	(Former Number[s])	Type	Design Code	Pool	Owner	Operator	Livery	Layout
40423	(40023)	TRBS	GK2040B	ICCT	Porterbrook	VT	VT	33S, 1TUS, WCS
40424	(40024)	TRBS	GK2030B	ICCT	Porterbrook	VT	VT	34S, 1TUS, WCS
40425	(40025)	TRBS	GK2040B	ICCT	Porterbrook	VT	VT	33S, 1TUS, WCS
40426	(40026)	TRBS	GK2040B	ICCT	Porterbrook	VT	VT	33S, 1TUS, WCS
40427	(40027)	TRBS	GK2040B	ICCT	Porterbrook	VT	VT	33S, 1TUS, WCS
40429	(40029)	TRBS	GK2040B	ICCT	Porterbrook	VT	VT	33S, 1TUS, WCS
40430	(40030)	TRBS	GK2040B	ICCT	Porterbrook	VT	VT	33S, 1TUS, WCS
40432	(40232,40032)	TRBS	GK2040B	ICCT	Porterbrook	VT	VT	33S, 1TUS, WCS
40433	(40233,40033)	TRBS	GK2040B	ICCT	Porterbrook	VT	VT	33S, 1TUS, WCS
40434	(40034)	TRBS	GK2040B	ICCT	Porterbrook	VT	VT	33S, 1TUS, WCS
40435	(40035)	TRBS	GK2040B	ICCT	Porterbrook	VT	VT	33S, 1TUS, WCS
40436	(40036)	TRBS	GK2040B	ICCT	Porterbrook	VT	VT	33S, 1TUS, WCS
40437	(40037)	TRBS	GK2040B	ICCT	Porterbrook	VT	VT	33S, 1TUS, WCS
40501		TRFK	GL1010A	SBXH	Porterbrook	HQ stored ZD IC		Kitchen no seats
40619	(40719,40319)	TRFM	GK1040A	ICCC	Porterbrook	VT	IC	17F, large kitchen
40700	(40300)	TRBF	GK1050B	IMLR	Porterbrook	MML	MM	17F, large kitchen
40701	(40301)	TRBF	GK1050B	IMLR	Porterbrook	MML	MM	17F, large kitchen
40702	(40302)	TRBF	GK1050B	IMLR	Porterbrook	MML	MM	17F, large kitchen
40703	(40303)	TRBF	GK1030A	IWRR	Angel Trains	FGW	FGW	17F, large kitchen
40704	(40304)	TRBF	GK1030A	IECD	Angel Trains	GNER	GNER	17F, large kitchen
40705	(40305)	TRBF	GK1030A	IECD	Angel Trains	GNER	GNER	17F, large kitchen
40706	(40306)	TRBF	GK1030A	IECD	Angel Trains	GNER	GNER	17F, large kitchen
40707	(40307)	TRBF	GK1030A	IWRR	Angel Trains	FGW	FGW	17F, large kitchen
40708	(40308)	TRBF	GK1050B	IMLR	Porterbrook	MML	MM	17F, large kitchen
40709	(40309)	TRBF	GK1030A	IWRR	Angel Trains	FGW	FGW	17F, large kitchen
40710	(40310)	TRBF	GK1030A	IWRR	Angel Trains	FGW	FGW	17F, large kitchen
40711	(40311)	TRBF	GK1030A	IECD	Angel Trains	GNER	GNER	17F, large kitchen
40712	(40312)	TRBF	GK1030A	IWRR	Angel Trains	FGW	FGW	17F, large kitchen
40713	(40313)	TRBF	GK1030A	IWRR	Angel Trains	FGW	FGW	17F, large kitchen
40714	(40314)	TRBF	GK1030A	IWRR	Angel Trains	FGW	FGW	17F, large kitchen
40715	(40315)	TRBF	GK1030A	IWRR	Angel Trains	FGW	FGW	17F, large kitchen
40716	(40316)	TRBF	GK1030A	IWRR	Angel Trains	FGW	FGW	17F, large kitchen
40717	(40317)	TRBF	GK1030A	IWRR	Angel Trains	FGW	FGW	17F, large kitchen
40718	(40318)	TRBF	GK1030A	IWRR	Angel Trains	FGW	FGW	17F, large kitchen
40720	(40320)	TRBF	GK1030A	IECD	Angel Trains	GNER	GNER	17F, large kitchen
40721	(40321)	TRBF	GK1030A	IWRR	Angel Trains	FGW	FGW	17F, large kitchen
40722	(40322)	TRBF	GK1030C	IWRR	Angel Trains	FGW	FGW	17F, large kitchen, BT10C bogies
40723	(40323)	TRBF	GK1030B	IWCT	Angel Trains	VT	VT	17F, large kitchen, BT10B bogies
40724	(40324)	TRBF	GK1030C	IWRR	Angel Trains	FGW	FGW	17F, large kitchen, BT10C bogies
40725	(40325)	TRBF	GK1030C	IWRR	Angel Trains	FGW	FGW	17F, large kitchen, BT10C bogies
40726	(40326)	TRBF	GK1030C	IWRR	Angel Trains	FGW	FGW	17F, large kitchen, BT10C bogies
40727	(40327)	TRBF	GK1030C	IWRR	Angel Trains	FGW	FGW	17F, large kitchen, BT10C bogies
40728	(40328)	TRBF	GK1050C	IMLR	Porterbrook	MML	MML	17F, large kitchen, BT10C bogies, DGS
40729	(40329)	TRBF	GK1050A	IMLR	Porterbrook	MML	MML	17F, large kitchen, BT10C bogies, DGS
40730	(40330)	TRBF	GK1050C	IMLR	Porterbrook	MML	MML	17F, large kitchen, BT10C bogies, DGS
40731	(40331)	TRBF	GK1030C	IWRR	Angel Trains	FGW	FGW	17F, large kitchen, BT10C bogies
40732	(40332)	TRBF	GK1030B	IWCT	Angel Trains	VT	VT	17F, large kitchen, BT10B bogies
40733	(40333)	TRBF	GK1030C	IWRR	Angel Trains	FGW	FGW	17F, large kitchen, BT10C bogies
40734	(40334)	TRBF	GK1030C	IWRR	Angel Trains	FGW	FGW	17F, large kitchen, BT10C bogies
40735	(40335)	TRBF	GK1031B	IECD	Angel Trains	GNER	GNER	17F, large kitchen, BT10B bogies
40736	(40336)	TRBF	GK1030C	IWRR	Angel Trains	FGW	FGW	17F, large kitchen, BT10C bogies
40737	(40337)	TRBF	GK1030B	IECD	Angel Trains	GNER	GNER	17F, large kitchen, BT10B bogies
40738	(40338)	TRBF	GK1030C	IWRR	Angel Trains	FGW	FGW	17F, large kitchen, BT10C bogies
40739	(40339)	TRBF	GK1030C	IWRR	Angel Trains	FGW	FGW	17F, large kitchen, BT10C bogies
40740	(40340)	TRBF	GK1030B	IECD	Angel Trains	GNER	GNER	17F, large kitchen, BT10B bogies
40741	(40341)	TRBF	GK1050C	IMLR	Porterbrook	MML	MML	17F, large kitchen, BT10C bogies, DGS
40742	(40342)	TRBF	GK1030B	IWCT	Angel Trains	VT	VT	17F, large kitchen, BT10B bogies
40743	(40343)	TRBF	GK1030C	IWRR	Angel Trains	FGW	FGW	17F, large kitchen, BT10C bogies
40744	(40344)	TRBF	GK1030C	IWRR	Angel Trains	FGW	FGW	17F, large kitchen, BT10C bogies
40745	(40345)	TRBF	GK1030C	IWRR	Angel Trains	FGW	FGW	17F, large kitchen, BT10C bogies
40746	(40346)	TRBF	GK1050A	IMLR	Porterbrook	MML	MML	17F, large kitchen, BT10C bogies, DGS
40747	(40347)	TRBF	GK1030C	IWRR	Angel Trains	FGW	FGW	17F, large kitchen, BT10C bogies
40748	(40348)	TRBF	GK1030B	IECD	Angel Trains	GNER	GNER	17F, large kitchen, BT10C bogies
40749	(40349)	TRBF	GK1050A	IMLR	Porterbrook	MML	MML	17F, large kitchen, BT10C bogies, DGS
40750	(40350)	TRBF	GK1030B	IECD	Angel Trains	GNER	GNER	17F, large kitchen, BT10B bogies
40751	(40351)	TRBF	GK1050C	IMLR	Porterbrook	MML	MML	17F, large kitchen, BT10C bogies, DGS

Number	(Former Number[s])	Type	Design Code	Pool	Owner	Operator	Livery	Layout
40752	(40352)	TRBF	GK1030B	IWRR	Angel Trains	FGW	FGW	17F, large kitchen, BT10B bogies
40753	(40353)	TRBF	GK1050C	IMLR	Porterbrook	MML	MML	17F, large kitchen, BT10C bogies, DGS
40754	(40354)	TRBF	GK1050C	IMLR	Porterbrook	MML	MML	17F, large kitchen, BT10C bogies, DGS
40755	(40355)	TRBF	GK1030B	IWRR	Angel Trains	FGW	FGW	17F, large kitchen, BT10B bogies
40756	(40356)	TRBF	GK1050C	IMLR	Porterbrook	MML	MML	17F, large kitchen, BT10C bogies, DGS
40757	(40357)	TRBF	GK1030B	IWRR	Angel Trains	FGW	FGW	17F, large kitchen, BT10B bogies

*40213 badly damaged in the Ladbroke Grove crash of 5 October 1999, awaiting disposal

Saloon Vehicles

Number (Former Number[s])	Type	Design Code	Pool	Owner	Operator	Livery	Layout
41003	TF	GH1022A	IWRR	Angel Trains	FGW	FGW	48F, 2L, Payphone
41004	TF	GH1020E	IWRR	Angel Trains	FGW	FGW	48F, 2L
41005	TF	GH1022A	IWRR	Angel Trains	FGW	FGW	48F, 2L, Payphone
41006	TF	GH1020E	IWRR	Angel Trains	FGW	FGW	48F, 2L
41007	TF	GH1022A	IWRR	Angel Trains	FGW	FGW	48F, 2L, Payphone
41008	TF	GH1020E	IWRR	Angel Trains	FGW	FGW	48F, 2L
41009	TF	GH1022A	IWRR	Angel Trains	FGW	FGW	48F, 2L, Payphone
41010	TF	GH1020E	IWRR	Angel Trains	FGW	FGW	48F, 2L
41011	TF	GH1022A	IWRR	Angel Trains	FGW	FGW	48F, 2L, Payphone
41012	TF	GH1020E	IWRR	Angel Trains	FGW	FGW	48F, 2L
41013	TF	GH1022A	IWRR	Angel Trains	FGW	FGW	48F, 2L, Payphone
41014	TF	GH1020E	IWRR	Angel Trains	FGW	FGW	48F, 2L
41015	TF	GH1022A	IWRR	Angel Trains	FGW	FGW	48F, 2L, Payphone
41016	TF	GH1020E	IWRR	Angel Trains	FGW	FGW	48F, 2L
41017	TF	GH1022A	IWRR	Angel Trains	FGW	FGW	48F, 2L, Payphone
41018	TF	GH1020E	IWRR	Angel Trains	FGW	FGW	48F, 2L
41019	TF	GH1022A	IWRR	Angel Trains	FGW	FGW	48F, 2L, Payphone
41020	TF	GH1020E	IWRR	Angel Trains	FGW	FGW	48F, 2L
41021	TF	GH1022A	IWRR	Angel Trains	FGW	FGW	48F, 2L, Payphone
41022	TF	GH1020E	IWRR	Angel Trains	FGW	FGW	48F, 2L
41023	TF	GH1022A	IWRR	Angel Trains	FGW	FGW	48F, 2L, Payphone
41024	TF	GH1020E	IWRR	Angel Trains	FGW	FGW	48F, 2L
41025	TF	GH1022A	IWRR	Angel Trains	FGW	FGW	48F, 2L, Payphone
41026	TF	GH1020E	IWCT	Angel Trains	VT	VT	48F, 2L
41027	TF	GH1022A	IWRR	Angel Trains	FGW	FGW	48F, 2L, Payphone
41028	TF	GH1020E	IWRR	Angel Trains	FGW	FGW	48F, 2L
41029	TF	GH1022A	IWRR	Angel Trains	FGW	FGW	48F, 2L, Payphone
41030	TF	GH1020E	IWRR	Angel Trains	FGW	FGW	48F, 2L
41031	TF	GH1022A	IWRR	Angel Trains	FGW	FGW	48F, 2L, Payphone
41032	TF	GH1020E	IWRR	Angel Trains	FGW	FGW	48F, 2L
41033	TF	GH1022A	IWRR	Angel Trains	FGW	FGW	48F, 2L, Payphone
41034	TF	GH1020E	IWRR	Angel Trains	FGW	FGW	48F, 2L
41035	TF	GH1020A	IWCT	Angel Trains	VT	VT	48F, 2L, 50% smoking
41036	TF	GH1020E	IWRR	Angel Trains	FGW	FGW	48F, 2L
41037	TF	GH1022A	IWRR	Angel Trains	FGW	FGW	48F, 2L, Payphone
41038	TF	GH1020E	IWRR	Angel Trains	FGW	FGW	48F, 2L
41039	TF	GH1020E	IECD	Angel Trains	GNER	GNER	48F, 2L
41040	TF	GH1020E	IECD	Angel Trains	GNER	GNER	48F, 2L
41041	TF	GH1050A	IMLR	Porterbrook	MML	MML	46F, 2L (1 DIS), BCF, PA Zone, WCS
41042	TF	GH1020A	SCXH	Angel Trains	(stored)	FGW	48F, 2L
41043	TF	GH1020A	IECD	Angel Trains	GNER	GNER	48F, 2L
41044	TF	GH1020E	IECD	Angel Trains	GNER	GNER	48F, 2L
41045	TF	GH1020C	ICCT	Porterbrook	VT	VT	47F, 2L, BCF, WCS, 50% smoking
41046	TF	GH1050A	IMLR	Porterbrook	MML	MML	46F, 2L (1 DIS), BCF, PA Zone, WCS
41051	TF	GH1020A	IWRR	Angel Trains	FGW	FGW	48F, 2L
41052	TF	GH1020E	IWRR	Angel Trains	FGW	FGW	48F, 2L
41055	TF	GH1020A	IWRR	Angel Trains	FGW	FGW	48F, 2L
41056	TF	GH1020E	IWRR	Angel Trains	FGW	FGW	48F, 2L
41057	TF	GH1040C	IMLR	Porterbrook	MML	MML	48F, 2L, PA Zone

Number (Former Number[s])	Type	Design Code	Pool	Owner	Operator	Livery	Layout
41058	TF	GH1050A	IMLR	Porterbrook	MML	MML	46F, 2L (1 DIS), BCF, PA Zone, WCS
41059	TF	GH1020C	ICCT	Porterbrook	VT	VT	47F, 2L, BCF, WCS, 50% smoking
41060	TF	GH1020E	SCXH	Angel Trains	(stored)	FGW	48F, 2L
41061	TF	GH1040C	IMLR	Porterbrook	MML	MML	48F, 2L, PA Zone
41062	TF	GH1040A	IMLR	Porterbrook	MML	MML	47F, 2L, PA Zone, WCS
41063	TF	GH1040C	IMLR	Porterbrook	MML	MML	48F, 2L, PA Zone
41064	TF	GH1050A	IMLR	Porterbrook	MML	MML	46F, 2L (1 DIS), BCF, PA Zone, WCS
41065	TF	GH1020E	IWRR	Angel Trains	FGW	FGW	48F, 2L
41066	TF	GH1022E	IWCT	Angel Trains	VT	VT	48F, 2L, Payphone
41067	TF	GH1050A	IMLR	Porterbrook	MML	MML	46F, 2L (1 DIS), BCF, PA Zone, WCS
41068	TF	GH1050A	IMLR	Porterbrook	MML	MML	46F, 2L (1 DIS), BCF, PA Zone, WCS
41069	TF	GH1050A	IMLR	Porterbrook	MML	MML	46F, 2L (1 DIS), BCF, PA Zone, WCS
41070	TF	GH1050A	IMLR	Porterbrook	MML	MML	46F, 2L (1 DIS), BCF, PA Zone, WCS
41071	TF	GH1040C	IMLR	Porterbrook	MML	MML	48F, 2L, PA Zone
41072	TF	GH1050A	IMLR	Porterbrook	MML	MML	46F, 2L (1 DIS), BCF, PA Zone, WCS
41075	TF	GH1040C	IMLR	Porterbrook	MML	MML	48F, 2L, PA Zone
41076	TF	GH1050A	IMLR	Porterbrook	MML	MML	46F, 2L (1 DIS), BCF, PA Zone, WCS
41077	TF	GH1040C	IMLR	Porterbrook	MML	MML	48F, 2L, PA Zone
41078	TF	GH1040C	IMLR	Porterbrook	MML	MML	48F, 2L, PA Zone
41079	TF	GH1040C	IMLR	Porterbrook	MML	MML	48F, 2L, PA Zone
41080	TF	GH1050B	IMLR	Porterbrook	MML	MML	46F, 2L (1 DIS), BCF, PA Zone, WCS
41081	TF	GH1020C	ICCT	Porterbrook	VT	VT	47F, 2L, BCF, WCS, 50% smoking
41083	TF	GH1040C	IMLR	Porterbrook	MML	MML	48F, 2L, PA Zone
41084	TF	GH1050A	IMLR	Porterbrook	MML	MML	46F, 2L (1 DIS), BCF, PA Zone, WCS
41085	TF	GH1020C	ICCT	Porterbrook	VT	VT	47F, 2L, BCF, WCS, 50% smoking
41086	TF	GH1020C	ICCT	Porterbrook	VT	VT	47F, 2L, BCF, WCS, 50% smoking
41087	TF	GH1020A	IECD	Angel Trains	GNER	GNER	48F, 2L
41088	TF	GH1020E	IECD	Angel Trains	GNER	GNER	48F, 2L
41089	TF	GH1020A	IWRR	Angel Trains	FGW	FGW	48F, 2L
41090	TF	GH1020E	IECD	Angel Trains	GNER	GNER	48F, 2L
41091	TF	GH1020A	IECD	Angel Trains	GNER	GNER	48F, 2L
41092	TF	GH1020E	IECD	Angel Trains	GNER	GNER	48F, 2L
41093	TF	GH1020A	IWRR	Angel Trains	FGW	FGW	48F, 2L
41094	TF	GH1020E	IWRR	Angel Trains	FGW	FGW	48F, 2L
41095	TF	GH1020C	ICCT	Porterbrook	VT	VT	47F, 2L, BCF, WCS, 50% smoking
41096	TF	GH1020C	ICCT	Porterbrook	VT	VT	47F, 2L, BCF, WCS, 50% smoking
41097	TF	GH1020A	IECD	Angel Trains	GNER	GNER	48F, 2L
41098	TF	GH1020G	IECD	Angel Trains	GNER	GNER	47F, 2L, WCS
41099	TF	GH1020A	IECD	Angel Trains	GNER	GNER	48F, 2L
41100	TF	GH1020G	IECD	Angel Trains	GNER	GNER	47F, 2L, WCS
41101	TF	GH1020A	IWRR	Angel Trains	FGW	FGW	48F, 2L
41102	TF	GH1020E	IWRR	Angel Trains	FGW	FGW	48F, 2L
41103	TF	GH1020A	IWRR	Angel Trains	FGW	FGW	48F, 2L
41104	TF	GH1020E	IWRR	Angel Trains	FGW	FGW	48F, 2L
41105	TF	GH1020A	IWRR	Angel Trains	FGW	FGW	48F, 2L
41106	TF	GH1020G	IWRR	Angel Trains	FGW	FGW	47F, 2L, WCS
41107	TF	GH1020C	ICCT	Porterbrook	VT	VT	47F, 2L, BCF, WCS, 50% smoking
41108	TF	GH1020C	ICCT	Porterbrook	VT	VT	47F, 2L, BCF, WCS, 50% smoking
41109	TF	GH1020C	ICCT	Porterbrook	VT	VT	47F, 2L, BCF, WCS, 50% smoking
41110	TF	GH1020A	IWRR	Angel Trains	FGW	FGW	48F, 2L
41111	TF	GH1040A	IMLR	Porterbrook	MML	MML	47F, 2L, PA Zone, WCS
41112	TF	GH1040C	IMLR	Porterbrook	MML	MML	48F, 2L, PA Zone
41113	TF	GH1050A	IMLR	Porterbrook	MML	MML	46F, 2L (1 DIS), BCF, PA Zone, WCS
41114	TF	GH1020C	ICCT	Porterbrook	VT	VT	47F, 2L, BCF, WCS, 50% smoking
41115	TF	GH1020E	ICCT	Porterbrook	VT	VT	48F, 2L
41116	TF	GH1020E	IWRR	Angel Trains	FGW	FGW	48F, 2L
41117	TF	GH1040C	IMLR	Porterbrook	MML	MML	48F, 2L, PA Zone
41118	TF	GH1020E	IECD	Angel Trains	GNER	GNER	48F, 2L
41119	TF	GH1020C	ICCT	Porterbrook	VT	VT	47F, 2L, BCF, WCS, 50% smoking
41120	TF	GH1020C	IECD	Angel Trains	GNER	GNER	47F, 2L, BCF, WCS, 50% smoking
41121	TF	GH1022D	IWRR	Angel Trains	FGW	FGW	48F, 2L, Payphone
41122	TF	GH1020D	IWRR	Angel Trains	FGW	FGW	48F, 2L
41123	TF	GH1022B	IWRR	Angel Trains	FGW	FGW	48F, 2L, Payphone
41124	TF	GH1020F	IWRR	Angel Trains	FGW	FGW	48F, 2L
41125	TF	GH1020F	IWRR	Angel Trains	FGW	FGW	48F, 2L

Number (Former Number[s])	Type	Design Code	Pool	Owner	Operator	Livery	Layout
41126	TF	GH1022B	IWRR	Angel Trains	FGW	FGW	48F, 2L, Payphone
41127	TF	GH1022B	IWRR	Angel Trains	FGW	FGW	48F, 2L, Payphone
41128	TF	GH1020F	IWRR	Angel Trains	FGW	FGW	48F, 2L
41129	TF	GH1022B	IWRR	Angel Trains	FGW	FGW	48F, 2L, Payphone
41130	TF	GH1020F	IWRR	Angel Trains	FGW	FGW	48F, 2L
41131	TF	GH1022B	IWRR	Angel Trains	FGW	FGW	48F, 2L, Payphone
41132	TF	GH1020F	IWRR	Angel Trains	FGW	FGW	48F, 2L
41133	TF	GH1022B	IWRR	Angel Trains	FGW	FGW	48F, 2L, Payphone
41134	TF	GH1020F	IWRR	Angel Trains	FGW	FGW	48F, 2L
41135	TF	GH1022B	IWRR	Angel Trains	FGW	FGW	48F, 2L, Payphone
41136	TF	GH1020F	IWRR	Angel Trains	FGW	FGW	48F, 2L
41137	TF	GH1022B	IWRR	Angel Trains	FGW	FGW	48F, 2L, Payphone
41138	TF	GH1020F	IWRR	Angel Trains	FGW	FGW	48F, 2L
41139	TF	GH1022B	IWRR	Angel Trains	FGW	FGW	48F, 2L, Payphone
41140	TF	GH1020F	IWRR	Angel Trains	FGW	FGW	48F, 2L
41141	TF	GH1022B	IWRR	Angel Trains	FGW	FGW	48F, 2L, Payphone
41142	TF	GH1020F	IWRR	Angel Trains	FGW	FGW	48F, 2L
41143	TF	GH1022B	IWRR	Angel Trains	FGW	FGW	48F, 2L, Payphone
41144	TF	GH1020F	IWRR	Angel Trains	FGW	FGW	48F, 2L
41145	TF	GH1022B	IWRR	Angel Trains	FGW	FGW	48F, 2L, Payphone
41146	TF	GH1020F	IWRR	Angel Trains	FGW	FGW	48F, 2L
41147	TF	GH1020J	ICCT	Porterbrook	VT	VT	47F, 2L, BCF, WCS, 50% smoking
41148	TF	GH1020J	ICCT	Porterbrook	VT	VT	47F, 2L, BCF, WCS, 50% smoking
41149	TF	GH1020J	ICCT	Porterbrook	VT	VT	47F, 2L, BCF, WCS, 50% smoking
41150	TF	GH1020F	IECD	Angel Trains	GNER	GNER	48F, 2L
41151	TF	GH1020B	IECD	Angel Trains	GNER	GNER	48F, 2L, 50% smoking
41152	TF	GH1020F	IECD	Angel Trains	GNER	GNER	48F, 2L
41153	TF	GH1040B	IMLR	Porterbrook	MML	MML	48F, 2L, PA Zone
41154	TF	GH1050B	IMLR	Porterbrook	MML	MML	46F, 2L (1 DIS), BCF, PA Zone, WCS
41155	TF	GH1040B	IMLR	Porterbrook	MML	MML	48F, 2L, PA Zone
41156	TF	GH1040B	IMLR	Porterbrook	MML	MML	48F, 2L, PA Zone
41157	TF	GH1020B	IWRR	Angel Trains	FGW	FGW	48F, 2L
41158	TF	GH1020F	IWRR	Angel Trains	FGW	FGW	48F, 2L
41159	TF	GH1020J	ICCT	Porterbrook	VT	VT	47F, 2L, BCF, WCS, 50% smoking
41160	TF	GH1020J	ICCT	Porterbrook	VT	VT	47F, 2L, BCF, WCS, 50% smoking
41161	TF	GH1020J	ICCT	Porterbrook	VT	VT	47F, 2L, BCF, WCS, 50% smoking
41162	TF	GH1020B	ICCT	Porterbrook	VT	VT	48F, 2L
41163	TF	GH1020J	ICCT	Porterbrook	VT	VT	47F, 2L, BCF, WCS, 50% smoking
41164	TF	GH1020B	IWCT	Angel Trains	VT	VT	48F, 2L
41165	TF	GH1020B	ICCT	Porterbrook	VT	VT	48F, 2L
41166	TF	GH1020B	ICCT	Porterbrook	VT	VT	48F, 2L
41167	TF	GH1020J	ICCT	Porterbrook	VT	VT	47F, 2L, BCF, WCS, 50% smoking
41168	TF	GH1020J	ICCT	Porterbrook	VT	VT	47F, 2L, BCF, WCS, 50% smoking
41169	TF	GH1020J	ICCT	Porterbrook	VT	VT	47F, 2L, BCF, WCS, 50% smoking
41170 (41001, 11002)	TF	GH1020B	IECD	Angel Trains	GNER	GNER	48F, 2L, 50% smoking
41179 (40505)	TF	GH1060A	IWRR	Angel Trains	FGW	FGW	48F, 2L
41180 (40511)	TF	GH1060B	IWRR	Angel Trains	FGW	FGW	48F, 2L
42003	TS	GH2030L	IWRR	Angel Trains	FGW	FGW	76S, 2L
42004	TS	GH2070A	IWRR	Angel Trains	FGW	FGW	65S, 2L (1 DIS), BCF, WCS, RA
42005	TS	GH2030L	IWRR	Angel Trains	FGW	FGW	76S, 2L
42006	TS	GH2030L	IWRR	Angel Trains	FGW	FGW	76S, 2L
42007	TS	GH2070A	IWRR	Angel Trains	FGW	FGW	65S, 2L (1 DIS), BCF, WCS, RA
42008	TS	GH2070A	IWRR	Angel Trains	FGW	FGW	65S, 2L (1 DIS), BCF, WCS, RA
42009	TS	GH2030L	IWRR	Angel Trains	FGW	FGW	76S, 2L
42010	TS	GH2030L	IWRR	Angel Trains	FGW	FGW	76S, 2L
42012	TS	GH2030L	IWRR	Angel Trains	FGW	FGW	76S, 2L
42013	TS	GH2030L	IWRR	Angel Trains	FGW	FGW	76S, 2L
42014	TS	GH2030M	IWRR	Angel Trains	FGW	FGW	76S, 2L
42015	TS	GH2070A	IWRR	Angel Trains	FGW	FGW	65S, 2L (1 DIS), BCF, WCS, RA
42016	TS	GH2030L	IWRR	Angel Trains	FGW	FGW	76S, 2L
42017	TS	GH2030M	IWRR	Angel Trains	FGW	FGW	76S, 2L
42018	TS	GH2070A	IWRR	Angel Trains	FGW	FGW	65S, 2L (1 DIS), BCF, WCS, RA
42019	TS	GH2030L	IWRR	Angel Trains	FGW	FGW	76S, 2L
42020	TS	GH2030M	IWRR	Angel Trains	FGW	FGW	76S, 2L
42021	TS	GH2070A	IWRR	Angel Trains	FGW	FGW	65S, 2L (1 DIS), BCF, WCS, RA

Number (Former Number[s])	Type	Design Code	Pool	Owner	Operator	Livery	Layout
42022	TS	GH2030L	IWRR	Angel Trains	FGW	FGW	76S, 2L
42023	TS	GH2030G	IWRR	Angel Trains	FGW	FGW	76S, 2L
42024	TS	GH2070A	IWRR	Angel Trains	FGW	FGW	65S, 2L (1 DIS), BCF, WCS, RA
42025	TS	GH2030H	IWRR	Angel Trains	FGW	FGW	76S, 2L
42026	TS	GH2030G	IWRR	Angel Trains	FGW	FGW	76S, 2L
42027	TS	GH2070A	IWRR	Angel Trains	FGW	FGW	65S, 2L (1 DIS), BCF, WCS, RA
42028	TS	GH2030H	IWRR	Angel Trains	FGW	FGW	76S, 2L
42029	TS	GH2030K	IWRR	Angel Trains	FGW	FGW	76S, 2L
42030	TS	GH2070A	IWRR	Angel Trains	FGW	FGW	65S, 2L (1 DIS), BCF, WCS, RA
42031	TS	GH2030H	IWRR	Angel Trains	FGW	FGW	76S, 2L
42032	TS	GH2030G	IWRR	Angel Trains	FGW	FGW	76S, 2L
42033	TS	GH2030H	IWRR	Angel Trains	FGW	FGW	76S, 2L
42034	TS	GH2030H	IWRR	Angel Trains	FGW	FGW	76S, 2L
42035	TS	GH2030K	IWRR	Angel Trains	FGW	FGW	76S, 2L
42036	TS	GH2030H	IWCT	Angel Trains	VT	VT	76S, 2L
42037	TS	GH2030H	IWCT	Angel Trains	VT	VT	76S, 2L
42038	TS	GH2030K	IWCT	Angel Trains	VT	VT	76S, 2L
42039	TS	GH2030H	IWRR	Angel Trains	FGW	FGW	76S, 2L
42040	TS	GH2030H	IWRR	Angel Trains	FGW	FGW	76S, 2L
42041	TS	GH2030K	IWRR	Angel Trains	FGW	FGW	76S, 2L
42042	TS	GH2030H	IWRR	Angel Trains	FGW	FGW	76S, 2L
42043	TS	GH2030H	IWRR	Angel Trains	FGW	FGW	76S, 2L
42044	TS	GH2030G	IWRR	Angel Trains	FGW	FGW	76S, 2L
42045	TS	GH2030H	IWRR	Angel Trains	FGW	FGW	76S, 2L
42046	TS	GH2030H	IWRR	Angel Trains	FGW	FGW	76S, 2L
42047	TS	GH2030K	IWRR	Angel Trains	FGW	FGW	76S, 2L
42048	TS	GH2030H	IWRR	Angel Trains	FGW	FGW	76S, 2L
42049	TS	GH2030H	IWRR	Angel Trains	FGW	FGW	76S, 2L
42050	TS	GH2030G	IWRR	Angel Trains	FGW	FGW	76S, 2L
42051	TS	GH2030H	IWCT	Angel Trains	VT	VT	76S, 2L
42052	TS	GH2030H	IWCT	Angel Trains	VT	VT	76S, 2L
42053	TS	GH2030K	IWCT	Angel Trains	VT	VT	76S, 2L
42054	TS	GH2070A	IWRR	Angel Trains	FGW	FGW	65S, 2L (1 DIS), BCF, WCS, RA
42055	TS	GH2030H	IWRR	Angel Trains	FGW	FGW	76S, 2L
42056	TS	GH2030K	IWRR	Angel Trains	FGW	FGW	76S, 2L
42057	TS	GH2030H	IECD	Porterbrook	GNER	GNER	76S, 2L
42058	TS	GH2030H	IECD	Porterbrook	GNER	GNER	76S, 2L
42059	TS	GH2030K	IECD	Porterbrook	GNER	GNER	76S, 2L
42060	TS	GH2030H	IWRR	Angel Trains	FGW	FGW	76S, 2L
42061	TS	GH2030K	IWRR	Angel Trains	FGW	FGW	76S, 2L
42062	TS	GH2070A	IWRR	Angel Trains	FGW	FGW	65S, 2L (1 DIS), BCF, WCS, RA
42063	TS	GH2030H	IECD	Porterbrook	GNER	GNER	76S, 2L
42064	TS	GH2030H	IECD	Porterbrook	GNER	GNER	76S, 2L
42065	TS	GH2030K	IECD	Porterbrook	GNER	GNER	76S, 2L
42066	TS	GH2070A	IWRR	Angel Trains	FGW	FGW	65S, 2L (1 DIS), BCF, WCS, RA
42067	TS	GH2030H	IWRR	Angel Trains	FGW	FGW	76S, 2L
42068	TS	GH2030G	IWRR	Angel Trains	FGW	FGW	76S, 2L
42069	TS	GH2070A	IWRR	Angel Trains	FGW	FGW	65S, 2L (1 DIS), BCF, WCS, RA
42070	TS	GH2070A	IWRR	Angel Trains	FGW	FGW	65S, 2L (1 DIS), BCF, WCS, RA
42071	TS	GH2030H	IWRR	Angel Trains	FGW	FGW	76S, 2L
42072	TS	GH2030H	IWRR	Angel Trains	FGW	FGW	76S, 2L
42073	TS	GH2030H	IWRR	Angel Trains	FGW	FGW	76S, 2L
42074	TS	GH2030K	IWRR	Angel Trains	FGW	FGW	76S, 2L
42075	TS	GH2070A	IWRR	Angel Trains	FGW	FGW	65S, 2L (1 DIS), BCF, WCS, RA
42076	TS	GH2030H	IWRR	Angel Trains	FGW	FGW	76S, 2L
42077	TS	GH2030H	IWRR	Angel Trains	FGW	FGW	76S, 2L
42078	TS	GH2030K	IWRR	Angel Trains	FGW	FGW	76S, 2L
42079	TS	GH2030H	IWRR	Angel Trains	FGW	FGW	76S, 2L
42080	TS	GH2030K	IWRR	Angel Trains	FGW	FGW	76S, 2L
42081	TS	GH2070A	IWRR	Angel Trains	FGW	FGW	65S, 2L (1 DIS), BCF, WCS, RA
42082	TS	GH2070A	IWRR	Angel Trains	FGW	FGW	65S, 2L (1 DIS), BCF, WCS, RA
42083	TS	GH2030H	IWRR	Angel Trains	FGW	FGW	76S, 2L
42084	TS	GH2030T	ICCT	Porterbrook	VT	VT	72S, 2L, BCF, CLS
42085	TS	GH2030S	ICCT	Porterbrook	VT	VT	72S, 2L, BCF, CLS
42086	TS	GH2030T	ICCT	Porterbrook	VT	VT	72S, 2L, BCF, CLS

Number (Former Number[s])	Type	Design Code	Pool	Owner	Operator	Livery	Layout
42087	TS	GH2030U	ICCT	Porterbrook	VT	VT	72S, 2L, BCF, CLS, Smoking
42088	TS	GH2030H	ICCT	Porterbrook	VT	VT	76S, 2L
42089	TS	GH2030H	IWRR	Angel Trains	FGW	FGW	76S, 2L
42090	TS	GH2030H	ICCT	Porterbrook	VT	VT	76S, 2L
42091	TS	GH2030K	ICCT	Porterbrook	VT	VT	76S, 2L, Smoking
42092	TS	GH2030T	ICCT	Porterbrook	VT	VT	72S, 2L, BCF, CLS
42093	TS	GH2030S	ICCT	Porterbrook	VT	VT	72S, 2L, BCF, CLS
42094	TS	GH2030T	ICCT	Porterbrook	VT	VT	72S, 2L, BCF, CLS
42095	TS	GH2030U	ICCT	Porterbrook	VT	VT	72S, 2L, BCF, CLS, Smoking
42096	TS	GH2070A	IWRR	Angel Trains	FGW	FGW	65S, 2L (1 DIS), BCF, WCS, RA
42097	TS	GH2030N	IWCT	Angel Trains	VT	VT	76S, 2L, WCS
42098	TS	GH2070A	IWRR	Angel Trains	FGW	FGW	65S, 2L (1 DIS), BCF, WCS, RA
42099	TS	GH2070A	IWRR	Angel Trains	FGW	FGW	65S, 2L (1 DIS), BCF, WCS, RA
42100	TS	GH2060A	IMLR	Porterbrook	MML	MML	72S, 2L, BCF, PA Zone
42101	TS	GH2060B	IMLR	Porterbrook	MML	MML	72S, 2L, WCS, PA Zone
42102	TS	GH2060A	IMLR	Porterbrook	MML	MML	72S, 2L, BCF, PA Zone
42103	TS	GH2030U	ICCT	Porterbrook	VT	VT	72S, 2L, BCF, CLS, Smoking
42104	TS	GH2030H	IECD	Porterbrook	GNER	GNER	76S, 2L
42105	TS	GH2030U	ICCT	Porterbrook	VT	VT	72S, 2L, BCF, CLS, Smoking
42106	TS	GH2030K	IECD	Porterbrook	GNER	GNER	76S, 2L
42107	TS	GH2030G	IWRR	Angel Trains	FGW	FGW	76S, 2L
42108	TS	GH2030H	ICCT	Porterbrook	VT	VT	76S, 2L
42109	TS	GH2030H	ICCT	Porterbrook	VT	VT	76S, 2L
42110	TS	GH2030H	ICCT	Porterbrook	VT	VT	76S, 2L
42111	TS	GH2060A	IMLR	Porterbrook	MML	MML	72S, 2L, BCF, PA Zone
42112	TS	GH2060A	IMLR	Porterbrook	MML	MML	72S, 2L, BCF, PA Zone
42113	TS	GH2060A	IMLR	Porterbrook	MML	MML	72S, 2L, BCF, PA Zone
42115	TS	GH2030S	ICCT	Porterbrook	VT	VT	72S, 2L, BCF, CLS
42116	TS	GH2030T	ICCT	Porterbrook	VT	VT	72S, 2L, BCF, CLS
42117	TS	GH2030U	ICCT	Porterbrook	VT	VT	72S, 2L, BCF, CLS, Smoking
42118	TS	GH2030G	IWRR	Angel Trains	FGW	FGW	76S, 2L
42119	TS	GH2060A	IMLR	Porterbrook	MML	MML	72S, 2L, BCF, PA Zone
42120	TS	GH2060A	IMLR	Porterbrook	MML	MML	72S, 2L, BCF, PA Zone
42121	TS	GH2060A	IMLR	Porterbrook	MML	MML	72S, 2L, BCF, PA Zone
42122	TS	GH2030K	IWCT	Angel Trains	VT	VT	76S, 2L, Smoking
42123	TS	GH2060A	IMLR	Porterbrook	MML	MML	72S, 2L, BCF, PA Zone
42124	TS	GH2060A	IMLR	Porterbrook	MML	MML	72S, 2L, BCF, PA Zone
42125	TS	GH2060A	IMLR	Porterbrook	MML	MML	72S, 2L, BCF, PA Zone
42126	TS	GH2030G	IWRR	Angel Trains	FGW	FGW	76S, 2L
42127	TS	GH2030T	ICCT	Porterbrook	VT	VT	72S, 2L, BCF, CLS
42128	TS	GH2030U	ICCT	Porterbrook	VT	VT	72S, 2L, BCF, CLS, Smoking
42129	TS	GH2030H	IWRR	Angel Trains	FGW	FGW	76S, 2L
42130	TS	GH2030H	ICCT	Porterbrook	VT	VT	76S, 2L
42131	TS	GH2060A	IMLR	Porterbrook	MML	MML	72S, 2L, BCF, PA Zone
42132	TS	GH2060A	IMLR	Porterbrook	MML	MML	72S, 2L, BCF, PA Zone
42133	TS	GH2060A	IMLR	Porterbrook	MML	MML	72S, 2L, BCF, PA Zone
42134	TS	GH2030H	IWCT	Angel Trains	VT	VT	76S, 2L
42135	TS	GH2060A	IMLR	Porterbrook	MML	MML	72S, 2L, BCF, PA Zone
42136	TS	GH2060A	IMLR	Porterbrook	MML	MML	72S, 2L, BCF, PA Zone
42137	TS	GH2060A	IMLR	Porterbrook	MML	MML	72S, 2L, BCF, PA Zone
42138	TS	GH2070A	IWRR	Angel Trains	FGW	FGW	65S, 2L (1 DIS), BCF, WCS, RA
42139	TS	GH2060A	IMLR	Porterbrook	MML	MML	72S, 2L, BCF, PA Zone
42140	TS	GH2060A	IMLR	Porterbrook	MML	MML	72S, 2L, BCF, PA Zone
42141	TS	GH2060A	IMLR	Porterbrook	MML	MML	72S, 2L, BCF, PA Zone
42143	TS	GH2030H	IWRR	Angel Trains	FGW	FGW	76S, 2L
42144	TS	GH2030H	IWRR	Angel Trains	FGW	FGW	76S, 2L
42145	TS	GH2030G	IWRR	Angel Trains	FGW	FGW	76S, 2L
42146	TS	GH2030H	IECD	Porterbrook	GNER	GNER	76S, 2L
42147	TS	GH2060A	IMLR	Porterbrook	MML	MML	72S, 2L, BCF, PA Zone
42148	TS	GH2060A	IMLR	Porterbrook	MML	MML	72S, 2L, BCF, PA Zone
42149	TS	GH2060A	IMLR	Porterbrook	MML	MML	72S, 2L, BCF, PA Zone
42150	TS	GH2030H	IECD	Porterbrook	GNER	GNER	76S, 2L
42151	TS	GH2060B	IMLR	Porterbrook	MML	MML	72S, 2L, WCS, PA Zone
42152	TS	GH2060A	IMLR	Porterbrook	MML	MML	72S, 2L, BCF, PA Zone
42153	TS	GH2060A	IMLR	Porterbrook	MML	MML	72S, 2L, BCF, PA Zone

Number (Former Number[s])	Type	Design Code	Pool	Owner	Operator	Livery	Layout
42154	TS	GH2030K	IECD	Porterbrook	GNER	GNER	76S, 2L
42155	TS	GH2060B	IMLR	Porterbrook	MML	MML	72S, 2L, WCS, PA Zone
42156	TS	GH2060A	IMLR	Porterbrook	MML	MML	72S, 2L, BCF, PA Zone
42157	TS	GH2060A	IMLR	Porterbrook	MML	MML	72S, 2L, BCF, PA Zone
42158(41177)	TS	GH2030H	IECD	Porterbrook	GNER	GNER	76S, 2L
42159	TS	GH2030H	ICCT	Porterbrook	VT	VT	76S, 2L
42160	TS	GH2030H	ICCT	Porterbrook	VT	VT	76S, 2L
42161	TS	GH2030H	ICCT	Porterbrook	VT	VT	76S, 2L
42162	TS	GH2030T	ICCT	Porterbrook	VT	VT	72S, 2L, BCF, CLS
42163	TS	GH2060B	IMLR	Porterbrook	MML	MML	72S, 2L, WCS, PA Zone
42164	TS	GH2060A	IMLR	Porterbrook	MML	MML	72S, 2L, BCF, PA Zone
42165	TS	GH2060A	IMLR	Porterbrook	MML	MML	72S, 2L, BCF, PA Zone
42166	TS	GH2030S	ICCT	Porterbrook	VT	VT	72S, 2L, BCF, CLS
42167	TS	GH2030T	ICCT	Porterbrook	VT	VT	72S, 2L, BCF, CLS
42168	TS	GH2030S	ICCT	Porterbrook	VT	VT	72S, 2L, BCF, CLS
42169	TS	GH2030T	ICCT	Porterbrook	VT	VT	72S, 2L, BCF, CLS
42170	TS	GH2030T	ICCT	Porterbrook	VT	VT	72S, 2L, BCF, CLS
42171	TS	GH2030H	IECD	Porterbrook	GNER	GNER	76S, 2L
42172	TS	GH2030H	IECD	Porterbrook	GNER	GNER	76S, 2L
42173	TS	GH2030U	ICCT	Porterbrook	VT	VT	72S, 2L, BCF, CLS, Smoking
42174	TS	GH2030U	ICCT	Porterbrook	VT	VT	72S, 2L, BCF, CLS, Smoking
42175	TS	GH2030T	ICCT	Porterbrook	VT	VT	72S, 2L, BCF, CLS
42176	TS	GH2030S	ICCT	Porterbrook	VT	VT	72S, 2L, BCF, CLS
42177	TS	GH2030T	ICCT	Porterbrook	VT	VT	72S, 2L, BCF, CLS
42178	TS	GH2030H	ICCT	Porterbrook	VT	VT	76S, 2L
42179	TS	GH2030H	IECD	Porterbrook	GNER	GNER	76S, 2L
42180	TS	GH2030H	IECD	Porterbrook	GNER	GNER	76S, 2L
42181	TS	GH2030H	IECD	Porterbrook	GNER	GNER	76S, 2L
42182	TS	GH2030H	IECD	Porterbrook	GNER	GNER	76S, 2L
42183	TS	GH2070A	IWRR	Angel Trains	FGW	FGW	65S, 2L (1 DIS), BCF, WCS, RA
42184	TS	GH2030H	IWRR	Angel Trains	FGW	FGW	76S, 2L
42185	TS	GH2030H	IWRR	Angel Trains	FGW	FGW	76S, 2L
42186	TS	GH2030H	IECD	Porterbrook	GNER	GNER	76S, 2L
42187	TS	GH2030S	ICCT	Porterbrook	VT	VT	72S, 2L, BCF, CLS
42188	TS	GH2030U	ICCT	Porterbrook	VT	VT	72S, 2L, BCF, CLS, Smoking
42189	TS	GH2030U	ICCT	Porterbrook	VT	VT	72S, 2L, BCF, CLS, Smoking
42190	TS	GH2030K	IECD	Porterbrook	GNER	GNER	76S, 2L
42191	TS	GH2030H	IECD	Porterbrook	GNER	GNER	76S, 2L
42192	TS	GH2030H	IECD	Porterbrook	GNER	GNER	76S, 2L
42193	TS	GH2030K	IECD	Porterbrook	GNER	GNER	76S, 2L
42194	TS	GH2060B	IMLR	Porterbrook	MML	MML	72S, 2L, WCS, PA Zone
42195	TS	GH2030T	ICCT	Porterbrook	VT	VT	72S, 2L, BCF, CLS
42196	TS	GH2070A	IWRR	Angel Trains	FGW	FGW	65S, 2L (1 DIS), BCF, WCS, RA
42197	TS	GH2030H	IWRR	Angel Trains	FGW	FGW	76S, 2L
42198	TS	GH2030H	IECD	Porterbrook	GNER	GNER	76S, 2L
42199	TS	GH2030K	IECD	Porterbrook	GNER	GNER	76S, 2L
42200	TS	GH2070A	IWRR	Angel Trains	FGW	FGW	65S, 2L (1 DIS), BCF, WCS, RA
42201	TS	GH2030H	IWRR	Angel Trains	FGW	FGW	76S, 2L
42202	TS	GH2070A	IWRR	Angel Trains	FGW	FGW	65S, 2L (1 DIS), BCF, WCS, RA
42203	TS	GH2030H	IWRR	Angel Trains	FGW	FGW	76S, 2L
42204	TS	GH2030G	IWRR	Angel Trains	FGW	FGW	76S, 2L
42205	TS	GH2060B	IMLR	Porterbrook	MML	MML	72S, 2L, WCS, PA Zone
42206	TS	GH2070A	IWRR	Angel Trains	FGW	FGW	65S, 2L (1 DIS), BCF, WCS, RA
42207	TS	GH2070A	IWRR	Angel Trains	FGW	FGW	65S, 2L (1 DIS), BCF, WCS, RA
42208	TS	GH2030H	IWRR	Angel Trains	FGW	FGW	76S, 2L
42209	TS	GH2030G	IWRR	Angel Trains	FGW	FGW	76S, 2L
42210	TS	GH2060A	IMLR	Porterbrook	MML	MML	72S, 2L, BCF, PA Zone
42211	TS	GH2070A	IWRR	Angel Trains	FGW	FGW	65S, 2L (1 DIS), BCF, WCS, RA
42212	TS	GH2030H	IWRR	Angel Trains	FGW	FGW	76S, 2L
42213	TS	GH2030H	IWRR	Angel Trains	FGW	FGW	76S, 2L
42214	TS	GH2030G	IWRR	Angel Trains	FGW	FGW	76S, 2L
42215	TS	GH2030H	IECD	Porterbrook	GNER	GNER	76S, 2L
42216	TS	GH2070A	IWRR	Angel Trains	FGW	FGW	65S, 2L (1 DIS), BCF, WCS, RA
42217	TS	GH2030S	ICCT	Porterbrook	VT	VT	72S, 2L, BCF, CLS
42218	TS	GH2030T	ICCT	Porterbrook	VT	VT	72S, 2L, BCF, CLS

Number (Former Number[s])	Type	Design Code	Pool	Owner	Operator	Livery	Layout
42219	TS	GH2030K	IECD	Porterbrook	GNER	GNER	76S, 2L
42220	TS	GH2060B	IMLR	Porterbrook	MML	MML	72S, 2L, WCS, PA Zone
42221	TS	GH2070A	IWRR	Angel Trains	FGW	FGW	65S, 2L (1 DIS), BCF, WCS, RA
42222	TS	GH2030S	ICCT	Porterbrook	VT	VT	72S, 2L, BCF, CLS
42223	TS	GH2030T	ICCT	Porterbrook	VT	VT	72S, 2L, BCF, CLS
42224	TS	GH2030U	ICCT	Porterbrook	VT	VT	72S, 2L, BCF, CLS, Smoking
42225	TS	GH2060A	IMLR	Porterbrook	MML	MML	72S, 2L, BCF, PA Zone
42226	TS	GH2030H	IECD	Porterbrook	GNER	GNER	76S, 2L
42227	TS	GH2060A	IMLR	Porterbrook	MML	MML	72S, 2L, BCF, PA Zone
42228	TS	GH2060A	IMLR	Porterbrook	MML	MML	72S, 2L, BCF, PA Zone
42229	TS	GH2060A	IMLR	Porterbrook	MML	MML	72S, 2L, BCF, PA Zone
42230	TS	GH2060A	IMLR	Porterbrook	MML	MML	72S, 2L, BCF, PA Zone
42231	TS	GH2030T	ICCT	Porterbrook	VT	VT	72S, 2L, BCF, CLS
42232	TS	GH2030S	ICCT	Porterbrook	VT	VT	72S, 2L, BCF, CLS
42233	TS	GH2030T	ICCT	Porterbrook	VT	VT	72S, 2L, BCF, CLS
42234	TS	GH2030U	ICCT	Porterbrook	VT	VT	72S, 2L, BCF, CLS, Smoking
42235	TS	GH2030N	IECD	Porterbrook	GNER	GNER	76S, 2L, WCS
42236	TS	GH2030H	IWRR	Angel Trains	FGW	FGW	76S, 2L
42237	TS	GH2030S	ICCT	Porterbrook	VT	VT	72S, 2L, BCF, CLS
42238	TS	GH2030T	ICCT	Porterbrook	VT	VT	72S, 2L, BCF, CLS
42239	TS	GH2030U	ICCT	Porterbrook	VT	VT	72S, 2L, BCF, CLS, Smoking
42240	TS	GH2030K	IECD	Porterbrook	GNER	GNER	76S, 2L
42241	TS	GH2030H	IECD	Porterbrook	GNER	GNER	76S, 2L
42242	TS	GH2030H	IECD	Porterbrook	GNER	GNER	76S, 2L
42243	TS	GH2030K	IECD	Porterbrook	GNER	GNER	76S, 2L
42244	TS	GH2030K	IECD	Porterbrook	GNER	GNER	76S, 2L
42245	TS	GH2030H	IWRR	Angel Trains	FGW	FGW	76S, 2L
42246	TS	GH2030T	ICCT	Porterbrook	VT	VT	72S, 2L, BCF, CLS
42247	TS	GH2030S	ICCT	Porterbrook	VT	VT	72S, 2L, BCF, CLS
42248	TS	GH2030T	ICCT	Porterbrook	VT	VT	72S, 2L, BCF, CLS
42249	TS	GH2030U	ICCT	Porterbrook	VT	VT	72S, 2L, BCF, CLS, Smoking
42250	TS	GH2030K	IWRR	Angel Trains	FGW	FGW	76S, 2L
42251	TS	GH2070B	IWRR	Angel Trains	FGW	FGW	65S, 2L (1 DIS), BCF, WCS, RA
42252	TS	GH2030E	IWRR	Angel Trains	FGW	FGW	76S, 2L
42253	TS	GH2030A	IWRR	Angel Trains	FGW	FGW	76S, 2L
42254	TS	GH2030X	ICCT	Porterbrook	VT	VT	72S, 2L, BCF, CLS
42255	TS	GH2070B	IWRR	Angel Trains	FGW	FGW	65S, 2L (1 DIS), BCF, WCS, RA
42256	TS	GH2030E	IWRR	Angel Trains	FGW	FGW	76S, 2L
42257	TS	GH2030A	IWRR	Angel Trains	FGW	FGW	76S, 2L
42258	TS	GH2030W	ICCT	Porterbrook	VT	VT	72S, 2L, BCF, CLS
42259	TS	GH2070B	IWRR	Angel Trains	FGW	FGW	65S, 2L (1 DIS), BCF, WCS, RA
42260	TS	GH2030E	IWRR	Angel Trains	FGW	FGW	76S, 2L
42261	TS	GH2030A	IWRR	Angel Trains	FGW	FGW	76S, 2L
42262	TS	GH2030X	ICCT	Porterbrook	VT	VT	72S, 2L, BCF, CLS
42263	TS	GH2030E	IWRR	Angel Trains	FGW	FGW	76S, 2L
42264	TS	GH2070B	IWRR	Angel Trains	FGW	FGW	65S, 2L (1 DIS), BCF, WCS, RA
42265	TS	GH2030A	IWRR	Angel Trains	FGW	FGW	76S, 2L
42266	TS	GH2030Y	ICCT	Porterbrook	VT	VT	72S, 2L, BCF, CLS
42267	TS	GH2070B	IWRR	Angel Trains	FGW	FGW	65S, 2L (1 DIS), BCF, WCS, RA
42268	TS	GH2070B	IWRR	Angel Trains	FGW	FGW	65S, 2L (1 DIS), BCF, WCS, RA
42269	TS	GH2030A	IWRR	Angel Trains	FGW	FGW	76S, 2L
42270	TS	GH2030X	ICCT	Porterbrook	VT	VT	72S, 2L, BCF, CLS
42271	TS	GH2070B	IWRR	Angel Trains	FGW	FGW	65S, 2L (1 DIS), BCF, WCS, RA
42272	TS	GH2030E	IWRR	Angel Trains	FGW	FGW	76S, 2L
42273	TS	GH2030A	IWRR	Angel Trains	FGW	FGW	76S, 2L
42274	TS	GH2030W	ICCT	Porterbrook	VT	VT	72S, 2L, BCF, CLS
42275	TS	GH2070B	IWRR	Angel Trains	FGW	FGW	65S, 2L (1 DIS), BCF, WCS, RA
42276	TS	GH2030E	IWRR	Angel Trains	FGW	FGW	76S, 2L
42277	TS	GH2030A	IWRR	Angel Trains	FGW	FGW	76S, 2L
42278	TS	GH2030X	ICCT	Porterbrook	VT	VT	72S, 2L, BCF, CLS
42279	TS	GH2070B	IWRR	Angel Trains	FGW	FGW	65S, 2L (1 DIS), BCF, WCS, RA
42280	TS	GH2030E	IWRR	Angel Trains	FGW	FGW	76S, 2L
42281	TS	GH2030A	IWRR	Angel Trains	FGW	FGW	76S, 2L
42282	TS	GH2030Y	ICCT	Porterbrook	VT	VT	72S, 2L, BCF, CLS, Smoking
42283	TS	GH2070B	IWRR	Angel Trains	FGW	FGW	65S, 2L (1 DIS), BCF, WCS, RA

Number (Former Number[s])	Type	Design Code	Pool	Owner	Operator	Livery	Layout
42284	TS	GH2030E	IWRR	Angel Trains	FGW	FGW	76S, 2L
42285	TS	GH2030J	IWRR	Angel Trains	FGW	FGW	76S, 2L
42286	TS	GH2030X	ICCT	Porterbrook	VT	VT	72S, 2L, BCF, CLS
42287	TS	GH2070B	IWRR	Angel Trains	FGW	FGW	65S, 2L (1 DIS), BCF, WCS, RA
42288	TS	GH2030E	IWRR	Angel Trains	FGW	FGW	76S, 2L
42289	TS	GH2030A	IWRR	Angel Trains	FGW	FGW	76S, 2L
42290	TS	GH2030W	ICCT	Porterbrook	VT	VT	72S, 2L, BCF, CLS
42291	TS	GH2070B	IWRR	Angel Trains	FGW	FGW	65S, 2L (1 DIS), BCF, WCS, RA
42292	TS	GH2070B	IWRR	Angel Trains	FGW	FGW	65S, 2L (1 DIS), BCF, WCS, RA
42293	TS	GH2030A	IWRR	Angel Trains	FGW	FGW	76S, 2L
42294	TS	GH2030X	ICCT	Porterbrook	VT	VT	72S, 2L, BCF, CLS
42295	TS	GH2070B	IWRR	Angel Trains	FGW	FGW	65S, 2L (1 DIS), BCF, WCS, RA
42296	TS	GH2030E	IWRR	Angel Trains	FGW	FGW	76S, 2L
42297	TS	GH2030A	IWRR	Angel Trains	FGW	FGW	76S, 2L
42298	TS	GH2030Y	ICCT	Porterbrook	VT	VT	72S, 2L, BCF, CLS, Smoking
42299	TS	GH2070B	IWRR	Angel Trains	FGW	FGW	65S, 2L (1 DIS), BCF, WCS, RA
42300	TS	GH2030E	IWRR	Angel Trains	FGW	FGW	76S, 2L
42301	TS	GH2030A	IWRR	Angel Trains	FGW	FGW	76S, 2L
42302	TS	GH2030X	ICCT	Porterbrook	VT	VT	72S, 2L, BCF, CLS
42303	TS	GH2030W	ICCT	Porterbrook	VT	VT	72S, 2L, BCF, CLS
42304	TS	GH2030X	ICCT	Porterbrook	VT	VT	72S, 2L, BCF, CLS
42305	TS	GH2030Y	ICCT	Porterbrook	VT	VT	72S, 2L, BCF, CLS, Smoking
42306	TS	GH2030H	ICCT	Porterbrook	VT	VT	76S, 2L
42307	TS	GH2030H	ICCT	Porterbrook	VT	VT	76S, 2L
42308	TS	GH2030H	ICCT	Porterbrook	VT	VT	76S, 2L
42309	TS	GH2030J	ICCT	Porterbrook	VT	VT	76S, 2L, Smoking
42310	TS	GH2030X	ICCT	Porterbrook	VT	VT	72S, 2L, BCF, CLS
42311	TS	GH2030W	ICCT	Porterbrook	VT	VT	72S, 2L, BCF, CLS
42312	TS	GH2030X	ICCT	Porterbrook	VT	VT	72S, 2L, BCF, CLS
42313	TS	GH2030Y	ICCT	Porterbrook	VT	VT	72S, 2L, BCF, CLS, Smoking
42314	TS	GH2030X	ICCT	Porterbrook	VT	VT	72S, 2L, BCF, CLS
42315	TS	GH2030W	ICCT	Porterbrook	VT	VT	72S, 2L, BCF, CLS
42316	TS	GH2030X	ICCT	Porterbrook	VT	VT	72S, 2L, BCF, CLS
42317	TS	GH2030Y	ICCT	Porterbrook	VT	VT	72S, 2L, BCF, CLS, Smoking
42318	TS	GH2030X	ICCT	Porterbrook	VT	VT	72S, 2L, BCF, CLS
42319	TS	GH2030W	ICCT	Porterbrook	VT	VT	72S, 2L, BCF, CLS
42320	TS	GH2030X	ICCT	Porterbrook	VT	VT	72S, 2L, BCF, CLS
42321	TS	GH2030Y	ICCT	Porterbrook	VT	VT	72S, 2L, BCF, CLS, Smoking
42322	TS	GH2030J	ICCT	Porterbrook	VT	VT	76S, 2L, Smoking
42323	TS	GH2030F	IECD	Porterbrook	GNER	GNER	76S, 2L
42324	TS	GH2060C	IMLR	Porterbrook	MML	MML	72S, 2L, WCS, PA Zone
42325	TS	GH2030F	IWRR	Angel Trains	FGW	FGW	76S, 2L
42326	TS	GH2030X	ICCT	Porterbrook	VT	VT	72S, 2L, BCF, CLS
42327	TS	GH2060C	IMLR	Porterbrook	MML	MML	72S, 2L, WCS, PA Zone
42328	TS	GH2060C	IMLR	Porterbrook	MML	MML	72S, 2L, WCS, PA Zone
42329	TS	GH2060C	IMLR	Porterbrook	MML	MML	72S, 2L, WCS, PA Zone
42330	TS	GH2030X	ICCT	Porterbrook	VT	VT	72S, 2L, BCF, CLS
42331	TS	GH2060C	IMLR	Porterbrook	MML	MML	72S, 2L, WCS, PA Zone
42332	TS	GH2070B	IWRR	Angel Trains	FGW	FGW	65S, 2L (1 DIS), BCF, WCS, RA
42333	TS	GH2070B	IWRR	Angel Trains	FGW	FGW	65S, 2L (1 DIS), BCF, WCS, RA
42334	TS	GH2030X	ICCT	Porterbrook	VT	VT	72S, 2L, BCF, CLS
42335	TS	GH2060C	IMLR	Porterbrook	MML	MML	72S, 2L, WCS, PA Zone
42336	TS	GH2030X	ICCT	Porterbrook	VT	VT	72S, 2L, BCF, CLS
42337	TS	GH2060C	IMLR	Porterbrook	MML	MML	72S, 2L, WCS, PA Zone
42338	TS	GH2030X	ICCT	Porterbrook	VT	VT	72S, 2L, BCF, CLS
42339	TS	GH2060C	IMLR	Porterbrook	MML	MML	72S, 2L, WCS, PA Zone
42340	TS	GH2030F	IECD	Porterbrook	GNER	GNER	76S, 2L
42341	TS	GH2060D	IMLR	Porterbrook	MML	MML	74S, 2L, BCF, PA Zone
42342(44082)	TS	GH2030D	IWCT	Angel Trains	VT	VT	76S, 2L
42343(44095)	TS	GH2030D	IWRR	Angel Trains	FGW	FGW	76S, 2L
42344(44092)	TS	GH2070B	IWRR	Angel Trains	FGW	FGW	65S, 2L (1 DIS), BCF, WCS, RA
42345(44096)	TS	GH2070B	IWRR	Angel Trains	FGW	FGW	65S, 2L (1 DIS), BCF, WCS, RA
42346(41053)	TS	GH2040A	IWRR	Angel Trains	FGW	FGW	76S, 2L
42347(41054)	TS	GH2070A	IWRR	Angel Trains	FGW	FGW	65S, 2L (1 DIS), BCF, WCS, RA
42348(41073)	TS	GH2070A	IWRR	Angel Trains	FGW	FGW	65S, 2L (1 DIS), BCF, WCS, RA

Number (Former Number[s])	Type	Design Code	Pool	Owner	Operator	Livery	Layout
42349(41074)	TS	GH2040A	IWRR	Angel Trains	FGW	FGW	76S, 2L
42350(41047)	TS	GH2040A	IWRR	Angel Trains	FGW	FGW	76S, 2L
42351(41048)	TS	GH2040A	IWRR	Angel Trains	FGW	FGW	76S, 2L
42352(41176,42142)	TS	GH2060A	IMLR	Porterbrook	MML	MML	72S, 2L, BCF, PA Zone
42353(41171,42001, 12002)	TS	GH2040E	ICCT	Porterbrook	VT	VT	72S, 2L, BCF, CLS
42354(41175,42114)	TS	GH2030P	IECD	Porterbrook	GNER	GNER	76S, 2L
42355(41172,42000 12000)	TS	GH2040C	IWCT	Angel Trains	VT	VT	76S, 2L
42356(41173,42002, 12003)	TS	GH2040D	IWRR	Angel Trains	FGW	FGW	76S, 2L
42357(41174,41002, 11003)	TS	GH2040C	IWCT	Angel Trains	VT	VT	76S, 2L
42360(45084,44084)	TS	GH2080A	IWRR	Angel Trains	FGW	FGW	76S, 2L
42361(44099)	TS	GH2080A	IWRR	Angel Trains	FGW	First	76S, 2L
42362(41178,42011)	TS	GH2080A	IWRR	Angel Trains	FGW	FGW	76S, 2L
42363 (41082)	TS	GH2040E	ICCT	Porterbrook	VT	VT	72S, 2L, BCF, CLS

Power Cars

Number	Design Code	Pool	Owner	Operator	Livery	Number	Design Code	Pool	Owner	Operator	Livery
43002	430HA	IWRP	Angel Trains	FGW	FGW	43039	430CA	IECP	Angel Trains	GNER	GNER
43003	430HA	IWRP	Angel Trains	FGW	FGW	43040	430HA	IWRP	Angel Trains	FGW	FGW
43004	430HA	IWRP	Angel Trains	FGW	FGW	43041	430HA	IWRP	Angel Trains	FGW	FGW
43005	430HA	IWRP	Angel Trains	FGW	FGW	43042	430HA	IWRP	Angel Trains	FGW	FGW
43006	430CA	IWCP	Angel Trains	VT	VT	43043	430CA	IMLP	Porterbrook	MML	MML
43007	430CA	IWCP	Angel Trains	VT	VT	43044	430CA	IMLP	Porterbrook	MML	MML
43008	430CA	IWCP	Angel Trains	VT	VT	43045	430CA	IMLP	Porterbrook	MML	MML
43009	430HA	IWRP	Angel Trains	FGW	FGW	43046	430CA	IMLP	Porterbrook	MML	MML
43010	430HA	IWRP	Angel Trains	FGW	FGW	43047	430LA	IMLP	Porterbrook	MML	MML
43011	430HA	IWRP	Angel Trains		GW	43048	430CA	IMLP	Porterbrook	MML	MML
			Withdrawn at, Bombardier Crewe			43049	430CA	IMLP	Porterbrook	MML	MML
43012	430HA	IWRP	Angel Trains	FGW	FGW	43050	430CA	IMLP	Porterbrook	MML	MML
43013	430FA	ICCS	Porterbrook	VT	VT	43051	430CA	IMLP	Porterbrook	MML	MML
43014	430FA	ICCS	Porterbrook	VT	VT	43052	430CA	IMLP	Porterbrook	MML	MML
43015	430HA	IWRP	Angel Trains	FGW	FGW	43053	430CA	IMLP	Porterbrook	MML	MML
43016	430HA	IWRP	Angel Trains	FGW	FGW	43054	430CA	IMLP	Porterbrook	MML	MML
43017	430HA	IWRP	Angel Trains	FGW	FGW	43055	430CA	IMLP	Porterbrook	MML	MML
43018	430HA	IWRP	Angel Trains	FGW	FGW	43056	430CA	IMLP	Porterbrook	MML	MML
43019	430HA	IWRP	Angel Trains	FGW	FGW	43057	430CA	IMLP	Porterbrook	MML	MML
43020	430HA	IWRP	Angel Trains	FGW	FGW	43058	430CA	IMLP	Porterbrook	MML	MML
43021	430HA	IWRP	Angel Trains	FGW	FGW	43059	430LA	IMLP	Porterbrook	MML	MML
43022	430HA	IWRP	Angel Trains	FGW	FGW	43060	430CA	IMLP	Porterbrook	MML	MML
43023	430HA	IWRP	Angel Trains	FGW	FGW	43061	430CA	IMLP	Porterbrook	MML	MML
43024	430HA	IWRP	Angel Trains	FGW	FGW	43062	430CA	ICCS	Porterbrook	VT	VT
43025	430HA	IWRP	Angel Trains	FGW	FGW	43063	430CA	ICCS	Porterbrook	VT	VT
43026	430HA	IWRP	Angel Trains	FGW	FGW	43064	430CA	IMLP	Porterbrook	MML	MML
43027	430HA	IWRP	Angel Trains	FGW	FGW	43065	430FA	ICCS	Porterbrook	VT	VT
43028	430HA	IWRP	Angel Trains	FGW	FGW	43066	430CA	IMLP	Porterbrook	MML	MML
43029	430HA	IWRP	Angel Trains	FGW	First	43067	430FA	ICCS	Porterbrook	VT	VT
43030	430HA	IWRP	Angel Trains	FGW	FGW	43068	430FA	ICCS	Porterbrook	VT	VT
43031	430HA	IWRP	Angel Trains	FGW	FGW	43069	430CA	ICCS	Porterbrook	VT	VT
43032	430HA	IWRP	Angel Trains	FGW	FGW	43070	430CA	ICCS	Porterbrook	VT	VT
43033	430HA	IWRP	Angel Trains	FGW	FGW	43071	430CA	ICCS	Porterbrook	VT	VT
43034	430HA	IWRP	Angel Trains	FGW	FGW	43072	430CA	IMLP	Porterbrook	MML	MML
43035	430HA	IWRP	Angel Trains	FGW	FGW	43073	430CA	IMLP	Porterbrook	MML	MML
43036	430HA	IWRP	Angel Trains	FGW	FGW	43074	430LA	IMLP	Porterbrook	MML	MML
43037	430HA	IWRP	Angel Trains	FGW	FGW	43075	430LA	IMLP	Porterbrook	MML	MML
43038	430CA	IECP	Angel Trains	GNER	GNER	43076	430CA	IMLP	Porterbrook	MML	MML

Number	Design Code	Pool	Owner	Operator	Livery
43077	430CA	IMLP	Porterbrook	MML	MML
43078	430CA	ICCS	Porterbrook	VT	VT
43079	430CA	ICCS	Porterbrook	VT	VT
43080	430FA	ICCS	Porterbrook	VT	VT
43081	430CA	IMLP	Porterbrook	MML	MML
43082	430CA	IMLP	Porterbrook	MML	MML
43083	430CA	IMLP	Porterbrook	MML	MML
43084	430FA	ICCS	Porterbrook	VT	VT
43085	430CA	IMLP	Porterbrook	MML	MM
43086	430CA	ICCS	Porterbrook	VT	VT
43087	430CA	ICCP	Porterbrook	VT	VT
43088	430CA	ICCP	Porterbrook	VT	VT
43089	430CA	ICCP	Porterbrook	VT	VT
43090	430CA	ICCP	Porterbrook	VT	VT
43091	430CA	ICCP	Porterbrook	VT	VT
43092	430CA	ICCS	Porterbrook	VT	VT
43093	430CA	ICCS	Porterbrook	VT	VT
43094	430CA	ICCS	Porterbrook	VT	VT
43095	430CA	IECP	Angel Trains	GNER	GNER
43096	430AA	IECP	Angel Trains	GNER	GNER
43097	430CA	ICCS	Porterbrook	VT	VT
43098	430CA	ICCS	Porterbrook	VT	VT
43099	430AA	ICCS	Porterbrook	VT	VT
43100	430CA	ICCS	Porterbrook	VT	VT
43101	430CA	ICCP	Porterbrook	VT	VT
43102	430CA	ICCP	Porterbrook	VT	VT
43103	430CA	ICCP	Porterbrook	VT	VT
43104	430AA	IWCP	Angel Trains	VT	VT
43105	430CA	IECP	Angel Trains	GNER	GNER
43106	430CA	IECP	Angel Trains	GNER	GNER
43107	430AA	IECP	Angel Trains	GNER	GNER
43108	430AA	IECP	Angel Trains	GNER	GNER
43109	430AA	IECP	Angel Trains	GNER	GNER
43110	430CA	IECP	Angel Trains	GNER	GNER
43111	430CA	IECP	Angel Trains	GNER	GNER
43112	430CA	IECP	Angel Trains	GNER	GNER
43113	430CA	IECP	Angel Trains	GNER	GNER
43114	430AA	IECP	Angel Trains	GNER	GNER
43115	430CA	IECP	Angel Trains	GNER	GNER
43116	430AA	IECP	Angel Trains	GNER	GNER
43117	430CA	IECP	Angel Trains	GNER	GNER
43118	430CA	IECP	Angel Trains	GNER	GNER
43119	430CA	IECP	Angel Trains	GNER	GNER
43120	430CA	IECP	Angel Trains	GNER	GNER
43121	430CA	ICCP	Porterbrook	VT	VT
43122	430CA	ICCP	Porterbrook	VT	VT
43123	430FA	ICCS	Porterbrook	VT	VT
43124	430JA	IWRP	Angel Trains	FGW	FGW
43125	430JA	IWRP	Angel Trains	FGW	FGW
43126	430JA	IWRP	Angel Trains	FGW	FGW
43127	430JA	IWRP	Angel Trains	FGW	FGW
43128	430JA	IWRP	Angel Trains	FGW	FGW
43129	430JA	IWRP	Angel Trains	FGW	FGW
43130	430JA	IWRP	Angel Trains	FGW	FGW
43131	430JA	IWRP	Angel Trains	FGW	FGW
43132	430JA	IWRP	Angel Trains	FGW	FGW
43133	430JA	IWRP	Angel Trains	FGW	FGW
43134	430JA	IWRP	Angel Trains	FGW	FGW
43135	430JA	IWRP	Angel Trains	FGW	FGW
43136	430JA	IWRP	Angel Trains	FGW	FGW
43137	430JA	IWRP	Angel Trains	FGW	FGW
43138	430JA	IWRP	Angel Trains	FGW	FGW
43139	430JA	IWRP	Angel Trains	FGW	FGW
43140	430JA	IWRP	Angel Trains	FGW	FGW
43141	430JA	IWRP	Angel Trains	FGW	FGW
43142	430JA	IWRP	Angel Trains	FGW	FGW
43143	430JA	IWRP	Angel Trains	FGW	FGW
43144	430JA	IWRP	Angel Trains	FGW	FGW
43145	430JA	IWRP	Angel Trains	FGW	FGW
43146	430JA	IWRP	Angel Trains	FGW	FGW
43147	430GA	IWRP	Angel Trains	FGW	FGW
43148	430GA	IWRP	Angel Trains	FGW	FGW
43149	430JA	IWRP	Angel Trains	FGW	FGW
43150	430JA	IWRP	Angel Trains	FGW	FGW
43151	430JA	IWRP	Angel Trains	FGW	FGW
43152	430HA	IWRP	Angel Trains	FGW	FGW
43153	430CA	ICCP	Porterbrook	VT	VT
43154	430CA	ICCP	Porterbrook	VT	VT
43155	430CA	ICCP	Porterbrook	VT	VT
43156	430CA	ICCP	Porterbrook	VT	VT
43157	430CA	ICCP	Porterbrook	VT	VT
43158	430CA	ICCP	Porterbrook	VT	VT
43159	430CA	ICCP	Porterbrook	VT	VT
43160	430CA	ICCP	Porterbrook	VT	VT
43161	430CA	ICCP	Porterbrook	VT	VT
43162	430CA	ICCP	Porterbrook	VT	VT
43163	430HA	IWRP	Angel Trains	FGW	FGW
43164	430HA	IWRP	Angel Trains	FGW	FGW
43165	430HA	IWRP	Angel Trains	FGW	FGW
43166	430HA	IWCP	Angel Trains	VT	VT
43167	430LA	IECP	Angel Trains	GNER	GNER
43168	430MA	IWRP	Angel Trains	FGW	FGW
43169	430MA	IWRP	Angel Trains	FGW	FGW
43170	430MA	IWRP	Angel Trains	FGW	FGW
43171	430HA	IWRP	Angel Trains	FGW	FGW
43172	430HA	IWRP	Angel Trains	FGW	FGW
43173	430HA	IWRP	Angel Trains		GW
			Withdrawn at DERA Shoeburyness		
43174	430HA	IWRP	Angel Trains	FGW	FGW
43175	430HA	IWRP	Angel Trains	FGW	FGW
43176	430HA	IWRP	Angel Trains	FGW	FGW
43177	430MA	IWRP	Angel Trains	FGW	FGW
43178	430CA	IWCP	Angel Trains	VT	VT
43179	430MA	IWRP	Angel Trains	FGW	FGW
43180	430CA	ICCS	Porterbrook	VT	VT
43181	430HA	IWRP	Angel Trains	FGW	FGW
43182	430HA	IWRP	Angel Trains	FGW	FGW
43183	430HA	IWRP	Angel Trains	FGW	FGW
43184	430CA	ICCS	Porterbrook	VT	VT
43185	430HA	IWRP	Angel Trains	FGW	FGW
43186	430HA	IWRP	Angel Trains	FGW	FGW
43187	430HA	IWRP	Angel Trains	FGW	FGW
43188	430HA	IWRP	Angel Trains	FGW	FGW
43189	430HA	IWRP	Angel Trains	FGW	FGW
43190	430HA	IWRP	Angel Trains	FGW	FGW
43191	430MA	IWRP	Angel Trains	FGW	FGW
43192	430HA	IWRP	Angel Trains	FGW	FGW
43193	430CA	ICCP	Porterbrook	VT	VT
43194	430CA	ICCP	Porterbrook	VT	VT
43195	430CA	ICCP	Porterbrook	VT	VT
43196	430CA	ICCP	Porterbrook	VT	VT
43197	430CA	ICCP	Porterbrook	VT	VT
43198	430CA	ICCP	Porterbrook	VT	VT

Saloon Vehicles (continued).

Number (Former Number[s])	Type Code	Design	Pool	Owner	Operator	Livery	Layout
44000	TGS	GJ2050D	ICCE	Porterbrook	VT	VT	61S, 1L, BCF
44001	TGS	GJ2050A	IWRR	Angel Trains	FGW	FGW	61S, 1TUS, 1L, WCS, BRF
44002	TGS	GJ2050A	IWRR	Angel Trains	FGW	FGW	61S, 1TUS, 1L, WCS, BRF
44003	TGS	GJ2050A	IWRR	Angel Trains	FGW	FGW	61S, 1TUS, 1L, WCS, BRF
44004	TGS	GJ2050A	IWRR	Angel Trains	FGW	FGW	65S, 1TUS, 1L, WCS, BRF
44005	TGS	GJ2050A	IWRR	Angel Trains	FGW	FGW	61S, 1TUS, 1L, WCS, BRF
44006	TGS	GJ2050A	IWRR	Angel Trains	FGW	FGW	61S, 1TUS, 1L, WCS, BRF
44007	TGS	GJ2050A	IWRR	Angel Trains	FGW	FGW	61S, 1TUS, 1L, WCS, BRF
44008	TGS	GJ2050A	IWRR	Angel Trains	FGW	FGW	65S, 1TUS, 1L, WCS, BRF
44009	TGS	GJ2050A	IWRR	Angel Trains	FGW	FGW	61S, 1TUS, 1L, WCS, BRF
44010	TGS	GJ2050A	IWRR	Angel Trains	FGW	FGW	61S, 1TUS, 1L, WCS, BRF
44011	TGS	GJ2050A	IWRR	Angel Trains	FGW	FGW	61S, 1TUS, 1L, WCS, BRF
44012	TGS	GJ2070A	IWCT	Angel Trains	VT	VT	63S, 1L, Smoking
44013	TGS	GJ2050A	IWRR	Angel Trains	FGW	FGW	61S, 1TUS, 1L, WCS, BRF
44014	TGS	GJ2050A	IWRR	Angel Trains	FGW	FGW	61S, 1TUS, 1L, WCS, BRF
44015	TGS	GJ2050A	IWRR	Angel Trains	FGW	FGW	61S, 1TUS, 1L, WCS, BRF
44016	TGS	GJ2050A	IWRR	Angel Trains	FGW	FGW	61S, 1TUS, 1L, WCS, BRF
44017	TGS	GJ2070A	IWCT	Angel Trains	VT	VT	63S, 1L, Smoking
44018	TGS	GJ2050A	IWRR	Angel Trains	FGW	FGW	61S, 1TUS, 1L, WCS, BRF
44019	TGS	GJ2050A	IECD	Angel Trains	GNER	GNER	63S, 1TUS, 1L, WCS
44020	TGS	GJ2050A	IWRR	Angel Trains	FGW	FGW	61S, 1TUS, 1L, WCS, BRF
44021	TGS	GJ2050D	ICCE	Porterbrook	VT	VT	61S, 1L, BCF
44022	TGS	GJ2050A	IWRR	Angel Trains	FGW	FGW	61S, 1TUS, 1L, WCS, BRF
44023	TGS	GJ2050A	IWRR	Angel Trains	FGW	FGW	61S, 1TUS, 1L, WCS, BRF
44024	TGS	GJ2050A	IWRR	Angel Trains	FGW	FGW	61S, 1TUS, 1L, WCS, BRF
44025	TGS	GJ2050A	IWRR	Angel Trains	FGW	FGW	61S, 1TUS, 1L, WCS, BRF
44026	TGS	GJ2050A	IWRR	Angel Trains	FGW	FGW	61S, 1TUS, 1L, WCS, BRF
44027	TGS	GJ2070A	IMLR	Porterbrook	MML	MML	63S, 1L, PA Zone, Smoking
44028	TGS	GJ2050A	IWRR	Angel Trains	FGW	FGW	61S, 1TUS, 1L, WCS, BRF
44029	TGS	GJ2050A	IWRR	Angel Trains	FGW	FGW	61S, 1TUS, 1L, WCS, BRF
44030	TGS	GJ2050A	IWRR	Angel Trains	FGW	FGW	61S, 1TUS, 1L, WCS, BRF
44031	TGS	GJ2070A	IWCT	Angel Trains	VT	VT	63S, 1L, Smoking
44032	TGS	GJ2050A	IWRR	Angel Trains	FGW	FGW	61S, 1TUS, 1L, WCS, BRF
44033	TGS	GJ2050A	IWRR	Angel Trains	FGW	FGW	61S, 1TUS, 1L, WCS, BRF
44034	TGS	GJ2050A	IWRR	Angel Trains	FGW	FGW	61S, 1TUS, 1L, WCS, BRF
44035	TGS	GJ2050A	IWRR	Angel Trains	FGW	FGW	61S, 1TUS, 1L, WCS, BRF
44036	TGS	GJ2050A	IWRR	Angel Trains	FGW	FGW	61S, 1TUS, 1L, WCS, BRF

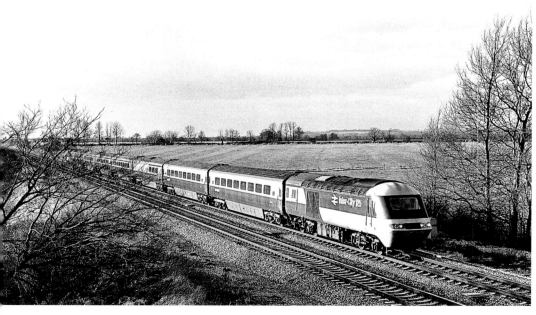

Left:
Running at the line speed of 125mph, the 12.45 Weston-super-Mare-Paddington, formed of set No 253032, passes near Challow between Didcot and Swindon on 5 January 1980. *CJM*

Number (Former Number[s])	Type Code	Design	Pool	Owner	Operator	Livery	Layout
44037	TGS	GJ2050A	IWRR	Angel Trains	FGW	FGW	61S, 1TUS, 1L, WCS, BRF
44038	TGS	GJ2050A	IWRR	Angel Trains	FGW	FGW	61S, 1TUS, 1L, WCS, BRF
44039	TGS	GJ2050A	IWRR	Angel Trains	FGW	FGW	61S, 1TUS, 1L, WCS, BRF
44040	TGS	GJ2050A	IWRR	Angel Trains	FGW	FGW	61S, 1TUS, 1L, WCS, BRF
44041	TGS	GJ2070A	IMLR	Porterbrook	MML	MML	63S, 1L, PA Zone, Smoking
44042	TGS	GJ2050D	ICCE	Porterbrook	VT	VT	61S, 1L, BCF
44043	TGS	GJ2040A	IWRR	Angel Trains	FGW	FGW	63S, 1TUS, 1L, WCS, BRF
44044	TGS	GJ2070A	IMLR	Porterbrook	MML	MML	63S, 1L, PA Zone, Smoking
44045	TGS	GJ2050A	IECD	Angel Trains	GNER	GNER	63S, 1TUS, 1L, WCS
44046	TGS	GJ2070A	IMLR	Porterbrook	MML	MML	63S, 1L, PA Zone, Smoking
44047	TGS	GJ2070A	IMLR	Porterbrook	MML	MML	63S, 1L, PA Zone, Smoking
44048	TGS	GJ2070A	IMLR	Porterbrook	MML	MML	63S, 1L, PA Zone, Smoking
44049	TGS	GJ2050A	IWRR	Angel Trains	FGW	FGW	61S, 1TUS, 1L, WCS, BRF
44050	TGS	GJ2070A	IMLR	Porterbrook	MML	MML	63S, 1L, PA Zone, Smoking
44051	TGS	GJ2070A	IMLR	Porterbrook	MML	MML	63S, 1L, PA Zone, Smoking
44052	TGS	GJ2070A	IMLR	Porterbrook	MML	MML	63S, 1L, PA Zone, Smoking
44053	TGS	GJ2050A	ICCE	Porterbrook	VT	VT	63S, 1TUS, 1L, WCS
44054	TGS	GJ2070A	IMLR	Porterbrook	MML	MML	63S, 1L, PA Zone, Smoking
44055	TGS	GJ2050D	ICCE	Porterbrook	VT	VT	61S, 1L, BCF
44056	TGS	GJ2050B	IECD	Angel Trains	GNER	GNER	63S, 1TUS, 1L, WCS, Buffers, DH/BE
44057	TGS	GJ2050D	ICCE	Porterbrook	VT	VT	61S, 1L, BCF
44058	TGS	GJ2050B	IECD	Angel Trains	GNER	GNER	63S, 1TUS, 1L, WCS, Buffers, DH/BE
44059	TGS	GJ2050B	IWRR	Angel Trains	FGW	FGW	63S, 1TUS, 1L, WCS, BRF, Buffers, DH/BE
44060	TGS	GJ2050D	ICCE	Porterbrook	VT	VT	61S, 1L, BCF
44061	TGS	GJ2050A	IECD	Angel Trains	GNER	GNER	63S, 1TUS, 1L, WCS
44062	TGS	GJ2050D	ICCE	Porterbrook	VT	VT	61S, 1L, BCF
44063	TGS	GJ2050A	IECD	Angel Trains	GNER	GNER	63S, 1TUS, 1L (DIS), WCS
44064	TGS	GJ2050A	IWRR	Angel Trains	FGW	FGW	61S, 1TUS, 1L, WCS, BRF
44065	TGS	GJ2050D	ICCE	Porterbrook	VT	VT	61S, 1L, BCF
44066	TGS	GJ2050A	IWRR	Angel Trains	FGW	FGW	61S, 1TUS, 1L, WCS, BRF
44067	TGS	GJ2050A	IWRR	Angel Trains	FGW	FGW	61S, 1TUS, 1L, WCS, BRF
44068	TGS	GJ2050D	ICCE	Porterbrook	VT	VT	61S, 1L, BCF
44069	TGS	GJ2050D	ICCE	Porterbrook	VT	VT	61S, 1L, BCF
44070	TGS	GJ2070A	IMLR	Porterbrook	MML	MML	63S, 1L, PA Zone, Smoking
44071	TGS	GJ2070A	IMLR	Porterbrook	MML	MML	63S, 1L, PA Zone, Smoking
44072	TGS	GJ2020A	ICCE	Porterbrook	VT	VT	61S, 1L, WCS
44073	TGS	GJ2070A	IMLR	Porterbrook	MML	MML	63S, 1L, PA Zone, Smoking
44074	TGS	GJ2050D	ICCE	Porterbrook	VT	VT	61S, 1L, BCF
44075	TGS	GJ2050D	ICCE	Porterbrook	VT	VT	61S, 1L, BCF
44076	TGS	GJ2050D	ICCE	Porterbrook	VT	VT	61S, 1L, BCF
44077	TGS	GJ2050A	IECD	Angel Trains	GNER	GNER	65S, 1TUS, 1L
44078	TGS	GJ2050D	ICCE	Porterbrook	VT	VT	61S, 1L, BCF
44079	TGS	GJ2050D	ICCE	Porterbrook	VT	VT	61S, 1L, BCF
44080	TGS	GJ2050A	IECD	Angel Trains	GNER	GNER	63S, 1TUS, 1L, WCS
44081	TGS	GJ2050D	ICCE	Porterbrook	VT	VT	61S, 1L, BCF
44083	TGS	GJ2070A	IMLR	Porterbrook	MML	MML	63S, 1L, PA Zone, Smoking
44085	TGS	GJ2070A	IMLR	Porterbrook	MML	MML	63S, 1L, PA Zone, Smoking
44086	TGS	GJ2050B	IWRR	Angel Trains	FGW	FGW	63S, 1TUS, 1L, WCS, BRF, Buffers, DH/BE
44087	TGS	GJ2050A	ICCT	Porterbrook	VT	VT	63S, 1TUS, 1L, WCS
44088	TGS	GJ2050A	ICCT	Porterbrook	VT	VT	63S, 1TUS, 1L, WCS
44089	TGS	GJ2050D	ICCE	Porterbrook	VT	VT	61S, 1L, BCF
44090	TGS	GJ2050D	ICCE	Porterbrook	VT	VT	61S, 1L, BCF
44091	TGS	GJ2050D	ICCE	Porterbrook	VT	VT	61S, 1L, BCF
44093	TGS	GJ2050A	IWRR	Angel Trains	FGW	FGW	61S, 1TUS, 1L, WCS, BRF
44094	TGS	GJ2050A	IECD	Angel Trains	GNER	GNER	63S, 1TUS, 1L, WCS
44097	TGS	GJ2050D	ICCE	Porterbrook	VT	VT	61S, 1L, BCF
44098	TGS	GJ2050B	IECD	Angel Trains	GNER	GNER	63S, 1TUS, 1L, WCS, Buffers, DH/BE
44100	TGS	GJ2050D	ICCE	Porterbrook	VT	VT	61S, 1L, BCF
44101	TGS	GJ2050D	ICCE	Porterbrook	VT	VT	61S, 1L, BCF

Appendix III. The Class 41/43 Power Car Fleet and Names

Number	Original Set No	Date Delivered*	Name Details
43000**	252001	10.6.72	
43001**	252001	10.8.72	
43002	253001	18.2.76	Top of the Pops 30.8.84-4.98, Techniquest 5.5.98
43003	253001	18.2.76	
43004	253002	18.3.76	Swan Hunter 30.11.90-2.95, Borough of Swindon 22.5.97
43005	253002	4.3.76	
43006	253003	13.5.76	
43007	253003	10.3.76	
43008	253004	18.3.76	
43009	253004	2.4.76	
43010	253005	15.4.76	TSW Today 17.10.90-1.93
43011	253005	14.4.76	Reader 125 4.6.92-10.99 (Leading power car in the Ladbroke Grove crash
43012	253006	11.5.76	
43013	253006	25.5.76	University of Bristol 17.10.86-8.89, CrossCountry Voyager 25.2.96-10.98
43014	253007	17.5.76	
43015	253007	21.5.76	
43016	253008	5.6.76	Garden Festival Wales 1992/ Gwyl Gerddi Cymru 1992 14.4.92-6.96
43017	253008	5.6.76	HTV West 6.5.87-5.89
43018	253009	19.6.76	The Red Cross 5.9.97
43019	253009	2.7.76	City of Swansea /Dinas Abertawe 1.5.87
43020	253010	9.7.76	John Grooms 25.8.93
43021	253010	9.7.76	
43022	253011	24.7.76	
43023	253011	7.8.76	County of Cornwall 30.11.89
43024	253012	31.7.76	
43025	253012	21.8.76	Exeter 25.4.94
43026	253013	14.8.76	City of Westminster 29.5.85
43027	253013	4.9.76	Westminster Abbey 29.5.85-5.90, Glorious Devon 25.4.94
43028	253014	28.8.76	
43029	253014	4.9.76	
43030	253015	23.9.76	Christian Lewis Trust 1.7.00
43031	253015	24.9.76	
43032	253016	18.10.76	The Royal Regiment of Wales 5.12.89
43033	253016	29.10.76	
43034	253017	13.11.76	The Black Horse 14.10.94
43035	253017	13.11.76	
43036	253018	20.11.76	
45037	253018	27.11.76	
43038	253019	4.12.76	National Railway Museum The First Ten Years 1975-1985 28.9.85-3.97
43039	253019	11.12.76	
43040	253020	18.12.76	Granite City 27.6.90-1.96
43041	253020	24.12.76	City of Discovery 27.6.90-2.00
43042	253021	24.2.77	
43043	253021	24.2.77	Leicestershire County Cricket Club 19.5.97
43044	253022	19.3.77	Borough of Kettering 22.10.93
43045	253022	19.3.77	The Grammar School Doncaster A.D. 1350 28.11.83-12.97
43046	253023	12.3.77	Royal Philharmonic 19.10.94
43047	253023	12.3.77	Rotherham Enterprise 27.3.84-6.91
43048	253024	26.3.77	
43049	253024	5.4.77	Neville Hill 21.1.84
43050	253025	7.5.77	
43051	253025	23.4.77	The Duke and Duchess of York 4.7.87-4.98
43052	253026	29.4.77	City of Peterborough 19.5.84-2.98
43053	253026	20.5.77	County of Humberside 10.4.84-4.94, Leeds United 6.4.94
43054	253027	28.5.77	
43055	253027	15.6.77	Sheffield Star 20.11.93
43056	254001	2.7.77	University of Bradford 9.11.83-10.97
43057	254001	5.7.77	Bounds Green 10.3.84-8.98
43058	254002	30.7.77	Midland Pride 9.2.97
43059	254002	13.8.77	
43060	254003	20.8.77	County of Leicestershire 12.3.85
43061	254003	26.8.77	City of Lincoln 12.5.84-11.97
43062	254004	20.9.77	
43063	254004	24.9.77	Maiden Voyager 6.1.97
43064	254005	15.10.77	City of York 20.9.83-2.98
43065	254005	15.10.77	City of Edinburgh 25.2.96-11.98
43066	254006	29.10.77	Nottingham Playhouse 24.8.95
43067	254006	29.10.77	
43068	254007	5.11.77	The Red Nose 3.3.97-3.99, The Red Arrows 11.00
43069	254007	12.11.77	
43070	254008	19.11.77	
43071	254008	19.11.77	Forward Birmingham 20.9.96
43072	254009	3.12.77	Derby Etches Park 20.7.93
43073	254009	8.12.77	
43074	254010	17.12.77	BBC East Midlands Today 5.97
43075	254010	17.12.77	
43076	254011	30.12.77	BBC East Midlands Today 5.1.91-3.97, The Master Cutler 1947-1997 6.10.97
43077	254011	30.12.77	County of Nottingham 20.9.84-5.97
43078	254012	14.1.78	Shildon County Durham 24.9.83-6.96, Golowan Festival Penzance 22.6.96
43079	254012	21.1.78	
43080	254013	28.1.78	
43081	254013	4.2.78	
43082	254014	11.2.78	Derbyshire First 10.11.97
43083	254014	18.2.78	
43084	254015	25.2.78	County of Derbyshire 17.7.86
43085	254015	25.3.78	City of Bradford 23.6.83-9.97
43086	254016	29.4.78	
43087	254016	6.5.78	
43088	254017	20.5.78	XIII Commonwealth Games Scotland 1986 27.3.85-12.99
43089	254017	20.5.78	
43090	254018	27.5.78	
43091	254018	27.5.78	Edinburgh Military Tattoo 5.8.85-4.99
43092	254019	3.6.78	Highland Chieftain 15.5.84-1.88, Highland Chieftain 3.93-4.93, Institution of Mechanical Engineers 150th Anniversary 1847-1997 25.4.97
43093	254019	10.6.78	York Festival '88 22.2.88-1.97, Lady In Red 3.2.97
43094	254020	17.6.78	
43095	254020	24.6.78	Heaton 4.2.84-3.91
43096	254021	1.7.78	The Queen's Own Hussars 14.5.85-3.97, The Great Racer 12.5.97-12.00
43097	254021	8.7.78	The Light Infantry 1.11.83-4.90
43098	254022	15.7.78	Tyne and Wear Metropolitan County 16.9.85-12.87, Railway Children 8.5.98

Number	Original Set No	Date Delivered*	Name Details
43099	254022	12.8.78	
43100	254023	19.8.78	*Craigentinny* 31.3.84-4.98, *Blackpool Rock* 25.5.98-7.00
43101	254023	7.10.78	*Edinburgh International Festival* 23.8.84-6.98, *The Irish Mail* 31.7.98-09.00
43102	254024	7.10.78	*City of Wakefield* 23.6.84-10.87
43103	254024	14.10.78	*John Wesley* 21.5.88-5.98
43104	254025	14.10.78	*County of Cleveland* 29.4.85-11.00 *City of Edinburgh* 29.3.01
43105	254025	28.10.78	*Hartlepool* 4.7.84-11.96, *City of Inverness* 2.01
43106	254026	28.10.78	*Songs of Praise* 13.6.89-5.97
43107	254026	11.11.78	*City of Derby* 7.5.86-12.88
43108	254027	18.11.78	*BBC Television Railwatch* 13.2.89-21.2.89, *Old Course St Andrews* 17.7.00
43109	254027	20.1.79	*Yorkshire Evening Press* 12.1.84-6.98
43110	254028	27.1.79	*Darlington* 5.5.84-4.97
43111	254028	3.2.79	
43112	254029	10.2.79	*Doncaster* 5.01
43113	254029	24.2.79	*City of Newcastle upon Tyne* 26.4.83-4.97
43114	254030	3.3.79	*National Garden Festival Gateshead 1990* 10.8.89-12.96
43115	254030	10.3.79	*Yorkshire Cricket Academy* 7.6.89-6.97
43116	254031	17.3.79	*City of Kingston upon Hull* 9.5.83-1.97
43117	254031	24.3.79	
43118	254032	31.3.79	*Charles Wesley* 21.5.88-11.96
43119	254032	7.4.79	
43120	Spare	3.9.77***	
43121	Spare	10.9.77***	*West Yorkshire Metropolitan County* 23.9.84-4.99
43122	Spare	7.4.79	*South Yorkshire Metropolitan County* 18.1.85
43123	Spare	14.4.79	
43124	Spare	6.6.81	*B.B.C Points West* 29.9.86-11.89
43125	253028	21.4.79	*Merchant Venturer* 17.4.85
43126	253028	5.5.79	*City of Bristol* 17.4.85
43127	253029	26.5.79	
43128	253029	9.6.79	
43129	253030	15.6.79	
43130	253030	7.7.79	*Sulis Minerva* 2.6.92
43131	253031	14.7.79	*Sir Felix Pole* 23.8.85
43132	253031	21.7.79	*Worshipful Company of Carmen* 6.10.87
43133	253032	28.7.79	
43134	253032	4.8.79	*County of Somerset* 1.7.92
43135	253033	18.8.79	
43136	253033	25.8.79	
43137	253034	15.9.79	*Newton Abbot 150* 11.4.97
43138	253034	20.9.79	
43139	253035	17.3.80	
43140	253035	17.3.80	
43141	253036	19.4.80	
43142	253036	24.5.80	*St Mary's Hospital Paddington* 4.11.86-3.89
43143	253037	31.12.80	
43144	253037	31.12.80	
43145	253038	20.2.81	
43146	253038	7.3.81	
43147	253039	11.4.81	*Red Cross* 3.5.88-2.91, *The Red Cross* 3.91-4.9.97
43148	253039	25.4.81	
43149	253040	16.5.81	*BBC Wales Today* 27.9.88
43150	253040	16.5.81	*Bristol Evening Post* 4.10.88
43151	Spare	23.5.81	*Blue Peter II* 11.5.87-11.89
43152	Spare	28.5.81	*St Peter's School York A.D. 627* 5.11.84-3.96
43153	254033	12.12.80	*University of Durham* 2.7.83-2.97, *The English Riviera Torquay, Paignton, Brixham* 25.6.97
43154	254033	6.12.80	*InterCity* 26.3.94
43155	254034	20.12.80	*BBC Look North* 13.6.85-4.97, *The Red Arrows* 12.5.97-4.6.98, *City of Aberdeen* 5.6.98
43156	254034	20.12.80	
43157	254035	13.2.81	*Yorkshire Evening Post* 12.1.84-6.98, *HMS Penzance* 13.7.98-3.00
43158	254035	13.2.81	*Dartmoor The Pony Express* 12.3.95
43159	254036	14.3.81	
43160	254036	28.3.81	*Storm Force* 27.4.91-9.97
43161	254037	2.5.81	*Reading Evening Post* 6.4.91-7.99
43162	254037	9.5.81	*Borough of Stevenage* 21.3.84-5.99
43163	253041	30.5.81	
43164	253041	6.6.81	
43165	253042	13.6.81	
43166	253042	20.6.81	
43167	253043	27.6.81	
43168	253043	2.7.81	
43169	253044	25.7.81	*The National Trust* 14.7.89
43170	253044	1.8.81	*Edward Paxman* 16.6.95
43171	253045	15.8.81	
43172	253045	22.8.81	
43173	253046	29.8.81	*Swansea University* 28.6.96-10.97 (Leading power car in the Southall crash)
43174	253046	29.8.81	*Bristol-Bordeaux* 26.4.97
43175	253047	19.8.81	
43176	253047	2.10.81	
43177	253048	10.10.81	*University of Exeter* 1.12.95
43178	253048	17.10.81	
43179	253049	31.10.81	*Pride of Laira* 15.9.91
43180	253049	14.11.81	*City of Newcastle upon Tyne* 13.5.98
43181	253050	21.11.81	*Devonport Royal Dockyard 1693-1993* 25.11.93
43182	253050	12.12.81	
43183	253051	19.12.81	
43184	253051	16.1.82	
43185	253052	20.2.82	*Great Western* 20.5.92
43186	253052	26.2.82	*Sir Francis Drake* 12.7.88
43187	253053	27.3.82	
43188	253053	17.4.82	*City of Plymouth* 8.5.86
43189	253054	17.4.82	*Railway Heritage Trust* 10.10.95
43190	253054	29.4.82	
43191	253055	15.5.82	*Seahawk* 12.10.88
43192	253055	18.5.82	*City of Truro* 12.10.88
43193	253056	21.5.82	*Yorkshire Post* 22.12.83-5.91, *Plymouth Spirit of Discovery* 12.3.95
43194	253056	5.6.82	*Royal Signals* 23.10.85-12.89
43195	253057	26.6.82	*British Red Cross 125th Birthday 1995* 11.12.95
43196	253057	3.7.82	*The Newspaper Society* 17.4.86-2.89, *The Newspaper Society Founded 1836* 2.91
43197	253058	13.8.82	*Railway Magazine Centenary 1897-1997* 22.11.96-17.10.00, *The Railway Magazine* 6.2.01
43198	253058	13.8.82	*HMS Penzance* 26.6.00

*Dates released from BREL Crewe, authorised for delivery to Derby for coach collection or home depot
**Originally numbered 41001 and 41002
***Delivered out of order, spare vehicles

Appendix IV. HST Stock Lot Numbers

Trailer Vehicles

Vehicle Nos	Builder	Lot No	Year
10000 (40000)	BR Derby	30849	1973
10100 (40500)	BR Derby	30850	1973
11000-11002 (41000-41001)	BR Derby	30848	1972
11003 (41002)	BR Derby	30833	1972
12000-12002 (42000-42001)	BR Derby	30847	1972
12003 (42002)	BR Derby	30832	1972
40001-40027	BREL Derby	30883	1976-77
40028-40037	BREL Derby	30899	1978-79
40204-40233	BREL Derby	Not issued — rebuild from TRSB	
40300-40321	BREL Derby	30921	1978-79
40322-40335	BREL Derby	30940	1978-79
40336-40353	BREL Derby	30948	1980-81
40354-40357	BREL Derby	30966	1982
40401-40437	BREL Derby	Not issued — rebuild from TRSB	
40501-40520	BREL Derby	30884	1976-77
40619	BREL Derby	Not issued — rebuild from TRUB	
40700-40757	BREL Derby	Not issued — rebuild from TRBF	
41003-41056	BREL Derby	30881	1976-77
41057-41120	BREL Derby	30896	1977-78
41121-41148	BREL Derby	30938	1979-80
41149-41166	BREL Derby	30947	1980
41167-41169	BREL Derby	30963	1982
41170-41174 (from prototype)	BREL Derby	30967	1982
41175-41177	BREL Derby	Not issued — rebuild from TS	
41178	BREL Derby	Not issued — rebuild from TS	
41179-41180	BREL Derby	Not issued — rebuild from TRUK	
42003-42090	BREL Derby	30882	1976-77
42091-42250	BREL Derby	30897	1977-79
42251-42305	BREL Derby	30939	1979-80
42306-42322	BREL Derby	30969	1982
42323-42341	BREL Derby	30983	1984-85
42342-42345	BREL Derby	Not issued — rebuild from TGS	
42346-42351	BREL Derby	Not issued — rebuild from TF	
42352-42357	BREL Derby	Not issued — rebuild from TF	
42358-42359	Numbers not issued		
42360	BREL Derby	Not issued — rebuild from TCSD	
42361	BREL Derby	Not issued — rebuild from TGS	
42362	BREL Derby	Not issued — rebuild from TF	
42363	BREL Derby	Not issued — rebuild from TF	
44000	BREL Derby	30953	1980
44001-44090	BREL Derby	30949	1980-82
44091-44094	BREL Derby	30964	1982
44095-44101	BREL Derby	30970	1982
45084	BREL Derby	Not issued — rebuild from TGS	

Power Cars

Vehicle Nos	Builder	Lot No	Year
41001-41002 (43000-43001)	BREL Crewe	30875	1972
43002-43055	BREL Crewe	30786	1973
43056-43123	BREL Crewe	30895	1976
43124-43152	BREL Crewe	30941	1979
43153-43190	BREL Crewe	30946	1980
43191-43198	BREL Crewe	30968	1982

Royal Train Vehicles

Vehicle Nos	Builder	Lot No	Year
2903 — rebuild from 11001	BREL Wolverton	30886	1977
2904 — rebuild from 12001	BREL Wolverton	30887	1977
2916 — rebuild from 40512	BREL Wolverton	31059	1986
2917 — rebuild from 40514	BREL Wolverton	31084	1989
2918 — rebuild from 40513	BREL Wolverton	31083	1989
2919 — rebuild from 40518	BREL Wolverton	31085	1989

Above:
The picturesque station of Dent on the Settle & Carlisle line played host to a photographic shoot by Virgin Trains on 4 January 1997 when the first red-liveried train worked empty from Neville Hill to Edinburgh Craigentinny in preparation for the high-profile take-over of the CrossCountry operation two days later. With power car No 43063 leading, the train is seen waiting to depart from Dent after a short break in its run. *CJM*